THE SCIENCE BENEATH THE SURFACE:

A VERY SHORT GUIDE TO THE MARCELLUS SHALE

BY
DON DUGGAN-HAAS, ROBERT M. ROSS,
AND WARREN D. ALLMON

WITH CONTRIBUTIONS BY
KELLY E. CRONIN, TRISHA A. SMRECAK, AND SARA AUER PERRY

Paleontological Research Institution
2013

INTRODUCTION

It is a common observation that the world has changed, that we today live in a very different world from the one in which our grandparents or parents, or even we, were born. What's usually meant by such statements, however, is the world of human culture and society. The "natural" world, by contrast, seems relatively constant, the epitome of stability. Yet this is no longer the case. Whatever one's political, economic, or social views, it is no longer reasonable to deny that the Earth's land, air, water, and life have been significantly altered by human activity. The *Anthropocene* is a name recently proposed by Earth scientists for the time interval since humanity became such a powerful force of change.[1] The term is usually assigned to start at the beginning of the Industrial Revolution, approximately 200 years ago.

Although any interval might seem historically significant as one is living through it, it's hard not to conclude that history will look back upon the early 21st century as a pivotal moment, at which the recognition and understanding of humanity's impacts on the Earth led to a global debate about what, if anything, should be done to change course. History will, of course, know whether humanity took steps that measurably slowed the rate of human impact, or it did not, and stuck to "business as usual," in which case accelerated environmental change led to a transformed planet, with major consequences for humans and other life.

Global environmental change is obviously not the only pressing concern for humanity right now. We are worried about how we will feed and otherwise provide for a population that will likely grow by at least 2 billion over the next 30–40 years. All of these people will want many of the things that most Americans take for granted, including reasonable levels of security, freedom, justice, prosperity, and the expectation that their children will have a better future. All of this takes resources, most importantly clean air, clean water, food, and energy. Solving the challenges of global environmental change must happen at the same time that we try to solve these other pressing social, political, and economic challenges. Solving one without solving the other will not work, at least not for very long.

Into this maelstrom has recently been thrust a means to extract vastly more fossil fuels than were forecasted even a decade ago, namely the extraction of natural gas and oil by a combination of two existing technologies—*horizontal drilling* and *hydraulic fracturing* (together often referred to as "high-volume hydraulic fracturing"

1

Figure 1.2. Artist's reconstruction of a typical Middle Devonian shallow sea environment, with crinoids (far left), trilobites and brachiopods (center), horn corals (right), and a nautiloid cephalopod (above).

The Marcellus Shale underlies more than 95,000 square miles (246,000 square kilometers) in parts of New York, Pennsylvania, West Virginia, Ohio, and in minor parts of New Jersey, Maryland, Virginia, Kentucky, and Tennessee (Figure 1.3). It takes its name from the town of Marcellus, New York, one of the locations where surface outcrops of the layers were first described by geologists. The Marcellus Shale is the bottom part of a thicker set of rocks known as the Hamilton Group (Figure 1.4), which accumulated during the middle part of the Devonian Period, between approximately 393 and 383 million years ago. The Marcellus is itself subdivided into different layers, including the Union Springs, Cherry Valley, and Oatka Creek.[1] This chapter provides an introductory look at the formation and subsequent geologic history of the Marcellus Shale.

FROM MUD TO ROCK

Approximately 390 million years ago, the area that is now the eastern United States lay south of the equator, and was largely under water (Figure 1.5).[2] It was part of an epicontinental sea that stretched for tens of thousands of square miles. On the northeastern shore of this sea, near what is now Albany, New York, *tectonic* forces were moving a small island chain westward, compressing the landscape to form what geologists call the *Acadian mountain range*. These same forces also caused the continental crust to bend downward, forming a depression, or *basin*, on the western

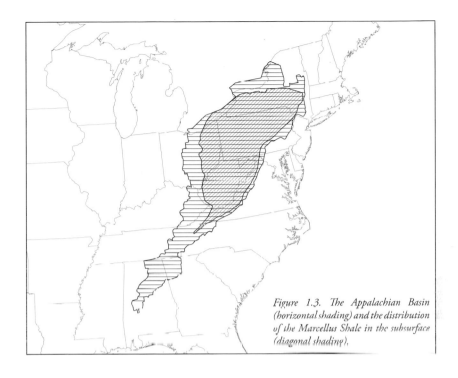

Figure 1.3. The Appalachian Basin (horizontal shading) and the distribution of the Marcellus Shale in the subsurface (diagonal shading).

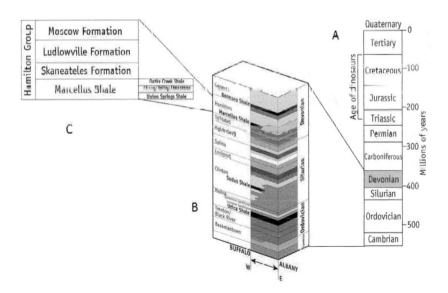

Figure 1.4. (A) Geological time scale, with Devonian Period shaded. (B) Block diagram showing the major units of sedimentary rock that accumulated in central New York State between approximately 500 million and 360 million years ago. Shales that contain significant amounts of natural gas are marked in black. (C) Detailed stratigraphy of the Hamilton Group, including the Marcellus Shale.

7

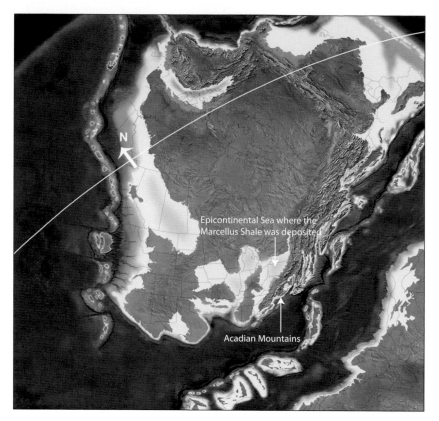

Figure 1.5. A paleogeographic map, showing what North America might have looked like during the middle part of the Devonian Period, approximately 390 million years ago. The curved line represents the Equator. Lighter-colored areas on the continental interior represent shallow epicontinental seas.

margin of the mountains. The deepest part of the sea was located in the eastern part of the basin, near the mountains, gradually becoming shallower to the west. The young Acadian mountains experienced intense erosional forces, and the eroded sediment was carried into the sea to the west. Phytoplankton and other organisms inhabited the surface waters of the sea. When they died and sank to the bottom, they mixed with the sediment that flowed in from the mountain erosion. The sediment and organic material that would become the Marcellus Shale was probably deposited over 2 to 4 million years.

The non-organic components of the Marcellus sediment were mostly fine-grained clay and silt, which together constitute what geologists call "mud." Sedimentary rock that forms from mud is called *shale*. When the mud originally accumulated, it contained lots of pores between the sediment grants. As the mud was compacted under the weight of additional layers of sediment, however, the sedimentary particles became reoriented so that they fit more snugly together, with very small pore spaces between grains and little or no connections between those spaces. The result was a rock with very low *permeability*.

For much of the time that the Marcellus Shale was being deposited, oxygen levels in the water near the sea floor were very low. This was probably because during a period of sea level rise, the deeper parts of the basin experienced poor water circulation from outside the basin and a lack of seasonal vertical mixing in the tropical setting.[3] An increase in phosphorus and nitrogen (from erosion from the land) stimulated the growth of primary producers in the water. As these populations of producers grew, died, and sank to the sea floor, they contributed to both the reduction in oxygen and the accumulation of organic matter.[4] Due to these low levels of oxygen, sea-floor dwelling organisms, like trilobites and brachiopods, could not survive well. The Marcellus Shale is therefore fossil-poor compared to the rock layers above it. There are occasional layers in the Marcellus containing small fossils similar to what might be found in other parts of the Hamilton Group (Figure 1.6), evidence that some life forms were adapted to the somewhat stressful bottom conditions, and even some short spans of time when a broad variety of fossils can be found, indicating occasionally more hospitable conditions with more oxygen. The vast majority of the organic material in the Marcellus thus came not from large bottom-dwelling animals, but from tiny planktonic organisms living near the sea surface.

Figure 1.6. Fossil brachiopods from the Oatka Creek Shale (left, top and bottom) and the Union Springs Shale (right). See Figure Credits for further details.

Over time, more sediment was carried into the basin, burying the Marcellus deposits. Water circulation in the sea also improved, creating a more oxygen-rich environment where decomposition could occur and where trilobites, coral, and other larger animals could live. The Marcellus Shale and the gray shales and siltstones that lie above it make up the Hamilton. The rest of the Hamilton Group is famously fossil-rich and has been studied by paleontologists for more than a century.

WHERE DID THE GAS COME FROM?

The combination of increased organic input and lack of oxygen in bottom waters was crucial to the accumulation of abundant organic matter that would eventually give rise to natural gas in the Marcellus Shale. Organic matter decomposes very slowly when oxygen is very low.[4] The organic matter that sank to the bottom of the sea mixed with the sediment, and as the basin continued to fill over time, this mixture was buried. The undecomposed organic matter, when subjected to the heat and pressure of burial and tectonic forces, eventually was transformed into natural gas.

During this process, the complex carbon-containing molecules in the organic matter were *cracked*, or broken down into simpler, lighter molecules containing only carbon and hydrogen atoms. These are called *hydrocarbons*. Methane (CH_4) is the simplest type of hydrocarbon molecule, with only a single carbon atom, surrounded by four hydrogen atoms. Other hydrocarbons, such as *ethane, propane,* and *butane,* contain two, three, and four carbon atoms, and six, eight, and ten hydrogen atoms, respectively. *Petroleum* ("oil") is a mix of heavier hydrocarbons, meaning hydrocarbons with more carbon atoms. Both oil and gas can be formed by the cracking of organic matter from heat and pressure underground. Oil is usually formed at shallower depths and lower temperatures, whereas natural gas is formed at higher temperatures and deeper in the crust (Figure 1.7).

The geological history of the Marcellus Shale helps explain many of its characteristics (as we will discuss further in Chapter 2). For example, to the east, where the Marcellus is buried relatively deeply, the natural gas found is almost pure methane. In the western part of the formation, other kinds of hydrocarbons can be found in addition to methane. Parts of the Marcellus along its eastern margin (generally in its thickest regions) are called *overmature*, meaning that the gas has started to be burned off by the heat and pressure.

Because of its high organic carbon content (referred to as *total organic carbon* or TOC), the Marcellus Shale is usually dark gray to black in color, in contrast to the light gray limestone below it. Shales of the Hamilton Group above it range from light to dark gray in color. The Marcellus Shale is the only part of the Hamilton Group to produce commercial quantities of natural gas.

The varying gas content of the Marcellus is also connected to its geological history. The most gas-rich portions of the Marcellus are the older Union Springs shale and the younger Oatka Creek shale (see Figure 1.4). Between these layers of shale is the

10

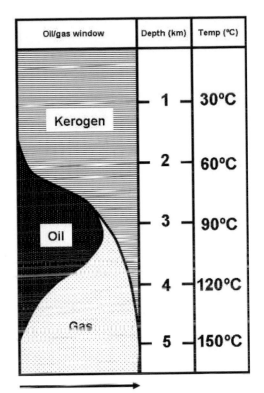

Oil/gas window	Depth (km)	Temp (°C)

1 — 30°C

Kerogen

2 — 60°C

3 — 90°C

Oil

4 — 120°C

Gas

5 — 150°C

Figure 1.7. Diagram showing how the formation of oil and gas depend on temperature and pressure. Kerogen is a rubbery organic material, made of a mixture of organic chemical compounds. It is the product of the initial stages of the alteration of once-living organic material as it is buried and becomes compressed and heated.

hydrocarbon formation

Cherry Valley limestone, which represents a time when oxygen levels (and bottom life) in the basin increased. The organic matter in the limestone decomposed before it could be buried and turned to natural gas. The current organic richness in the Marcellus Shale is a result of the balance between the rate of planktonic organisms and sediment settling to the bottom, and the rate of decomposition of the organic matter.

The TOC of portions of the Marcellus Shale is higher than most rocks—from 1% to 17% by weight.[6] The same sea-level rise associated with low oxygen levels also shifted the shoreline to the east; sediment eroding from the Acadian mountains didn't travel as far west into the basin and so did not dilute the concentration of organic matter. The Marcellus as a whole is thicker in the east (roughly 250 feet or 76 meters) than it is in the west (roughly 50 feet or 15 meters), because of this pattern of sediment input. Somewhere between the eastern part of the basin where sediment input was high, and the western part of the basin, which had little sediment input but also had more oxygen-rich water, is a zone in which the preserved TOC is greatest. In the lowest layer of the Marcellus—the Union Springs shale—that zone is farther east than it is in the highest rocks—the Oatka Creek shale. Thus the combination

11

Figure 1.8. Flame from a natural gas seep under a waterfall at Chestnut Ridge County Park, Erie County, New York.

of subsurface conditions (heat and pressure) and the amount of organic material trapped in the shale during deposition dictates the quantity of natural gas present in the rock today.

NATURAL FRACTURES IN THE MARCELLUS

People first discovered natural gas when they encountered it seeping naturally out of the rock, and such seeps still occur today (Figure 1.8). Natural gas, however, generally has a hard time escaping from shale. This is because shale is not very permeable—that is, gases and fluids do not move easily through it—unless it is fractured. The Marcellus Shale is a naturally fractured rock because of the combination of the quantity of organic matter trapped within it and the historical tectonic activity that occurred in eastern North America. The conversion from organic material to natural gas created pressure in the fluids trapped in the rocks, which helped to create natural *fractures* in the rock, called *joints*.[7] These joints were further propagated by the collision of plates during a mountain-building event that began around 350 million years ago, which geologists call the *Alleghanian Orogeny*. This combination of forces created and spread the majority of the joints in the Marcellus Shale. Because the joints were formed from the same processes, most of the joints in the Marcellus Shale occur in "sets" that run in only two directions (Figure 1.9); one east-northeast and one north-northwest.

12

Figure 1.9. Aerial view of the creek near Taughannock Falls north of Ithaca, New York. Note the joint pattern in the rocks. The two joint sets intersect at roughly 90°, creating a pattern of repeating "corners" in the rock. Above these surface joints, the overlying rock has eroded away, but beneath Earth's surface, the joints are planar cracks that exist within the rock mass. This same jointing pattern is exhibited at depth in the Marcellus Shale.

These naturally-occurring fractures in the Marcellus Shale are not homogeneous. For example, some geologists suggest that the lower part of the Marcellus—the Union Springs shale—which has higher TOC and larger quantities of pyrite than the rest of the Marcellus, could have more jointing. It would thus have a higher natural interconnection of fractures through which gas can move, creating a higher natural gas yield. Because the eastern part of the Marcellus Shale has been subjected to greater tectonic forces, jointing could be more abundant in the east. On the other

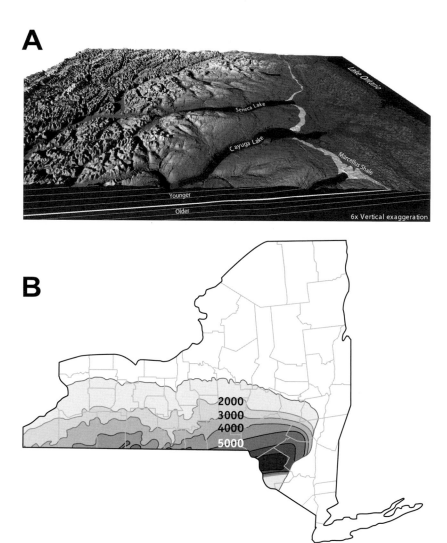

Figure 1.10. (A) Surface of central New York State (north at right, south at left), showing how the Marcellus Shale layer (the irregular light-colored band across the land surface near the northern edge of the Finger Lakes) outcrops at the surface. The Marcellus can also be seen in a south-to-north cross section, tilting slightly toward the south and thus progressively further beneath the surface toward Pennsylvania. The tilt is exaggerated; the actual tilt is no more than 10 degrees. Other layers shown in the cross section are drawn for heuristic purposes. (B) The Marcellus Shale in New York is beneath the surface in most of the southern tier and is exposed near Buffalo, Rochester, and Syracuse. Contour intervals on this map indicate the depth of the Marcellus Shale below the surface.

14

hand, thinner layers within the formation are generally more fractured than thicker layers, and the Marcellus is thinner in the west than it is in the east, so jointing could be more prevalent in the western portion of the Marcellus Shale.[8]

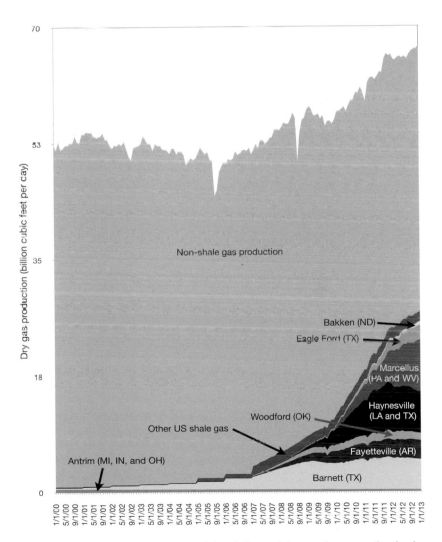

Figure 1.11. Between the beginning of 2000 and the end of 2012, shale gas production grew from less than 2% of U.S. dry gas production to more than 40%. Over that time, the Marcellus Shale became the largest producing shale gas play in the country, providing almost 12% of U.S. dry gas production.

GEOGRAPHY OF THE MARCELLUS SHALE

The Marcellus Shale is the lowest (oldest) unit of the Hamilton Group (Figure 1.4). Beneath it lies the Onondaga Limestone, and above it lies the Skaneateles Formation and the rest of the Hamilton Group. The rock layers below central New York tilt gently southward, and so the Marcellus Shale is deeper underground to the south and shallower to the north, which is why it outcrops at the surface to the north but not the south (Figure 1.10). Of the states underlain by the Marcellus Shale (Figure 1.3), Pennsylvania, Ohio, West Virginia, and New York contain economically recoverable natural gas. The *Appalachian Basin* is the geological term that describes the entire area covered by shallow sea and sediments in which the Marcellus Shale and other rock layers formed.

HOW MUCH GAS IS THERE IN THE MARCELLUS?

Estimates of the amount of natural gas in the Marcellus have been rising for the last 30 years. Before the late 1980s, geologists estimated that the Marcellus contained around 5 trillion cubic feet (tcf) of natural gas. In 1988, that estimate was increased to 26.5 tcf, and in 2008, revised further to 50 tcf. From there, still higher numbers were put forward, reaching as high as 516 tcf. More recently, the U.S. Geological Survey and the U.S. Department of Energy (Energy Information Agency, EIA) have estimated that the Marcellus contains between 85 and 141 tcf of recoverable natural gas.[9] For perspective, total U.S. consumption of natural gas in 2012 was approimately 25.5 tcf.[10] The actual production of natural gas from the Marcellus Shale is presently the largest among shale gas basins in the U.S., producing over 2 tcf/year (Figure 1.11), primarily from Pennsylvania.

Chapter 1 Summary

- The Marcellus Shale was deposited approximately 390 million years ago in a warm, shallow sea with little bottom oxygen. Organic matter accumulated on the sea floor as microscopic organisms that lived near the surface of the water died and were buried. Over time and with great heat and pressure, the organic matter was transformed into natural gas, which is now the object of extraction efforts.

- Tectonic activity created natural fractures (joints) in the Marcellus Shale. These occur in sets, and allow gas to flow through an otherwise impermeable rock. Current natural gas development in the Marcellus creates very large numbers of additional, closely spaced fractures to increase gas flow.

- Today, gas bearing portions of the Marcellus Shale underlie parts of Pennsylvania, New York, West Virginia, and Ohio. The Marcellus contains a very large amount of recoverable natural gas, although the exact amount remains unknown.

Figure 2.1. A waste container on a drill pad being filled with drill cuttings—finely ground rock pieces removed from the well bore during drilling—near Towanda, Pennsylvania.

CHAPTER 2

WHY THE GEOLOGY MATTERS

The geological history of the Marcellus Shale matters because properties of the sediment that was deposited on the bottom of the shallow sea 390 million years ago and intervening events in Earth history have determined the current properties of the rocks. These properties affect both how natural gas is extracted from the Marcellus and the potential environmental risks resulting from that extraction.

For example, the surface waters of the Marcellus Sea were well-oxygenated and richly populated by algae and other plankton, but if the deeper waters had not been oxygen-deficient, the organic matter that settled to the bottom of the sea would have decomposed. Without the heat and pressure provided by the combination of mountain building and the pressure of the overlying sediment eroded from mountains and deposited on top of Marcellus sediment, the undecomposed organic matter would not have become natural gas. Without the subsequent tectonic pressure, the joint sets that drillers exploit to extract that gas would not exist. Similarly, the nature of the sediments affects what naturally-occurring chemicals they contain, as well as how the rocks are treated by drillers, and therefore the environmental consequences of that treatment.

This chapter will discuss the implications of the geological history of the Marcellus Shale for both natural gas exploitation and environmental issues connected with that exploitation.

19

GEOLOGY MAKES THE MARCELLUS "UNCONVENTIONAL"

Recall from Chapter 1 that the Marcellus Shale is a *sedimentary rock* made of the clay, silt, and organic matter that was deposited in a shallow sea. The small, closely packed nature of the sediments of the Marcellus Shale have contributed to its ability to hold onto organic matter and prevent it from being washed away or oxidized by water moving through the sediments. This is why natural gas usually forms in such fine-grained sediments. The grain size of shale, however, means that there is little opportunity for the natural gas to move through the rock. Such a rock is said to have low *permeability*, or to be a *tight* shale.[1] Although gas frequently forms in such shales, it is relatively difficult to extract natural gas from them, compared to more permeable rocks, because the gas cannot be easily drawn through the rock to collecting points.

As discussed in further detail in Chapter 3, in *conventional* exploitation of natural gas, the gas originates in a rock that is high in organic material, which is then subjected to the appropriate degrees of heat and pressure—like the Marcellus Shale. This is called a *source* rock. If geological conditions are right, over millions of years, some of this gas can then migrate—for example, through natural cracks or fractures—to another adjacent layer of rock with greater *permeability*. Because gas can move more easily through such a rock, it is easier to extract it, by drilling a well into the reservoir and releasing or pumping out the gas. If the gas does not migrate into an accessible reservoir, however, it cannot usually be extracted using conventional drilling technology. In the case of the Marcellus Shale, although some gas has migrated to other layers, huge amounts of gas remain trapped in the rock itself. This gas cannot be extracted by the techniques commonly used in more porous gas reservoirs, and *unconventional* methods are therefore required.[2]

Shale gas, such as is contained in the Marcellus, is not the only source of fossil fuel considered to be unconventional. Oil forms in shales as well as gas. Lower, although still substantial, amounts of heat and pressure will transform organic matter into oil, which is comprised of larger hydrocarbons, while higher amounts of heat and pressure transform organic matter into natural gas, formed of smaller molecules. Oil-bearing shales (*oil shales*) are, like gas shales, an unconventional petroleum source. *Tar sands* are another kind of unconventional fossil fuel resource, consisting of very thick, viscous oil found in loosely consolidated sandstone. Natural gas can also be found in association with coal in the form of *coal bed methane* (discussed further in Chapter 6). The common feature of all of these unconventional fossil fuel sources is that their extraction requires unconventional methods, discussed in Chapter 3.

Recall from Chapter 1 that tectonic and other geological forces cause a network of fractures, or joints, to form naturally in the Marcellus Shale. The shale is most permeable along this network of fractures, and they contribute to extraction of natural gas from the rock. The purpose of creating additional, artificial fractures in the shale is to increase permeability still further. To do this most efficiently, drillers try to connect the *well* with as many of the existing natural fractures as possible by drilling in particular directions that intersect the most of these natural fractures.[3]

NATURALLY OCCURRING RADIOACTIVE MATERIAL (NORM)

Radioactivity is present throughout all Earth systems, although the degree of radioactivity varies greatly among different materials. Organic-rich shales are *naturally occurring radioactive material* (NORM), containing relatively high concentrations of certain radionuclides. Under natural conditions, such shales are exposed at the surface primarily in relatively small outcrops of Marcellus, which would release correspondingly small amounts of radioactivity to the environment. In the process of drilling, however, larger quantities of shale can be brought to the surface via drill *cuttings*, which are the fragments of rock displaced from a well during drilling (Figure 2.1), and also in *wastewater* from a well.

Radioactivity is caused by the spontaneous decay of unstable atoms. Atoms are comprised of a nucleus, formed from protons and neutrons, surrounded by electrons. A chemical element is defined by the number of protons in the nucleus, for instance, hydrogen has one proton, helium has two protons, and carbon has six. The number of neutrons present in a nucleus determines the *isotope*. Some isotopes are called *radioisotopes* because they are unstable, meaning they spontaneously decay, or break down into other elements. When radioisotopes decay, they emit particles and energy, which is radioactivity. The new particles that are left after radioactive decay occurs are called the *daughter products* of the original or *parent element*. NORM contains naturally occurring unstable isotopes, which emit radiation when they decay.

Radiation is a health concern because the particles and energy released can damage molecules inside the body. We are exposed to radiation all the time, but at higher levels of chronic exposure, radiation can cause cell damage and lead to cancer or other serious conditions. Death can occur at extremely high levels of acute exposure.

NORM AND THE MARCELLUS SHALE

All rock contains some radioactive material, but the concentrations of isotopes vary in different types of rock. Organic-rich black shales, such as the Marcellus Shale, often contain levels of the radioisotopes uranium-238 (^{238}U), uranium-235 (^{235}U), potassium-40 (^{40}K), and thorium-232 (^{232}Th) that are higher than the concentrations found in less organic-rich gray shales, sandstone, or limestone (Figure 2.2A). This is because in low oxygen conditions ^{238}U and ^{235}U precipitate out of solution and bond to organic matter derived from the organisms that died and settled to the bottom of the sea in which the Marcellus Shale was deposited.[4] ^{40}K occurs commonly in the mineral feldspar and also in numerous clay minerals. ^{232}Th preferentially bonds to clays, which compose much of the sediment on the sea floor.[5] These elements and their daughter products are thus abundant in the Marcellus and remain bound to its clay and organic matter.

Geologists actually use these higher radioactivity readings to identify, map, and measure the thickness of organic-rich shales when they drill test wells (Figure 2.2B).[6]

21

Such radioactivity can be measured with sensitive equipment at outcrops or a detector can be lowered into a well.

The daughter products of ^{40}K (argon-40 or ^{40}Ar, and calcium-40 or ^{40}Ca) are stable isotopes, and not radioactive. ^{238}U, however, decays to radium-226 (^{226}Ra) and ^{232}Th decays to radium-228 (^{228}Ra), and both of these daughter products are *soluble* in water and radioactive. Uranium and thorium, on the other hand, are generally *insoluble*, and more likely to adhere to rock and soil than to be carried along in fluids, both naturally occurring and human-made.

The New York State Department of Environmental Conservation (NYSDEC), for example, considers ^{226}Ra to be the primary radioisotope of concern in shale-gas drilling.[7] When it enters an organism's body, radium is processed in a way that is very similar to how calcium is processed. This causes the radium to accumulate in the body. This *bioaccumulation* is especially common in mineralized tissues within organisms, such as the shells of clams, which are made of calcium carbonate, and the bones of vertebrates (such as fish and humans), which are made of calcium phosphate. The radium atoms accumulated in these tissues will continue to emit radiation from within the body as the radium decays.[8]

Box 2.1. Units of Radioactivity

Radioactivity is measured in different ways. One unit of the amount of radioactivity emitted by a substance is the *curie*, which describes the number of decay events per second in a substance. The higher the number, the more decay events per second, and the more radioactive the substance. The unit used most often in reports cited in this book is the *picocurie per gram* (pCi/g) or *picocurie per liter* (pCi/L), which describes the amount of radioactivity per unit of weight of a solid (*e.g.*, rock) or unit of volume of liquid (*e.g.*, wastewater).[9] A second commonly used unit is the *rem*, which expresses the biological effect of an absorbed dose of gamma radiation. Some of the reports discussed here use *milirems* (mrem) per unit time. A higher value of mrem per unit time means that there is a larger effect of radiation on an exposed person. Federal and State regulations allow up to 100 mrem/year radiation dose to members of the general public from the licensed use of radiation-producing equipment or radioactive materials. This level is adopted as a conservative limit, and is many times below levels demonstrated to cause measurable harmful effects.

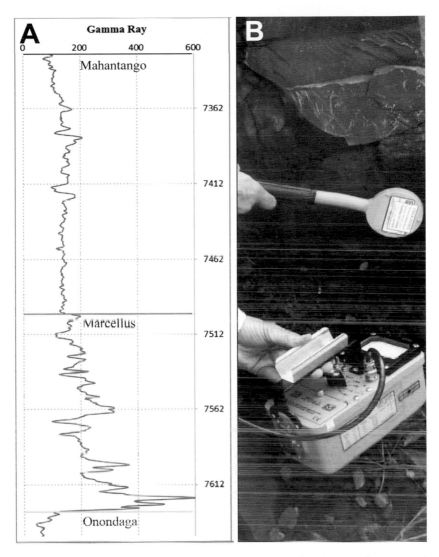

Figure 2.2. (A) A composite gamma-ray log for the Marcellus Shale and overlying Hamilton Group rock layers (in Pennsylvania, all of the Hamilton above the Marcellus is sometimes called the Mahantango Formation). The intensity of gamma rays is a measure of the uranium content of the sediment. (B) A Geiger counter being applied to an outcrop of Union Springs Shale. The level of radioactivity is sufficiently low that the geiger counter only registers it as noticeably different from background level if the detector is held very close to the rock.

Radon-222 (^{222}Rn) is a daughter product of the decay of ^{226}Ra. ^{222}Rn is a gas and is itself radioactive. It can accumulate in closed spaces, like basements of buildings, and is the second leading cause of lung cancer, after cigarette smoke, in the U.S. It is a concern in some areas where houses are built on bedrock with abundant

23

uranium-238.[10] Radon-222 can also accumulate in enclosed spaces in association with gas drilling, for example, near stored drill cuttings and wastewater. It can also be present in the natural gas itself.

Drilling activities can concentrate NORM radionuclides in wastewater and scale, because the radioisotopes ^{226}Ra and ^{228}Ra are water soluble. Cuttings pile up black shale, although radionuclides are not necessarily concentrated relative to Marcellus Shale in natural surface outcrops.[11]

CUTTINGS

When wells are drilled, rock is displaced and brought to the surface in small pieces called *cuttings* (Figure 2.1). The vertical portion of the well will contain cuttings from all of the various formations between the surface and the Marcellus Shale (which would be more than 3,000 feet or 915 meters; see Figure 1.10B) below the surface for much of the area likely to be drilled in New York State). The horizontal portion of the well (see Chapter 3) will pass through the Marcellus Shale for at least several thousand feet, and all of the rock displaced from this portion will be from the Marcellus Shale. NYSDEC estimates that there will be approximately 40% more cuttings generated from a horizontal well than from a vertical well.[12] The actual amount is, of course, dependent upon the length of the horizontal portion of the well bore. Because the Marcellus Shale is on average 20–25 times more radioactive than the rock in surrounding formations, horizontal wells will on average produce more radioactive cuttings than non-horizontal wells through the same rock layers.[13]

NYSDEC has tentatively concluded that Marcellus drill cuttings will not pose a significant risk to human health.[14] Proposed New York drilling regulations nevertheless include a requirement that cuttings be stored on the *well pad* either in a *closed loop tank system*, in which the cuttings are held in containers at all times, or in a pit lined to prevent the cuttings from spreading into the underlying soil or off of the well site. If drilling was done without drilling mud (*i.e.*, by compressed air or lubricated only with water; see Chapter 3), then cuttings can be disposed of onsite. If drilling mud was used, then cuttings would be required to be disposed of in a municipal solid waste facility.[15] Critics of the NYSDEC assessment have expressed concern that even if it is not higher than "background," the radioactivity in cuttings could still be released into the soil surrounding the well pad or solid waste facility, potentially leading to contamination of future crops grown on this land or of wildlife in the years after natural gas development.[16] NORM containing radionuclides that have been concentrated, however, such as in wastewater and scale, would present more risk than NORM as the original rock (such as in cuttings).

WASTEWATER

Wastewater that comes out of the well in the first few days after hydrofracking is similar in composition to the fluid used to fracture the well (see Chapter 3). After this initial period of *flowback*, the water that the well produces, called *produced water* (also referred to as *production brine* or simply *brine*), becomes saltier and includes more of the chemicals found in the Marcellus Shale pore fluids. Experts differ as to how much pore water is in the Marcellus formation. Whether it is *formation water* or altered *fracturing fluid*, the result is the same—more dissolved metals and salts are present. Produced water can continue to flow out of the well at low levels for the entire life of the well, and radionuclide levels in this brine are high. Radioactivity from radium in produced water from Marcellus wells in New York and Pennsylvania has been reported to be 2,460 pCi/L. This is almost double the radium radioactivity in produced water from other formations in the Appalachian Basin. New York radium radioactivity was higher, at 5,490 pCi/L. This is many times the levels allowed by the Environmental Protection Agency (EPA) in either drinking water or industrial effluent.[17]

The risk posed to human health by radionuclides in Marcellus wastewater depends upon how much is released into the surrounding environment. Radionuclides that have not precipitated out of flowback fluid and produced water, but remains dissolved, can be released into soil and ground- or surface waters in the event of a leak or spill. Because radium bioaccumulates, it can affect humans not only through drinking water, but also through plants and animals used for human consumption. Sometimes brine from other rock formations is spread on roads for ice control during the winter and dust control during the summer. Due to the potentially high radium levels, NYSDEC proposes not to allow this practice with Marcellus wastewater until more is known about radionuclide content in brines. For more information on wastewater disposal practices, see Chapter 4.

SCALE

Scale is a mineral deposit (mostly calcium carbonate) that precipitates out of water and adheres to the inside of pipes, heaters, and other drilling equipment (Figure 2.3). The minerals in scale accumulate certain radionuclides. Radium, for example, can react with barium sulfate in scale to precipitate out of the produced water and adhere to equipment. There are no available data on the radionuclide concentrations in scale from the Marcellus Shale; however, measurements of scale from 10 gas wells from other rock formations across New York show maximum ^{226}Ra concentrations of 11 pCi/g and ^{228}Ra concentrations of 3.8 pCi/g, with average concentrations of 1.46 and 0.64 pCi/g.[18] NYSDEC is recommending that pipes and equipment be monitored periodically for radiation associated with scale, to protect workers from excessive radiation exposure and to ensure proper disposal of scale.

VOLATILE ORGANIC COMPOUNDS

Volatile organic compounds (VOCs) are relatively light hydrocarbons that readily evaporate under normal conditions. They can be toxic to humans and sometimes persist in drinking water.[19] Four of these compounds—*benzene, toluene, ethylbenzene, and xylene* (collectively referred to as BTEX compounds)—are of particular concern in Marcellus Shale drilling. These VOCs are found in the produced water that comes to the surface after hydrofracking.

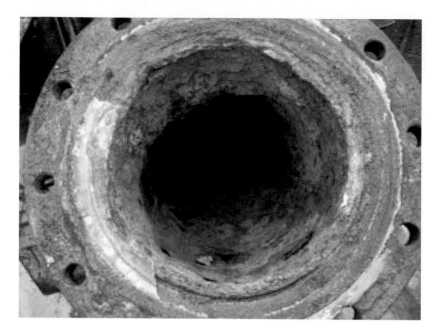

Figure 2.3. Scale, typically in the form of calcium carbonate, can build up in drilling pipes, reducing drilling efficiency and accumulating certain naturally occurring radionuclides.

BTEX compounds represent threats to human health. Benzene is a known carcinogen, and also causes numerous other health problems. For this reason, the EPA has determined that there should be no benzene at all in drinking water, although its accepted maximum level is 5 parts per billion (ppb). Benzene naturally occurs in petroleum, gasoline, and tobacco smoke and is used in the production of plastics and synthetic fabrics. Toluene, ethylbenzene, and xylene are not suspected carcinogens, but prolonged exposure above the levels set by the EPA has been shown to cause liver, kidney, and nervous system damage.[20]

TOTAL DISSOLVED SOLIDS

Large quantities of *salts*, typically measured as *total dissolved solids* (TDS), are found in Marcellus Shale wastewater.[21] These salts are solids dissolved in water that a normal household filter cannot remove. They break apart; for example, table salt (NaCl) breaks down into sodium ions (Na+) and clorine ions (Cl-) when dissolved in water.

Seawater has approximately 35,000 parts per million (ppm) TDS, and drinking (potable) water is defined as having less than 1,000 ppm TDS, although the EPA recommends a maximum concentration of 500 ppm TDS.[22] Measured levels of TDS detected in flowback water from Marcellus wells in Pennsylvania and West Virginia are much higher than those of seawater. One study found a median concentration of 93,200 ppm, another of approximately 157,000 ppm.[23] Maximum TDS levels from these wells can be even higher. The TDS concentration in produced water, and with it the radioactivity, increases over the lifetime of the well.[24]

Although contact with radionuclide-free salts is not directly associated with negative human health effects, changes in environmental TDS concentrations can cause harm to aquatic organisms, especially plants and invertebrate animals such as mollusks and insects. High TDS can also cause buildup of scale, damaging well casings, clogging fractures, and causing NORM to build up in pipes and equipment. As with BTEX and NORM, the high TDS concentration makes it important that Marcellus wastewater is disposed of in ways that involve minimal release to the environment.

INDUCED SEISMICITY

An earthquake (seismic activity) is generated by a sudden movement in the outer layer or crust of the Earth, which releases stress that has built up over time due to tectonic forces (see Chapter 1). This movement most often occurs along pre-existing faults, which are fractures in the crust of the Earth. This, in turn, releases energy that is transmitted by vibrations, known as seismic waves. These seismic waves move through and along the surface of the Earth. The San Andreas Fault System in California is a well-known example of a group of faults along which movement often occurs, triggering earthquakes. Like the San Andreas, most active fault systems are located along the boundaries of the plates that make up the crust and upper mantle of the Earth.

The strength of an earthquake is determined by the amount of energy released by the movement along the fault. Large earthquakes result in ground shaking and movement that can be felt for thousands of miles from the *epicenter*, the point on the Earth's surface directly above the earthquake's origin. Small earthquakes are significantly more common, but are almost never felt, even by the residents living close to epicenters of the earthquakes. These can only be detected by sensitive equipment. The relative size of an earthquake has been historically measured by the *Richter scale*, which expresses the magnitude of an earthquake relative to the size of the recorded seismic waves that travel through the Earth from the epicenter.[25] The Richter scale is logarithmic, which means that a 1-unit increase in magnitude on the scale corresponds to a 10-fold increase in the size of the recorded wave.[26]

New York is far from the current boundaries of the North American plate, but has been near plate boundaries repeatedly during the geological past. As a result, it has a series of fault systems of different ages. Some of these fault systems, like the one underlying the Appalachian Mountains, contain individual faults that can extend for hundreds of miles (Figure 2.4). The densest concentration of faults is on the eastern side of the Appalachian Basin (and eastern margin of the Marcellus Shale). Relatively inactive today, many of these faults originated during the continental plate collisions that formed the supercontinent Pangea approximately 300 million years ago.

27

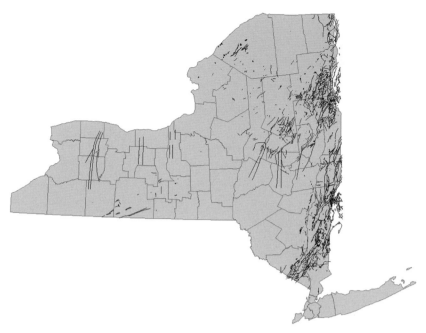

Figure 2.4. The location of active and inactive faults within New York State. Lines denote the location of faults, usually found beneath the surface. Note the high concentration of faults near the eastern state boundary.

Induced seismicity refers to earthquakes triggered by human activity (Figure 2.5). Natural earthquakes occur when two bodies of rock slip suddenly past one another along an existing fracture, or a new fracture is generated by crustal movements. Induced seismicity frequently involves adding lubrication to, or changing the stresses on, old locations of movement beneath the ground. This can be thought of as "reactivating" a location that had formed naturally but in a case of induced seismicity, the sudden energy release would be the result of human actions.

There have been three instances in which seismic events have been confidently linked to hydrofracking in shale. One occurred in Blackpool, England, in 2011, one in Oklahoma in 2011, and the other in northeastern British Columbia in 2009–2011. All three of these events appear to have been caused by the sort of "high-volume" hydrofracking associated with horizontal drilling in gas shales such as the Marcellus. Most of these events were smaller than magnitude 3.0; the largest was magnitude 3.8.[27] To date, there is no instance of a seismic event in New York State or Pennsylvania having been credibly inferred as a result of hydrofracking for natural gas.

What does this mean for the potential for induced seismicity associated with HVHF in the Marcellus Shale? Very small natural earthquakes occur frequently in New York and Pennsylvania, with only a few of them being large enough to be felt. It is clear

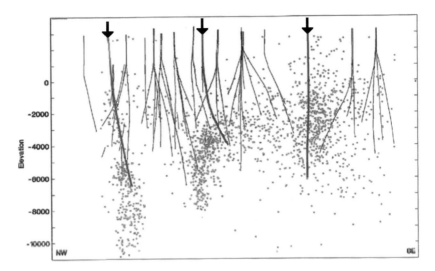

Figure 2.5. Schematic cross section through the Earth's crust, showing the potential connection between injection wastewater wells and induced seismicity. The arrows point to the locations of injection wells, and the other lines show production gas wells. The dots show the location of earthquakes.

that minor earthquakes could be caused by HVHF, but it appears that the risk of such events in the Marcellus is small.

Injection wells (Figure 2.6) make use of deep geological formations, sometimes depleted oil and gas wells, to store large quantities of gases or liquids underground.[28] They are one of the ways currently being used to dispose of wastewater from shale gas drilling from the Marcellus Shale and other formations. The most important objective of an injection well is that the fluid will stay in the formation into which it is being injected, without migrating to other formations. Proponents of injection wells claim that if they are properly sited and executed, underground injection wells are currently the only disposal option that completely prevents wastewater from entering surface and groundwater. There is, however, considerable evidence that injection wells carry significant seismic risks; more about injection wells can be found in Chapter 4.

Injection wells involve pumping billions of gallons of fluid into rock formations, thousands of times more than hydraulically fractured wells for natural gas extraction. High pressures are sustained for weeks at a time for fluid injection, as opposed to hours or days for hydraulic fracturing. High pressure is sustained so that the well can be used over years to dispose of the fluids. This is potentially hazardous, however, because it means that injection wells have a greater potential to cause induced seismicity (see above). For example, *earthquake swarms*—large numbers of very small earthquakes in a restricted geographic area—were caused in central New York as a result of injection wells in Avoca, New York (Steuben County) in 2001 and Dale, New York (Wyoming County) in 1970.[29]

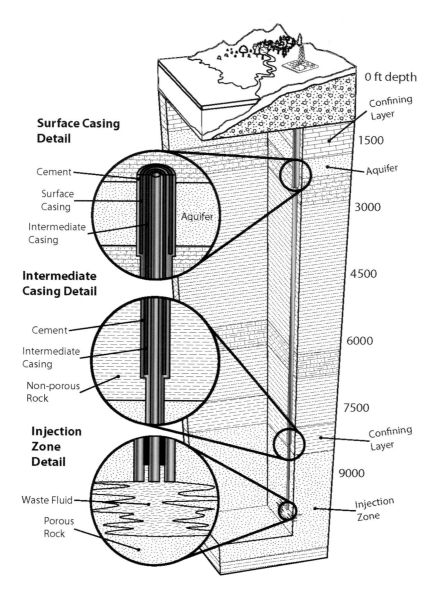

Surface Casing Detail

Cement

Surface Casing

Intermediate Casing

Aquifer

Intermediate Casing Detail

Cement

Intermediate Casing

Non-porous Rock

Injection Zone Detail

Waste Fluid

Porous Rock

0 ft depth

Confining Layer

1500

Aquifer

3000

4500

6000

7500

Confining Layer

9000

Injection Zone

Figure 2.6. Schematic diagram (not to scale) of an injection well, of the type used for the disposal of wastewater from HVHF operations in deep geological formations. Injections wells are typically many thousands of feet deep in rock that is hundreds of millions of years old. Disposal in injection wells is thought to be permanent.

More recently, seismic activity has been seen in other parts of the country as a result of injection wells. Alabama, Arkansas, California, Colorado, Illinois, Louisiana, Mississippi, Nebraska, Nevada, New Mexico, Ohio, Oklahoma, and Texas have all experienced detectable seismic events in connection with injection wells.[30] A study in Texas correlated the occurrence of numerous small earthquakes between 2009 and 2011 with certain injection wells used for fluid disposal from the Barnett Shale.[31] Numerous small earthquakes near Youngstown, Ohio, were linked to an injection well there, which has since been shut down.[32] A magnitude 5.7 earthquake in Arkansas in 2011 was linked to a nearby injection well. Most injection wells operate without seismic incidents, but small earthquakes are a potential consequence of a well that is improperly sited or used. Inadequate information about nearby fault systems or underground stresses, for example, could result in an injection well that causes swarms of small earthquakes.

Chapter 2 Summary

- The geological history of the Marcellus Shale has significant impacts on the natural gas drilling process and environmental issues associated with gas drilling today.

- The Marcellus Shale is considered an unconventional natural gas resource because the gas is distributed throughout the shale instead of migrating into porous rocks and being trapped under impermeable rock layers, and thus gas can be extracted through conventional drilling approaches. The Marcellus Shale has low porosity and permeability.

- Because of its history as an ancient ocean, the Marcellus Shale contains naturally occurring radionuclides and is thus considered naturally occurring radioactive material (NORM). It also contains high levels of salts (total dissolved solids, TDS), and volatile organic compounds (VOCs), some of which can threaten human health and the environment at certain exposures.

- Earthquakes can be induced by subsurface disposal of drilling wastewater, although most scientific studies have concluded that HVHF itself is unlikely to cause significant seismic events.

Figure 3.1. A Marcellus Shale drilling rig outside Towanda, Pennsylvania. A drilling rig stays on site for only the duration of the drilling of the well or wells, and can be assembled or disassembled in the course of a few days. The drilling operation itself lasts several weeks for each well; several wells could be drilled on the same well pad, so the duration that a drilling rig stays on site can vary.

CHAPTER 3

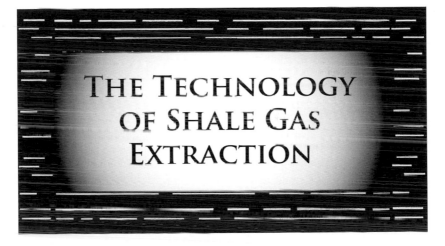

THE TECHNOLOGY OF SHALE GAS EXTRACTION

Methods for extracting and utilizing natural gas have varied greatly over the past 200 years, and continue to evolve today. Indeed, it is the recent combination of two existing technologies that led to the dramatic expansion of activity in the Marcellus and other similar rock layers, in the northeastern U.S. and around the world. In this chapter, we will briefly outline the history of gas development in New York, as well as the history of the technologies (horizontal drilling and hydrofracking) that have recently been combined to access the gas in the Marcellus Shale. We then give a more detailed overview of the current processes of developing a Marcellus well by high-volume hydraulic fracturing.

A SHORT HISTORY OF NATURAL GAS DEVELOPMENT IN NEW YORK

The first recorded human knowledge of natural gas in New York was a seep in what is now Ontario County, which Native Americans showed to French explorers in the 1660s. A century and a half later, in 1825, a gunsmith named William Aaron Hart dug a hole attempting to increase the flow of gas from another natural seep in Fredonia, New York. That hole, dug to 27 feet (8.3 meters) with shovels, then drilled to 70 feet (21 meters), is credited with being the world's first natural gas well. New York was the site of a number of other natural gas "firsts." As early as the late 1820s, Fredonia's streetlights were powered by natural gas. In 1857, Preston Barmor induced artificial fractures in rock to speed the flow of gas for the first time, using not water but a canister of gunpowder. The Fredonia Gas and Light Company—the first natural gas company in the U.S.—was formed in 1858. New York also saw the world's first natural gas pipeline in 1870. Made of pine logs and iron, it stretched 25 miles (40 kilometers) from Bloomfield to Rochester. In 1916, the nation's first natural gas storage facility was created from a depleted gas field south of Buffalo.[1]

Throughout the 1800s and early 1900s, most of the natural gas was used relatively close to where it was produced due to limited transportation technology. After World War II, an extensive national pipeline system to transport natural gas was developed, and by the 1960s, thousands of miles of pipeline had been built across the U.S. With the development of pipelines, natural gas began to be used in ways with which we are familiar today—from home heating and appliances to manufacturing and electricity generation.

Thousands of natural gas wells have been drilled into various formations in New York since the early 1800s.These wells have tapped gas in both geologically older formations—such as the Trenton-Black River from the Ordovician and the Silurian-aged Medina Sandstone—and younger formations, such as the Geneseo and Middlesex shales from the Upper Devonian (Figure 1.4). After depletion of the relatively shallow gas discovered in the 1800s and early 1900s, deeper wells were drilled into reservoirs of gas in sandstones like the Oriskany. By the 1940s, New York State gas production was insufficient to meet local demand. A resurgence of natural gas production in New York occurred in the 1970s and 1980s, however, when hydrofracking in vertical wells came into widespread use.[2]

New York's gas production places it roughly nineteenth among the states that produce natural gas. It is fifteenth in the density of gas wells per square mile, with about one well every 8 square miles (21 square kilometers). (This number is misleading, because most of the wells are clustered in the southern and western parts of the state; see Figure 3.2.) West Virginia and Pennsylvania have the highest gas well densities in the U.S., at just over two wells per square mile, and just less than one well per square mile, respectively.

Despite all of this production, wells in New York produced less than 3% of the gas consumed in the state.[3] In 2011, New York was the the fifth largest consumer of natural gas in the country behind Texas, California, Louisiana, and Florida. Per capita it ranks 29th. New York's natural gas consumption is split into approximately equal thirds among residential use, commercial and industrial use, and electric power generation.[4]

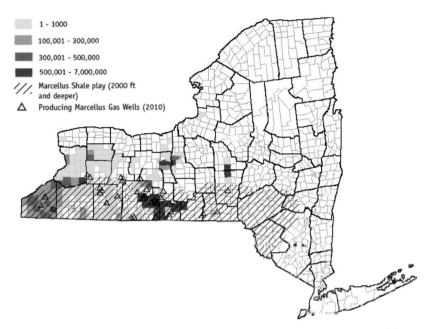

Figure 3.2. Gas production in New York is clustered in the southern and southwestern parts of the state. 2010 gas production in New York State by town (mcf), overlain on the Marcellus gas play and the few currently producing (conventional) Marcellus wells.

CONVENTIONAL VS UNCONVENTIONAL NATURAL GAS DRILLING

As mentioned in Chapter 2, *conventional* natural gas extraction is the combination of processes used in most wells over the past century to extract natural gas from spaces within rocks where natural gas has accumulated, after migrating underground from a source rock. Such porous rocks containing natural gas are called *reservoirs*. Conventional drilling techniques require geologists to locate such reservoirs, and then drill vertically into them to extract the gas. Once these underground "pockets" of gas have been located and drilled into, the gas inside them flows or is pumped into the well and to the surface to be collected.

Unconventional natural gas drilling, at least as this term is usually used with respect to the Marcellus Shale, is a combination of technologies used to extract natural gas from settings in which conventional drilling does not work. This combination of technologies is technically referred to as *slickwater horizontal high-volume hydraulic fracturing* (HVHF), usually shortened to *hydrofracking*, or just *fracking*. Natural gas that remains distributed throughout its source rock, such as in the Marcellus Shale, rather than collecting in subterranean pockets, is an example of an unconventional natural gas resource. Extracting natural gas from this sort of rock requires additional surface area contact between the well and the source rock, which is provided by

35

drilling horizontal wells along the layer of rock, parallel to bedding. It also requires the creation of abundant pathways for the natural gas to flow out of the source rock and into the well, which is done by hydrofracking.

HISTORY OF DIRECTIONAL DRILLING & HYDROFRACKING

Directional drilling is used in both conventional and unconventional natural gas drilling operations. It has long been used in the oil and gas industry when it is difficult or impossible to set up drilling operations directly above a reservoir, such as in an urban area. Directional drilling is the drilling of a well at anything other than a 90-degree angle relative to the surface. One version of directional drilling—*horizontal drilling*—starts with a vertical *well bore* (the hole the well makes under the surface), which is then angled until it is oriented horizontally (Figure 3.3B). From there, the well can be drilled horizontally underground for thousands of feet. Horizontal drilling can provide access to reservoirs that are too thin or compacted to be accessed with conventional vertical wells. The first horizontal well was drilled into the Antrim Shale in Michigan in 1988, and this technology was first used in New York in 1989.[5]

Fracturing source rock to increase gas well production also has a long history. Beginning in the 1860s, the explosive nitroglycerin was used, sometimes illegally, to fracture rocks in shallow wells. The first commercial use of hydraulic fracturing—using water or other fluid to fracture rocks by hydrostatic pressure—occurred in 1947, and the first successful commercial use was in 1949 in Oklahoma and Texas.[6] A variety of different fluids have been used in hydrofracking over the years, including plain water, acid, water and acid combined, gasoline, and even napalm and other gelled fossil fuels.[7] Water is currently the main fracture fluid in Marcellus wells in Pennsylvania, West Virginia, and Ohio, and would likely be in New York as well. Hydrofracking was first combined commercially with horizontal drilling in the Barnett Shale in Texas in the late 1990s. This technique came to the Marcellus Shale in 2004 with the hydrofracking of a well in Washington County, Pennsylvania.[8]

DIFFERENCES BETWEEN HVHF AND CONVENTIONAL DRILLING

Slickwater horizontal high-volume hydraulic fracturing differs from the methods of gas drilling that have previously occurred in New York in several important ways:

Recall that for horizontal drilling, the well bore is drilled vertically, then turns to travel horizontally through the *target formation* (the rock from which gas is being extracted; Figure 3.3B). The portion of the well that is drilled horizontally is called a *lateral*. The lateral allows the well to come into contact with, and therefore fracture, a larger amount of the formation. This is especially important in thinner rock layers, like the Marcellus Shale. Because they tend to be longer, horizontal hydrofracked wells

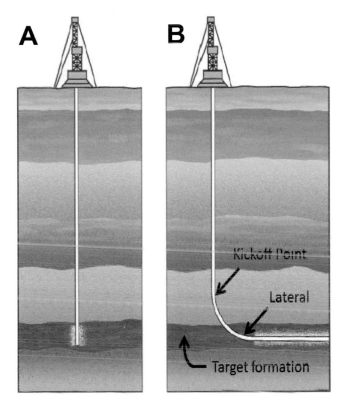

Figure 3.3. A conventional vertical well (A), and an unconventional horizontal well (B). Horizontal drilling allows the well to come into contact with more of the target formation than vertical drilling. Not to scale.

require far more water than it takes to hydrofrack a vertical well—millions of gallons compared to tens or hundreds of thousands of gallons; *high-volume* hydrofracking refers to this large volume of water that is needed. The term *slickwater* refers to the addition of chemicals to the well (Table 3.1), to reduce the friction of the fluid relative to the well bore and the internal friction of the fluid itself, decreasing the amount of energy required at the surface to create enough pressure to fracture the shale thousands of feet underground.

The amount of water and chemicals used in a horizontal well that is hydrofracked is greatly increased (by up to 100-fold) over vertical wells that are hydraulically fractured. Vertical wells typically use 20,000–80,000 gallons of water for hydraulic fracturing, and New York State regulations state that any well fractured with more than 300,000 gallons of water is considered a "high-volume" well.[9] Horizontal Marcellus wells in Pennsylvania use 3–5 million gallons of water per well, with a 2011 average of 4.3 million gallons.[10]

Table 3.1. Chemicals used in hydraulic fracturing.[11]

Chemical	Purpose	Common Additive(s)
Acids	Clear the wellbore of excess cement, make the formation rock easier to break	Hydrochloric acid (HCl), 3% to 28% concentrations
Gels	Increase fracturing fluid viscosity, allowing it to hold more proppant to deliver to the fractures	Guar gum
Cross-linkers	Maintain fracture fluid viscosity at high heat and pressure found at depth	Sodium pervorate and acetic anhydride
Breakers	Break the links created by the gels and the cross-linkers so that the proppant stays in the fractures and more fluid comes back out of the well	Peroxydisulfates
Friction reducers	Reduce the internal friction of the fluid to reduce the amount of pressure that needs to be exerted at the surface to fracture the well	Heavy naptha
Surfactants	Reduce the surface tension of the fluid and increase the amount of water that comes back out of the well	Methanol
Corrosion inhibitors	Reduce the damage to steel casing and other equipment that would be caused by acid	N,n-dimethylforamide
Biocides	Prevent growth of bacteria and other microorganisms in the well bore and fractures	Gluteraldehyde, bleach, DA-ZOMET, and 2,2,-dibromo3-nitrilopropionamide
Clay stabilizers (salts)	Prevent clay in the formation from swelling when the fracture fluid is added	Potassium chloride (KCl)
pH adjusters	Keep the pH of the fluid within the correct range for all of these chemicals to react as needed	Sodium or potassium carbonate

Vertical well operations also differ from horizontal well drilling operations in geographic scale. The well pad for a typical vertical well is smaller than a horizontal well pad—a fraction of an acre up to approximately 3 acres (1.2 hectares) compared to 3–6 acres (1.2–2.4 hectares). The difference is a result of the need for on-site storage for equipment and fluid for hydrofracked wells.

WHY THE SUDDEN INTEREST IN THE MARCELLUS?

As mentioned above, horizontal drilling combined with the combination of chemicals used to do slickwater hydraulic fracturing was successfully used to develop a gas shale in Texas called the Barnett Shale starting in the late 1990s. These technological developments made it possible for natural gas companies to extract natural gas from other tight shales like the Marcellus on a commercial scale. This technology, combined with high natural gas prices and increased estimates of available natural gas in the Marcellus Shale (see Figure 1.10), led to the rapid development of the Marcellus Shale in Pennsylvania starting in 2005.

The Marcellus Shale is also located very close to major population centers, in an area of the country that had a pipeline system already in place. These two factors reduce the cost of getting gas from the well to the customer.

Pennsylvania overlies a larger amount of Marcellus Shale than any other state, and the vast majority of the *fairway* (the region regarded as most commercially viable for gas extraction) is under Pennsylvania. Natural gas companies and land speculators therefore focused most of their early effort on Pennsylvania. The first few years of drilling saw rapid growth of well development. In 2007, 112 Marcellus wells were drilled in Pennsylvania. In 2008, 324 wells were drilled, in 2009 807, in 2010 1,575, and in 2011 1,937.[12] In 2012, the number of unconventional wells in Pennsylvania declined to 1,365.[13] Smaller numbers of wells have been drilled in other states. As of 2012, there have been 14 wells drilled into the Marcellus Shale in Ohio, all concentrated in the easternmost portion of the state.[14] In West Virginia, there were 282 producing horizontal Marcellus wells in 2011.[15]

Since 2008, *wellhead prices* for natural gas have fallen, in part because HVHF dramatically increased the amount of natural gas available for extraction (Figure 3.4). From its peak of $8 per tcf in 2002, the wellhead price of natural gas hovered around $4 per thousand cubic feet (mcf) from 2009 through 2011, and dropped to $2.66 in 2012.

When *wellhead* prices for methane were high, it made economic sense to drill most of the wells in the parts of the Marcellus Shale that exclusively produced this dry gas, and drilling activity focused on these areas. In recent years, an increased supply of methane on the market coupled with warm winters drove wellhead prices down, and the industry has changed strategy. The natural gas found in the eastern section of the Marcellus might be dry, but the Marcellus wells in western Pennsylvania and Ohio produce wet gas. The propane and butane produced along with the methane from these wells can be separated out and sold at higher prices. Natural gas companies have found recently that it is more profitable to concentrate on producing these products while methane prices remain low, and many of the new wells that are drilled into the Marcellus formation are drilled in areas that might produce these substances as well as methane.

The drop in methane prices has also caused the drilling and permitting of new wells to slow down more generally. The portion of the Marcellus fairway that underlies New York is expected to produce the same dry gas that is produced in the northeastern part of the Pennsylvania potion of the fairway, and the pace and scale of Marcellus Shale development in New York would likely follow a trajectory similar to that area.

GETTING MARCELLUS GAS OUT OF THE GROUND

Extracting natural gas from the Marcellus Shale is a complicated, multi-step process (Figure 3.5).

LEASING

Drilling companies must have an agreement with the owner of the land on and under which they intend to drill. This is done in the form of *leases*, with the gas companies paying the landowner some agreed-upon amount of money for access to either the surface of their land, the rock underneath it, or both. Leasing land for gas drilling has many complicating factors that are outside the scope of this book. These factors are tremendously important in determining where wells are drilled and how natural gas resources are developed.[16]

SITING

After a gas company has leased land for drilling, they must choose a site on which to drill. Each well, or each group of wells in the case of a multiwell pad, must have a well pad. A well pad is the area on the ground surface where drilling and hydrofracking takes place. Legally mandated setbacks, which vary from state to state, help determine well pad sites. In some cases, landowners have specified in their leases where on their property a well pad can be placed.

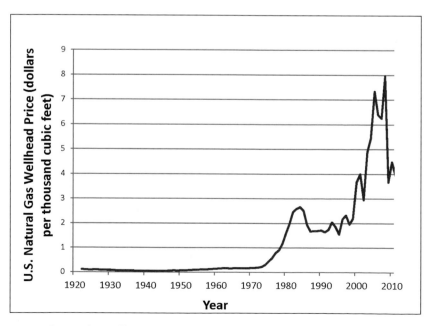

Figure 3.4. Natural gas wellhead prices have varied substantially in the last several years, falling sharply as gas from HVHF wells in shale formations came to market.

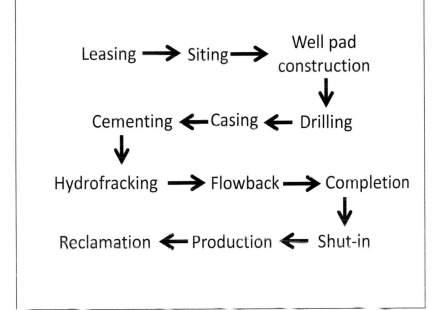

Figure 3.5. Simplified and generalized summary of the stages by which hydrofracked wells are developed.

WELL PAD CONSTRUCTION

Once a site has been chosen for the well pad, but before any drilling takes place, the access roads and well pad must be established. The access roads will be the pathway by which materials and equipment travel to and from a well site, which is often not directly adjacent to a main road. The well pad must be large enough to support all of the equipment needed to drill and hydrofrack a well, or multiple wells in the case of expected drilling patterns in the Marcellus Shale. On average, approximately 8.8 acres (3.6 hectares) are cleared to construct a single well pad for a horizontal Marcellus well in Pennsylvania. This includes approximately 3.1 acres (1.2 hectares) for the well pad itself and approximately 5.7 for the support structures, including access roads (Figure 3.6).[17] NYSDEC estimates that this would be reduced to approximately 5.5 acres (2.2 hectares) when drilling and hydrofracking activities cease, and the well is producing natural gas.[18] The well pad consists of a cleared and leveled patch of land. Topsoil is removed and often stockpiled for reclamation efforts. The ground is leveled, typically lined with a tough fabric known as *geotextile*, then covered with gravel or another substance appropriate for moving large and heavy equipment. The equipment includes the drill apparatus, storage equipment, and office trailers.

Erosion and sedimentation controls are constructed around access roads at well pads, and can include berms, ditches, sediment traps, sumps, or fencing. Berms are raised mounds of soil, often constructed in conjunction with a ditch, that help prevent erosion. Sediment traps help catch eroded soil before it enters nearby surface waters, and silt fences are actual fences designed to trap sediment before it washes offsite. These are the flexible black plastic fences commonly seen at construction sites. All of these measures will reduce, but not eliminate, soil erosion. Stormwater Pollution Prevention Plans, required for each well site, typically include plans for erosion control.

THE DRILL RIG

Oil and gas drilling has changed a great deal since the first oil well was drilled in Pennsylvania in 1859.[19] Since the early 20th century, however, the basic technology has remained the rotary drill rig, which drives a toothed bit on the end of a long hollow pipe (Figures 3.7–3.10). Much of the technology used for conventional wells is also used in horizontal drilling. Special drill bits are used to create different parts of the well bore, and as the well is being drilled, steel casing secured with *cement* is used to isolate the well from the surrounding rock (Figure 3.10).

Figure 3.7 shows a typical drilling rig (oil and gas rigs are generally quite similar to one another). There are two commonly used drive systems used to turn the drill string (the series of pipes used to drive the drill bit, circulate the drilling mud, and

Figure 3.6. Marcellus Shale well pad during drilling operations. On the well pad, typically five or more acres in size during drilling operations, sit the drill rig, temporary offices and housing for workers, and diesel generators.

42

bring the drill cuttings back to the surface)—kelly drives and top drives. A kelly drive (shown in Figure 3.7) uses a motorized rotary table to rotate the kelly bushing—typically a square or hexagonal hole in which the kelly pipe sits. The kelly pipe has the same square or rectangular cross section as the bushing and the drill pipe passes through the kelly pipe. In a top drive system, there is no rotary table and the drive sits atop the pipe. Top drives are more expensive, but allow for both faster and deeper drilling.

The drill rig is a system designed to use pipe, a drill bit, and drilling mud to make a hole down to the target formation. The rig moves massive amounts pipe and drilling mud in the completion of this task. Three pipe sections are connected to make a *stand* of drill pipe. Stands are hoisted up the rig by a block and tackle system, and temporarily stored along the derrick before being connected to the drill bit and then to successive other pipe stands. The set of drill pipe, drill bit, and the drive is known as the *drill string*. The weight and spinning of the drill string drive it into the ground. If the weight is too great, the derrick can bear weight and the flow and composition of the drilling mud can be adjusted to facilitate drilling. The drilling mud system serves multiple purposes, including lubricating and cooling the bit and carrying the drill cuttings back to the surface (Table 3.2).

DRILLING AND CASING

Drillers use different fluids to lubricate the drill bit and carry cuttings back to the surface during drilling. These fluids are called *drilling mud*. Drilling muds have as their base any of a number of fluids (Table 3.2). Water can be used as the base fluid. Sometimes chemicals such as potassium chloride mixed with mineral oil and/or synthetic oil are used. Drillers usually use compressed air or freshwater mixed with mud until the *well bore* has extended beyond the aquifers and has been sealed off from the surrounding rock. This reduces the chance that the drilling muds will come into contact with potable water.[20]

Drilling muds are often recovered, treated, and reused in other wells, especially if getting the mud to and from different well sites is convenient, as it might be if multiple wells were drilled on a single well pad. Compressed air, rather than drilling muds, can be used as a lubricant when there are few *water zones* (rock formations that are saturated with water) between the groundwater and the target formation, or when drilling muds might interfere with the fracturing. (It can be problematic if shale absorbs the water from drilling muds, sloughs off, and clogs the bottom of the well bore; shale can also lose permeability if drilling muds are forced into spaces around the well bore.[21]) Compressed air drilling is a common practice in New York State.[22]

Drilling a well creates cuttings. If fluid, rather than air, has been used to drill the well, then these cuttings are wet and slurry-like (Figure 2.1). If the well has been drilled using air, they will be drier, although they might contain some water from the formations themselves. Cuttings from the Marcellus Shale itself will represent half or more of the total cuttings, because the lateral well legs within the Marcellus are

Figure 3.7 (at right). Components of a typical drilling rig. Gas and oil drilling rigs are generally similar in design. The rig shown here uses a kelly drive. Some rigs, especially those for deeper or longer holes, have a top-drive rather than a kelly drive. The diagram does not include a doghouse—the multipurpose room often connected to the rig at the level of the drill floor.

Key:

(1) mud tank: an open-top container, typically made of square steel tube and steel plate, to store drilling fluid on a drilling rig. They are also called mud pits, because they used to be nothing more than pits dug out of the earth.

(2) shale shakers: components of drilling equipment used in many industries, including coal cleaning, mining, and oil and gas drilling. They are considered to be the first phase of a solids-control system on a drilling rig. They are used to remove large solids (cuttings) from the drilling fluid, more commonly called "mud" due to its similar appearance.

(3) mud pump & suction line: The pump circulates drilling fluid under high pressure (up to 7,500 psi, or 52,000 kPa) down the drill string and back up the annulus. The suction line draws the mud in from the mud tank.

(4) motor or power source: Typically the power on a well pad is provided by large diesel generators that are used to power electric motors essential to much of the operation. For example, motors are central to turning the drill bit and operating the pumps.

(5) vibrating hose: large diameter hose that passes drilling mud from the mud pump into the hoses and drilling pipe on the drilling rig. Like all hoses that transport drilling mud within the rig, the vibrating hose can accommodate very high pressure.

(6) standpipe: a solid metal pipe attached to the side of a drilling rig's derrick that is a part of its drilling mud system. It is used to conduct drilling fluid from the mud pumps to the kelly hose. Plugs, valves, and pressure sensors are found on the rig standpipe.

(7) kelly hose (also known as mud hose or rotary hose): a flexible, steel reinforced, high-pressure hose that connects the standpipe to the kelly (or more specifically to the goose-neck on the swivel above the kelly) and allows free vertical movement of the kelly while facilitating the flow of drilling fluid through the system and down the drill string.

(8) goose-necks: thick, hollow metal elbows that support and provide a downward angle from which the kelly hose hangs.

(9) derrick: the towerlike framework over a well that supports the drill pipe and drilling equipment.

(10) stand (of drill pipe): two or three joints (sections of drill pipe) connected and stood in the derrick vertically, usually while "tripping" pipe. Tripping pipe is the process of sending drill pipe up or down the well.

(11) kelly drive: well-drilling device that uses a section of pipe, typically with four or six sides, which passes through the matching four- or six-sided kelly (mating) bushing and rotary table. This bushing is rotated via the rotary table and thus the pipe and the attached drill string turn while the square or hexagonal pipe is free to slide vertically in the bushing as the bit digs the well deeper. When drilling, the drill bit is attached at the end of the drill string and thus the kelly drive provides the means to turn the bit (assuming that a downhole motor is not being used).

(12) rotary table: mechanical device on the drilling rig that provides rotational force to the drill string to facilitate the process of drilling.

(13) blowout preventer (BOP): a large, specialized valve or similar mechanical device, usually installed redundantly in stacks, to seal, control, and monitor oil and gas wells. Blowout preventers were developed to cope with extreme erratic pressures and uncontrolled flow emanating from the well during drilling. Erratic pressure changes can lead to a potentially catastrophic event known as a blowout.

(14) drill string: column of drill pipe that transmits drilling fluid (via the mud pumps) and torque (via the kelly drive or top drive) to the drill bit. The term is loosely applied to the assembled collection of the drill pipe, tools, and drill bit. The drill string is hollow so that drilling fluid can be pumped down through it and circulated back up the annulus (the void between the drill string and the casing/open hole).

(continued at right)

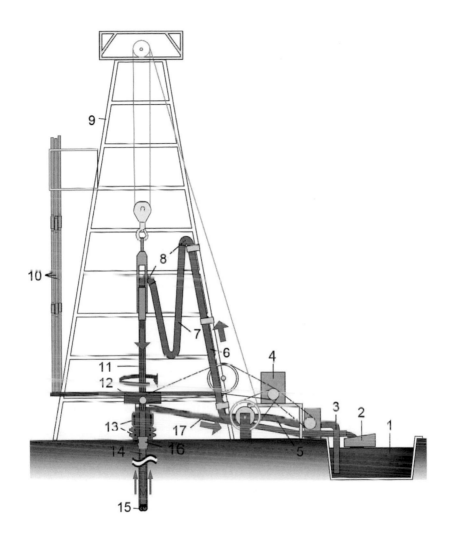

Figure 3.7 (continued).

(15) drill bit: device attached to the end of the drill string that breaks apart, cuts, or crushes the rock formations when drilling a well bore, such as those drilled to extract water, gas, or oil.

(16) casing head (wellhead): simple metal flange, welded or screwed to the top of the casing, which forms part of the wellhead system for the well.

(17) flow line: large diameter pipe (typically a section of casing), connected under the drill floor and extending to the mud tanks, that acts as a return line for the drilling fluid as it comes out of the hole.

Figure 3.8. A fixed cutter drill bit. Different kinds of bits are used for different parts of the operation, and certain bit types are more effective for drilling in different kinds of rock.

in some cases longer than the vertical well length to the Marcellus. This means that the drill cuttings will contain the same minerals and trace elements that are found in the Marcellus Shale. NYSDEC estimates that a well drilled to a depth of 7,000 feet (2,134 meters) with a single horizontal lateral of 4,000 feet (1,219 meters) will produce cuttings totaling 217 cubic yards, or 5,859 cubic feet (166 cubic meters)—enough to fill two to three school busses.[23]

As the well is being drilled, it is lined with steel *casing* to prevent collapse of the hole (Figure 3.11). Casings also prevent drilling fluids and gas from escaping through the sides of the well. Steel casing is inserted into the drilled hole, cemented in place, and then the well is drilled deeper with a slightly smaller drill bit. Then another, slimmer casing is hung in the deeper well hole and cemented in place.[24] Marcellus wells are drilled and cased in multiple stages in a process called a *casing program*.

The first piece of casing, called the *conductor pipe*, has the largest diameter, sometimes as large as 20 inches (51 centimeters).[25] Its primary job is to prevent the collapse of the top of the well. It also prevents the exchange of fluids between the well and nearby shallow water and gas reserves and provides a path for drilling muds. *Blowout*

Figure 3.9. Drill pipe stacked below the rig. The pipe for a single well can total more than 10,000 feet and many tons.

preventers (valves that help regulate erratic pressure changes that can be found while drilling) are attached to this level of casing.[76]

Surface casing is the next level of casing, and is commonly roughly 13¾ inches (35 centimeters) in diameter. Its job is similar to the conductor pipe; it prevents contamination of groundwater by drilling muds and keeps sediment from caving into the well. Intermediate casing, which is typically 9 inches (23 centimeters) in diameter, is added to mitigate potential problems at greater depths, like areas of unusually high pressure due to shallow gas pockets.[27]

In the case of horizontal wells, a special drill bit is used to turn the well bore at an angle at a predetermined depth, referred to as the *kickoff point*. To turn a well fully horizontal takes approximately 1,000 vertical feet (305 meters) of drilling.

The last casing to be inserted into the well is the thinnest in diameter (approximately 5 inches or 13 centimeters) and is called the production casing.[28] It is run through the portion of the well that will be producing natural gas. In the Marcellus, this is the horizontal portion of the well, also called the *lateral* or leg.

Because casing lines the entire well, it must have holes punctured into it to allow a pathway for natural gas into the well. These holes are created by perforation guns that are positioned in the lateral with a wire line or drill pipe and guiding wheels. There are many varieties of *perf guns*, but they all function in a similar way. Once in position, the perf gun shoots small projectiles (called shaped charges), which are essentially armor-piercing bullets, directly into the casing. These charges punch through the steel casing and the cement-filled *annulus*, which is the space between the casing and the drilled well.

Devices called *guiding shoes* on the ends of the casing help the lengths of casing move down the well safely, and a spring-like *centralizer* positions the casing in the center of the well hole. After the casing is complete, it is secured with *cement*. Eight types of cement are classified by the American Petroleum Institute (API) for use in well casings, and the cement chosen is commonly mixed with cement additives that modify its setting time and density. The cement is pumped down the well inside the casing. When it reaches the bottom of the hole, it flows out and back up into the annulus. To ensure that the cement in the casing is pushed fully into the annulus, a *wiper plug* is inserted behind the wet cement to force the cement out of the well bore, clean the inside walls of the casing, and separate the cement from additional

Figure 3.10 (at right). Drilling and casing a well. The process of drilling and casing vertical and horizontal wells is the same in the initial drilling depths. (1) The drill initially bores with a large diameter drill bit to accommodate the conductor casing. In the first several hundred feet of drilling, the bit is typically lubricated with air. (2) After the initial hole is drilled, a steel casing is inserted into the hole, guided by a spring-like "guiding shoe" that positions the casing in the center of the hole. The space between the casing and the rock on the outside of the hole is called the "annulus." (3) Cement is poured into the casing from the surface. It flows to the bottom of the hole and begins to infill the annulus. (4) When enough cement has been poured into the well to line the casing, wiper plugs are inserted into the casing to wipe the inside clean of wet cement. The plugs are pushed down by drilling muds, which are later used to lubricate the drill bit. The cement is allowed to dry. (5–6) The new well hole is now the only void space in the well. A drill is re-inserted into the well where it drills through a layer of cement and into deeper rock. (7) The process of drilling, casing, and cementing the casing is repeated with thinner and thinner casings that are intended to prevent any exchange between fluid flowing through the well and surrounding groundwater sources. The production casing lines the length of the well and is intended to be porous in the region where natural gas is to be extracted (in this diagram, the horizontal portion will undergo small blasts to puncture the steel and allow fracture fluid out and natural gas in).

48

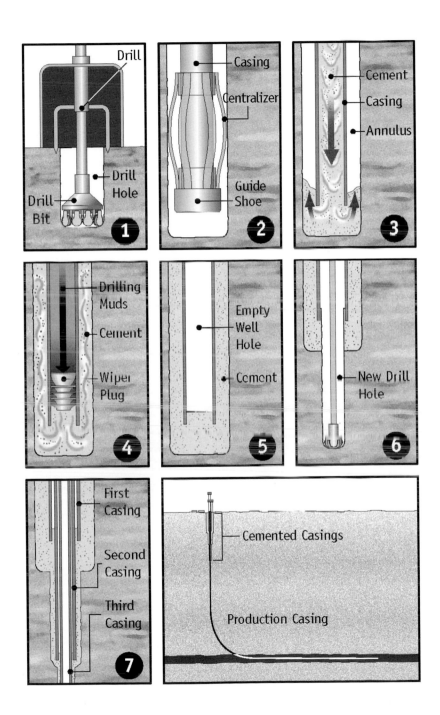

Table 3.2. Chemicals used in drilling fluids. Drilling fluids (also known as drilling mud) is a circulating fluid used during the drilling process to lift cuttings out of the well bore to the surface, to stabilize the borehole, to prevent fluids from the formation from entering the well bore, and to cool and lubricate the drill bit. The chemical makeup of drilling fluids has changed substantially over time, and varies in accordance with the nature of formations being drilled and with changes in technology and regulation.[29]

Base Fluid – material used for lubrication, cooling and to carry cuttings
Water or brine: *Solid particles are suspended in water or brine.*[30]
Potassium chloride/polymer-based with a mineral oil lubricant: *Clay-sized grains within shales can swell in the presence of water in water-based fluids and this can lead to instability within the wellbore. Potassium ions prevent water adsorption of clays, reducing swelling and therefore well instability.*[31]
Oil: *Solid particles are suspended in oil. Petroleum oil, such as diesel fuel, has been used in the past, but would not be permitted under proposed regulation in New York, and is not permitted for drilling in Pennsylvania.*[32]
Synthetic oil: *Solid particles are suspended in oil. Synthetic oil-based muds are described as "food-grade" or "environmentally friendly."*[33]
Gas: *Drill cuttings are removed by high velocity streams of air or natural gas. This is commonly used for drilling above the water table.*

Additive Type	Purpose	Common Additive(s)
Weighting Agent	Controls fluid density.	Barite, sodium chloride.
Clay	Changes viscosity and filtering properties. Clays allow the mud to behave as a non-Newtonian fluid—a substance that behaves as a liquid in some pressure situations and as a solid in others.	Bentonite (a material of clay minerals that swells in the presence of water).
Deflocculent, thinner	Thinning agent that prevents flocculation (clumping of clays, polymers, or other small charged particles); helps in controlling fluid loss.	Iron or calcium lignosul-fonates (by-products of paper manufacturing that are then treated with iron or calcium). Lignite (a type of coal) was once commonly used, but is now little used in the U.S. due to environmental concerns.

drilling muds. After the wiper plug is inserted, drilling mud is pumped into the well to continue to force the cement into lining the outside of the casing wall.[34]

After the well has been completed, a series of pressure tests is run on the well, commonly called *shut ins*. These tests, which usually last 72 hours, assess whether the newly drilled well has been drilled and cased correctly. After these tests, a device known as a "Christmas Tree" is placed on the top of the well at the surface. This device allows gas to be pumped into production pipelines. It also monitors production of natural gas and holds the regulating blowout valve that is designed to control erratic pressures in the well and to seal the well in an emergency.

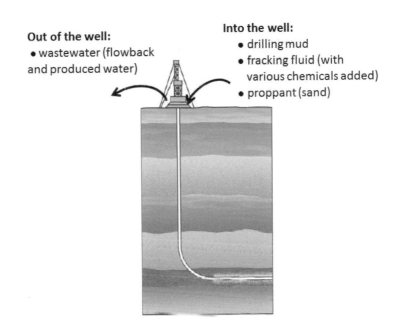

Out of the well:
- wastewater (flowback and produced water)

Into the well:
- drilling mud
- fracking fluid (with various chemicals added)
- proppant (sand)

Figure 3.11. Schematic summary of the fluids added to a typical hydrofracked well, and the fluids that typically come back out.

Because horizontal wells are so much longer than vertical wells, they are drilled by larger pieces of equipment, take more time to drill, and require more hydrofracking fluid to be hydraulically fractured, or stimulated, successfully. During the horizontal drilling process, a far greater amount of rock must be drilled through, which generates more cuttings that must be disposed of. The amount of time taken to complete a horizontal well—and therefore the total local impact of drilling—can also be much greater than the time for a vertical well.

The direction and length of the lateral depends on the local geology, the amount of land available to the driller, and the available technology. Laterals in shale gas wells have commonly been 4,000–5,000 feet (1,219–1,524 meters) in length, and have begun reaching as much as 10,000 feet (3,048 meters), as the limits of the technology are more widely tested. Recall that the directions in which the laterals extend from the vertical part of the well bore are determined by analysis of the current underground stresses and the predicted effects of existing and stimulated fractures.

HYDROFRACKING

Hydrofracking a horizontal well in the Marcellus Shale requires approximately 4 million gallons of water (Figure 4.1), which is mixed with a variety of chemicals and sand (Table 3.1). The chemicals aid the fracture process by keeping the fractures free

51

of bacteria, transporting the sand grains, etc. Sand of various grain-sizes, referred to as *proppant*, hold open the fractures created by this process.

Because the horizontal portion of a Marcellus well is typically at least 4,000–5,000 feet (1,219–1,524 meters) in length, the well is hydrofracked section by section. The section farthest away from the vertical part of the well is fractured first, and then closed off from the remainder of the well. Then the process is repeated with the next section, and so on until the full lateral length of the well has been fractured; during the process, each section is closed off from each other section, as well as the vertical portion of the well bore. A multistage fracture commonly has three or four sections of fracturing, but as lateral lengths of the wells increase, so could the number of stages in the full hydrofracking of a well.

The actual process of fracturing occurs in three phases. First, *fracturing fluid*, consisting of water and chemicals, is injected into the well, creating fractures near the well bore (Table 3.1). Generally, acid precedes the fracturing fluid to clear the well bore of excess cement, to weaken the target rock formation, and/or to mitigate buildup of mineral deposits.[35] If acid is used, a *corrosion inhibitor* is usually included in the fracture fluid so that the steel in the casing is not damaged.[36] The amount of corrosion inhibitor depends upon the type of casing used, and the temperatures at depth in the well. If temperatures are sufficiently high, another chemical, called a *booster*, is added to allow the corrosion inhibitor to work effectively.

Second, more fracturing fluid is mixed with proppant and injected into the well. During this phase, the initial fractures are elongated and the proppant is forced into the fractures to hold them open after the pressure from hydrofracking is released. To be effective, the fluid must be viscous or thick enough to hold and deliver proppant to the fractures rather than letting it settle to the bottom of the well bore, but friction must be reduced so that the fluid can maintain enough speed and pressure while reducing the still considerable amount of force needed at the surface to fracture the rock. A variety of *gels* are therefore used to increase the viscosity of the fluid. At the temperatures and pressures present deep inthe well, these gels can break down, so other additives, called *cross-linkers*, are added. Cross-linkers maintain viscosity even as the heat increases at depth.[37] *Friction reducers*, which give slickwater fracturing its name, reduce the friction of the fracture fluid. This allows the fluid to travel at higher speeds with lower surface pressures.[38]

Still other chemicals, called *surfactants*, reduce surface tension and, like breakers, increase the amount of fracture fluid recovered from the well. The gels added to drilling fluid are largely organic compounds—that is, carbon-containing molecules (not to be confused with pesticide-free farming)—and as such provide an environment in which bacteria can thrive.[39] Bacterial growth can clog fractures and produce metabolic byproducts that can corrode equipment.[40] Chemicals that kill bacteria, called *biocides*, are therefore added to the fracture fluid to inhibit the growth of microorganisms. Salts, called *clay stabilizers*, are generally added to the fracture solution to prevent clay in the target formation from swelling, migrating, and blocking fractures. A *pH adjuster* might also be used to regulate the acidity of the fluid at the correct level for the surfactants, cross-linkers, and friction reducers to interact properly.[41]

Finally, the well is flushed out to remove excess fracturing fluid.[42] For the hydrofracking to be successful, the proppant needs to stay in the fractures, and the gel must break down to release the proppant. If the gel does not break down, chemicals called *breakers* are pumped down the well at the end of the fracture treatment to break down the gels and decrease the viscosity of the fluid. This allows the proppant to stay in the well rather than be carried back up with the flowback fluid, and it also increases the amount of fluid that will flow back out of the well after the fracture treatment.[43] In the Marcellus Shale, only 9–35% of the fracturing fluids return to the surface.[44] Soon after well stimulation, wastewater that returns to the surface after hydrofracking is similar in chemical composition to the fracture fluid itself. This is called *flowback fluid*. Over time, the wastewater takes on more of the chemical characteristics of the Marcellus Shale, notably its salts and radioactive material. The amount of this *production brine* that flows back to the surface decreases over time, but some wells produce small amounts of water throughout the entire lifetime of the well.

Although the fate of the fracturing fluid that remains underground after the Marcellus Shale is fractured is not yet fully understood (see Chapter 4), geologists and engineers hypothesize that the remaining 65–89% of fracturing fluid is trapped in the multiple, tiny fractures due to a combination of capillary action and the swelling of clays.[45]

The characteristics of the target formation determine what specific techniques will be used to extract gas. For instance, the friction reducers used in slickwater fracturing are not necessarily used in coal bed methane wells.[46] Data must be collected for every new region and formation that is developed for gas drilling. The stresses on the rock at the depth of gas extraction and the rock permeability help determine which fluid and propping agent characteristics are needed to fracture wells most effectively. More, larger fractures yield more natural gas produced from the unit, but are costlier to create. It takes time for drillers to develop information on each region, but engineers in charge of each well use existing data to establish the optimum fracture treatment for each well.[47] Should a portion of the well become damaged, or should the well perform beneath the expectations of the company, a portion of the well or the whole well can be hydrofracked again. To what extent this will occur is not yet known, because most wells in the Marcellus region are less than a few years old.

THE GEOLOGY OF HYDRAULIC FRACTURES

To understand how hydraulic fractures could behave in Marcellus Shale natural gas drilling, geologists and engineers must understand the forces acting upon the rock (Figure 3.12). Today in the Appalachian Basin, the biggest force is due to the weight of the overlying rock, which is oriented vertically. The horizontal forces acting on the rocks at depth are due to a variety of processes, such as the tectonics of the North American plate due to spreading at the Mid-Atlantic Ridge, and even minor bending of the plate due moving over irregularities. For example, the largest horizontal force in the Ithaca area today is oriented approximately east-west and the smallest force is approximately north-south.

The outcome of a hydraulic fracturing operation depends on several different factors, including the difference between the largest and smallest forces, the amount of fluid pressure used during the operation, and the pre-existing weaknesses in the rock mass such as old joints, faults, and layering of the sediments. The first thing that usually happens when force is applied to rocks is that movement occurs along the pre-existing weaknesses oriented appropriately to the new force. This could result in further opening of some of them or, especially where there is a significant difference between the greatest and least horizontal force, faults could be reactivated (meaning that they could move). This latter process is the source of "induced seismicity" (discussed in Chapter 2).

If no pre-existing fractures are present in the proper orientation, and the fluid pressure continues to increase, new fractures will eventually be created. If the difference between the greatest and least forces is large, these fractures will be faults—cracks along which movement occurs; if the difference is small, the fractures will be vertical joints, and not experience movement. The joints will be parallel to the plane perpendicular to the smallest force; in Ithaca, for example, this would be a vertical plane oriented east-west. In this case, the most successful horizontal drilling orientation would be in a direction perpendicular to the maximum number of created or reactivated east-west fractures, and thus drillers would want parcels of land leased for drilling to be arranged in a north-south direction.[48]

EVALUATING THE EFFECTIVENESS OF HVHF

Because HVHF occurs beneath Earth's surface, the only way to track fractures resulting from HVHF is to use proxy or indirect evidence, in the form of models, field tests, and monitoring of wells, and incorporating that information into a body of knowledge that grows as more wells are drilled in the region. Although there is consensus on basic fracture patterns likely to occur in the Marcellus Shale as a result of stimulation, the shale is not homogeneous, and different areas within the Marcellus region will react differently to the same hydrofracking treatment.

MODELING

Scientific models are theoretical constructs—often mathematical—that scientists use to figure out how a natural phenomenon behaves. Models use known (or hypothesized) relationships between variables and "plug in" various values for these variables to see what happens. If the result agrees with observations, then scientists have greater confidence that they understand what is going on and why.

Models are used to predict the effectiveness of wells using HVHF in shale gas layers like the Marcellus Shale, and to inform future hydrofracking in nearby wells. These

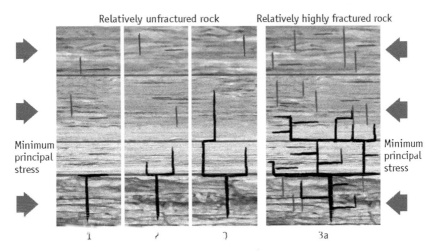

Figure 3.12 Fracture propagation. Scenarios 1, 2, and 3 represent theoretically likely directions of fracture propagation resulting from increasingly higher levels of fracture-inducing force. As force increases in relatively unfractured rock, fractures propagate perpendicular to the direction of maximum principle force. When they encounter a rock layer boundary (which is naturally weaker), the energy forcing the fracture dissipates laterally, making it harder for a fracture to continue across boundaries. In more fractured rock (3a), even with the same pressures as seen in (3), pre-existing fractures can cause energy forcing a fracture to dissipate in other directions. Because of the many boundaries between rock layers and pre-existing fractures in (3a), the fractures propagated are wider and shorter than they would normally be if the same rock was relatively unfractured.

models are based on data gathered in the field, which are imported into computer programs to predict the characteristics of the rock at depth. Field data usually incorporated into HVHF models include seismic and microseismic data, well log data, expected pressures throughout the subsurface, and other rock characteristics. Models predict how fracture fluid (and the associated pressures and fractures already present in the rock) will act during hydrofracking. When measured values differ significantly from the modeled values, the fluids are not behaving in the way the model predicted they would and one or more characteristics of the rock have not been adequately modeled. This can occur if the model itself needs to be revised or if estimates of rock properties where the hydrofracking is done were not accurate. Thus, to understand what is happening in the rock below the surface, modeling is used in concert with field testing to assess the most effective hydrofracking treatment for different regions in the Marcellus Shale.[49]

FIELD TESTS

Common field tests used initially to inform and eventually to confirm fracture propagation models include observing various *well logs* and monitoring fluid injection and pressures in the well during HVHF, among other techniques.[50]

Seismic testing is a technique that can be run on the surface of the Earth, but most techniques require an observational well to be drilled for monitoring purposes. A few field techniques will be discussed below. Seismic testing uses seismic waves, created by "thumping" the ground with heavy weights, to understand the subsurface. The waves travel through the ground, hit different layers of rock, fractured zones, and other variations in density beneath the surface of the Earth, and return to the surface at different times. The waves are recorded and analyzed to create an image of the rock layers beneath the surface. These tests are usually run along roads or other straight paths, and interpreted with other seismic tests to search for existing fractures and other structures in the subsurface that could potentially interact with a hydrofracking treatment. Because seismic testing can be done from Earth's surface, it is sometimes used after HVHF to explore the accuracy of the model of fracturing in predicting actual fracture patterns.

Microseismic testing works in much the same way as seismic testing, but small seismic monitors are shallowly buried or are placed at the surface above the area undergoing hydraulic fracturing. These monitors record small seismic changes and relay them, frequently in real time, to the engineers conducting the hydrofracking treatment. This is the most effective way to visualize the fractures that are created during hydrofracking and to evaluate model effectiveness.[51]

Observation wells are sometimes drilled near a well undergoing HVHF while a region is being established to collect data on the effectiveness of hydrofracking. A similar suite of field tests and observations can be conducted on an observation well to more objectively test the effectiveness of a hydrofracking treatment, the model used to predict the fracture behavior, and other parameters.[52]

WELL COMPLETION

After a well has been hydraulically fractured, there are a number of other steps that must be taken before the well can produce natural gas. Collectively, these steps are known as *completion* of a well. Recall that a horizontal well is fractured in sections, starting with the section farthest from the vertical portion of the well bore, each section sealed off before the next section is fractured. Before gas can be produced from the well, the seals between the sections must be drilled to open them up to the rest of the well. After the seals are broken, flowback fluid is released from the well. Most of the fluid that will flow out of a well will return to the surface within a few days. As the fluid amount decreases, the natural gas will begin to flow from the newly created and expanded fractures into the well bore and to the surface. Once enough natural gas flow is achieved, a separator is put in place and used to remove the wastewater from the flow of gas.[53] The gas that flows out of the well up to this point can either be captured and put into the pipeline, or *flared* off, depending upon the infrastructure available at the site. Measures taken during completion to reduce the amount of natural gas flared or vented to the atmosphere are called *green completion* (AKA *reduced emission completion*).[54] A series of tests are run on the gas to check its chemical composition, then the well is hooked up to gathering lines, which connect to the broader pipeline system to send the natural gas to processing plants and eventually to market.

Production and Reclamation

The most active periods on a well site are the drilling and hydrofracking phases. After the well begins producing natural gas and the gas is being collected, it enters what is called the production phase. Gas production in conventional drilling often lasts years to decades, and for horizontal wells that have been hydrofracked, it might (or might not) be similar. The production phase for an entire shale gas play will certainly extend for decades. In 2013, average daily production of natural gas from Marcellus wells in Pennsylvania is over 2,000 tcf.[55]

Production from an individual well is highest immediately following hydrofracking. After this initial period, natural gas production declines sharply, but wells continue to produce natural gas for years. Sometimes, wells are re-hydrofracked, to increase production. This could happen in the Marcellus Shale. This can be done with water-based hydrofracking fluids, although it can also be done with other fluids, such as acids or carbon dioxide (CO_2).[56] This process is sometimes called a *workover*.

During the production phase, well pads do not need as much storage and equipment on site, and need not take up as much space as when wells are being drilled or hydrofracked. During this period, regulations in Pennsylvania and proposed regulations in New York require that gas extraction companies do partial site restoration, or *reclamation*. This involves removing equipment from the well pad, removing some of the well pad to reduce its footprint, restoring topsoil and vegetation, and ensuring that soil compaction from heavy equipment will be remediated so that plants will grow.[57] In certain designated grassland and forested areas in New York, reclamation requirements would be more stringent and specific.[58] When wells stop producing gas economically, the well must be properly plugged and capped to prevent further gas leakage.

Processing

The natural gas that comes out of the ground through wells must usually undergo some processing before it goes to market. Natural gas is mostly comprised of methane, but can also include hydrogen sulfide and heavier hydrocarbons such as pentane, butane, and propane. These are removed before the gas is used as an energy source. In much of the Marcellus Shale, especially the eastern portions, wells produce what is called dry, sweet gas. When gas is called *dry*, it means that there is almost pure methane being produced from that well, without heavier hydrocarbons like propane and butane. Natural gas that contains these other kinds of hydrocarbons is called *wet*. Gas is called *sweet* when it contains very little to no hydrogen sulfide; otherwise it is called *sour*. Marcellus wells produce natural gas that is mostly methane, and which requires very little processing before it goes to market.

Emerging hydrofracking technologies

Natural gas extraction technology has progressed from shovels in the 1820s to the complicated procedure described in this chapter. Even as the technology associated with unconventional gas drilling in the Marcellus Shale is being refined, newer technologies are also being developed and tested in the hopes of making natural gas extraction more efficient and reducing its environmental impacts.

Water recycling

Water plays an extremely important role in hydrofracking as it is currently practiced. In Chapter 4, the many ways that water interacts with this process will be discussed. One of the recent developments in shale gas extraction is the ability of drilling companies to reuse the flowback fluid from one well in another well after treating it and mixing it with freshwater. This ultimately creates less fluid waste that must be treated and disposed of, and somewhat reduces the amount of water ultimately needed for HVHF. In Pennsylvania, several companies already recycle some portion of their flowback fluid. The extent to which this occurs is dependent upon the infrastructure in place to treat the fluid, the cost of transporting the recycled fluid, among other factors.

Different chemicals

Some drilling companies are investigating alternatives to some of the common hydrofracking additives. These alternatives can be as simple as swapping one chemical additive in the fracture fluid for a less toxic substitute, or as complicated as developing an entirely different fluid system. For example, Haliburton, a company that was initially strongly opposed to the disclosure of chemical additives, has created a chemical formula for hydrofracking called CleanStim, which began undergoing field testing in 2010.[59] CleanStim boasts a formula "made entirely of materials sourced from the food industry."[60] Chesapeake, one of the largest companies currently developing the Marcellus Shale, has a program called GreenFrac, which it says is intended to reduce the number of chemical additives used in their hydrofracking treatments. They claim a 25% reduction thus far. Ecosphere Technologies has successfully used ozone in place of biocides in hydrofracking formulas.[61]

Different base fluids

A few companies are experimenting with the technology used to hydrofrack a formation using non-water hydrofracking fluids. The company Baker Hughes has developed a system that delivers proppant using compressed nitrogen and carbon dioxide. The Canadian company GasFrac is using gelled propane. Early testing suggests that the quantity of gas extractable from an unconventional unit using propane to hydrofrack a well is considerably more than with water-based hydrofracking technology. In principle, the idea behind hydrofracking a well with propane is based on the physical properties of the propane. Surface tension is defined as the ability of a liquid to resist an external force. Because propane has approximately ten times less surface tension than water, frictional forces associated with pushing propane through a well are far lower than when pushing water through a well.[62] Propane is also only one eighth the viscosity of water, and is also less dense.

There are a number of predictable advantages to hydrofracking with propane, including less truck traffic than is currently seen hauling water, fewer chemical additives than are used in hydrofracking, and no hydrofracking wastewater issues. There are, of course, also drawbacks to using liquid propane. Compressing large quantities of propane on a regular basis increases the potential for explosions and fire. Propane itself is a fossil fuel that might need to be produced in larger quantities beyond existing production if it is to be directed to hydrofracking.

Currently, the process of hydrofracking with propane is not widespread, and the intellectual property rights belong to only one company. The initial cost of propane is also much higher than water. As a result, it may take years for widespread industrial use of hydrofracking with propane (or other alternatives) to occur.

REDUCED DIESEL EMISSIONS

Diesel engines are used to power the process of drilling and hydraulic fracturing. This process has large energy requirements, and the *emissions* from these engines are non-trivial. Halliburton has developed a machine that they call SandCastle, a solar-powered device that uses gravity to move proppant around the well pad, rather than a diesel engine. They are also researching ways to initiate fractures with lasers to reduce the diesel required to hydrofrack.[63]

Chapter 3 Summary

- Natural gas has been known to exist in the Appalachian Basin for hundreds of years. New York was home to the nation's first natural gas well, and has been producing gas commercially since the 19th century.

- New natural gas extraction technologies—developed in other shale gas basins, and already being employed in the Marcellus Shale in Pennsylvania, West Virginia, and Ohio—allow gas extraction from shales with low porosity and permeability, like the Marcellus Shale. The new techniques are the combination of horizontal directional drilling, which has been used since the 1980s, and hydraulic fracturing (hydrofracking), which has been used in its current form since the 1960s.

- The purpose of hydrofracking, or stimulating, a well is to increase the permeability of the shale to allow the natural gas to flow into the well bore and up to the surface. This is accomplished by fracturing the rock using a mixture of water and chemicals at high pressure to expand existing fractures and create new ones, and deliver proppant to the fractures to keep them open so natural gas can flow out of the shale.

- The results of well stimulation can be modeled and tracked with field tests to try to ensure effective hydrofracking treatments.

- Wells are completed to remove flowback fluid and start producing natural gas. Production can last for years, even decades.

- A number of new technologies are being developed to address some of the environmental concerns with drilling, but these could be years in development and implementation.

Figure 4.1. *The broad, shallow Reflecting Pool on the National Mall in Washington, DC, holds approximately 4 million gallons, comparable to the amount of water used to fracture one Marcellus HVHF well. (The Reflecting Pool averages 18 inches in depth.)*

CHAPTER 4

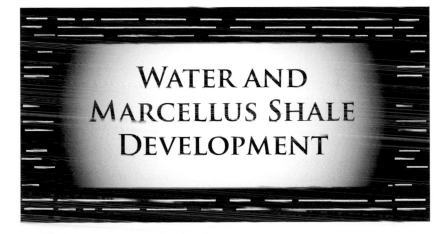

WATER AND MARCELLUS SHALE DEVELOPMENT

More than 20 million people get their water from areas potentially affected by Marcellus Shale development. Water is also an important part of that shale gas development. Water is therefore one of the principal environmental issues associated with extracting gas from the Marcellus Shale (Table 4.1).

In this chapter, we describe the path of water used for Marcellus Shale drilling from source to disposal, the amount of water that this process requires, and how that amount compares to other uses. We also consider the potential for ground and surface water contamination from gas development using HVHF.

USE OF WATER IN MARCELLUS SHALE DEVELOPMENT

Water is used in two primary ways in HVHF: as a lubricant in the well drilling process, and as the main component of the fracture fluid in hydrofracking. It takes about 80,000-100,000 gallons of water to drill a well (conventional or unconventional), an amount that would fill 4-5 school busses.[1] HVHF itself uses far more water, an average of approximately 4 million gallons per well. Water is used as the fluid that

Table 4.1. Potential environmental problems associated with large-scale water use by hydrofracking in the Marcellus Shale.

I. Water supply (withdrawal)
    A. Volume
    B. Source (groundwater vs surface water)
    C. Location
II. Water contamination
    A. Health risks of specific chemicals
    B. The fate of wastewater
    C. The fate of fluids remaining in the ground
    D. Wastewater disposal
    E. Methane migration into groundwater
III. Water transportation

exerts pressure on the shale to fracture it. It also carries the proppant, and it is the delivery mechanism for the other chemicals used in the hydrofracking process.

Human water use is called *consumptive* when the water withdrawn is "evaporated, transpired, incorporated into products or crops, consumed by humans or livestock, or otherwise removed from the immediate water environment."[2] Non-consumptive uses, in contrast, return the water to, or close to, its original environment.

Most energy production is very water-intensive; in the U.S., energy is second only to agriculture in terms of water use. Water is part of the extraction processes for fuels (*e.g.*, mining of fossil fuels, irrigation for biofuels), frequently involved in transportation, and generally required for power production, especially in thermoelectric power plants (those that use heat to create electricity). A coal-fired power plant with a cooling system that withdraws and releases water will consume ten times more water (by weight) than it does coal; thus coal and other thermoelectric plants are typically sited on bodies of water.

WATER USE PER WELL

Generally, between 3 and 5 million gallons of water are used to hydrofrack one horizontal well in the Marcellus Shale.[3] The exact amount of water used in a particular well depends upon a number of factors.

First, the length of the lateral portion of the well determines how much water is used to fracture that well. Conventional vertical wells are also commonly hydrofracked, but they use far less water than horizontal wells—tens to hundreds of thousands of gallons of water rather than millions. They use less water because they come in contact with less of the target formation and they fracture less rock (see Figure 3.3). The amount of water required to hydrofrack an individual horizontal well depends upon the length of the laterals (horizontal portions) of that well (Figure 3.3). It takes between 300,000 and 500,000 gallons of water to fracture each 500 feet (152 meters) of well bore.[4] So, a well with relatively short (*e.g.*, 2,000-foot) laterals might use between 1.2 million and 2 million gallons of water. Laterals in Marcellus wells are commonly 4,000–5,000 feet (1,219–1,524 meters) in length and accordingly use between 3.2 million and 5 million gallons. The length of laterals in the Marcellus Shale continues to increase as the limits of the technology are tested.[5] This would result in the average amount of water used per well increasing over time.

Second, different companies have slightly different procedures and techniques to stimulate wells. They might drill longer or shorter laterals or use different chemical mixtures in the hydrofracking fluid. For instance, Chesapeake Energy, one of the largest operators in Pennsylvania, reports that it uses an average of 5.5 million gallons of water to fracture their wells.[6] In contrast, an analysis of 831 Marcellus wells drilled by multiple companies in Pennsylvania between June 2008 and August 2011 found an average of 4.2 million gallons used per well, with a maximum of 6.1 million gallons per well.[7]

WATER USE REGIONALLY

Estimating total water requirements for Marcellus HVHF requires estimating total number of wells. If, as has been suggested, Marcellus Shale development in Pennsylvania is still early in its development, then the number of wells could increase significantly in the near future.[8] The first four years of drilling in Pennsylvania (2007–2010) saw, respectively, 18, 165, 703, and 1,373 wells. According to industry estimates used by NYSDEC, 2,462 Marcellus wells could be drilled in New York State during a peak development year.[9] NYSDEC estimates the total water use for such a peak year to be 9 billion gallons.[10]

Water can be obtained for use in natural gas drilling from two sources: surface water and groundwater. Surface water is the water found in lakes, streams, and rivers. Groundwater is found below the Earth's surface in the pore spaces within soil and rock, including the water that is found in aquifers that supply potable water. Currently most of the water used for Marcellus Shale drilling is being withdrawn from surface waters. In the Susquehanna River Basin in Pennsylvania between 2008 and 2011, 80% of the water used for Marcellus development came from direct surface water withdrawals—from a stream, river, or lake. The remaining 20% of water used for natural gas drilling came from purchases from public water suppliers, such as municipal water suppliers.[11]

Judgment of how large Marcellus water use is or could be depends in part on what it is compared to. For example, New York State as a whole withdraws approximately 10 billion gallons of freshwater from surface and groundwater each day. That is 3.6 trillion gallons per year. More than 70% of this water is used for cooling in thermoelectric power generation and returned to the watershed (and so is not considered consumptive withdrawal). Of the remaining consumptive withdrawals, approximately 2.6 billion gallons per day are withdrawn for public water supplies and domestic use. The rest is divided among livestock and agricultural uses, mining, and industrial uses.[12] At 9 billion gallons of water used per year, water withdrawn

Table 4.2. Water use per energy produced by various major energy sources in North America. One MMBTU is approximately equivalent to the energy released by burning eight gallons of gasoline. One MWh is slightly more electricity than the average U.S. household uses in one month. Different energy units are used as reflections of the standards within each energy sector.[13]

Energy source	Resource extraction or production (gal/MMBTU)	Processing and transportation (Gal/MMBTU)	Electricity production (gal/MWh)
Solar (photovoltaic)	~ 0	~ 0	~ 0
Concentrating solar power	~ 0	~ 0	20–1,000
Wind	~ 0	0	0
Biofuels	1,155–50,000+*	2–15,000	primarily transportation fuel
Hydroelectric	-	-	4,500†
Geothermal	-	-	0–1,400‡
Natural gas (conventional)	~ 0	0–2§	0–200
Natural gas (shale gas)	0.6–1.8		
Petroleum (conventional, primary-secondary production)	1.4–62**	petroleum processing and transporation impacts vary more broadly than any of the other fuels listed here	primarily transportation fuel
Petroleum [Enhanced Oil Recovery (EOR)]	39–94††		
Oil sands	14–33		
Oil shale	7.2–38		
Coal	1–8††	11–24 (slurry pipeline)	0–500
Uranium/nuclear power	1–6	4–8	0–650

* These figures refer only to irrigation during growing of corn for ethanol and soy for biodiesel, respectively. Cellulosic ethanol (produced from plant waste material, wood, and grass) does not require irrigation, so producing the raw material requires no additional water. Processing the plant material into fuel, however, requires 119 gallons per MMBTU.
† This is the average amount of evaporation per MMBTU produced in the U.S.
‡ Most of the water used for geothermal energy is not potable or fresh.
§ Pipeline transportation requires an additional 1 gallon per MMBTU.
** Primary production requires little water, but constitutes less than 1% of production, whereas nearly 80% of oil wells in the U.S. are in secondary production. This water does not necessarily have to be fresh. EOR accounts for the remaining 20%.
†† For mining and washing.

66

for Marcellus Shale drilling would account for approximately 0.25% of total annual New York freshwater withdrawals, equal to less than 1% of all water withdrawn for drinking and domestic use. Shale gas production and transportation, furthermore, consumes less water per unit of energy produced than development of many other energy sources. If natural gas offsets coal for power production (see Chapter 6), overall water usage for the energy sector could decrease. However, wind and solar photovoltaic are more water-efficient than any fossil fuel or nuclear power (Table 4.2). See more on comparisons of energy sources in Chapter 7.

On the other hand, such freshwater withdrawals over the projected multidecadal lifetime of natural gas production in the Marcellus might not be considered small at all. For example, a recent analysis suggested that surface water availability in all but the largest rivers in the region underlain by the Marcellus Shale is likely inadequate to support the drilling of hundreds of gas production wells per year over the coming decades.[14] This region includes the watersheds that supply water to New York City, and the potential effects of freshwater withdrawals for Marcellus development have therefore been the subject of considerable attention and concern. For example, one projection suggests that the higher end of potential water withdrawal estimates represents one thousand times the amount of water anticipated to be required for expansion of New York City's water supply storage for maintaining supply into the future.[15]

Furthermore, not all water withdrawals have equal impact on watersheds and the overall environment. For example, withdrawing equal amounts of water from a small stream and a larger river would have a much greater impact on the aquatic ecology of the small stream (see Chapter 5).

One way of envisioning this is to consider the amount of time that it takes for the 4.2 million gallons to flow past a specific point on a river. For example, the average flow of the Chenango River (a headwater tributary of the Susquehanna River), at the U.S. Geological Survey monitoring point at Sherburne, New York is 105 cubic feet per second (cfs), or 785.4 gallons per second.[16] At this rate, it would take just under 2.5 hours, capturing all of the water that flowed past, to collect enough water to fracture an average horizontal Marcellus well. In contrast, at the mouth of the Susquehanna River in Conowingo, Maryland, the mean flow is 40,863 cfs, or 305,656 gallons per second. At this rate, it would take just over 14 seconds to collect enough water to fracture a well.

Rivers, of course, do not always flow at the same rates. Seasonal changes in precipitation and snow melt, for example, cause the amount of water flowing through rivers to vary from month to month and year to year. In the northeastern U.S., including New York and Pennsylvania, the months of August, September, and October see the lowest flow rate in rivers.[17] Even when there are no drought conditions, seasonal variation in precipitation makes these months drier. Just as withdrawing water from a smaller river would have greater impact than withdrawing the same amount of water from a larger one, withdrawing water during periods of low flow would have a larger impact than withdrawing the same amount of water in a period of higher flow.

This is why regulators require that withdrawals cease in Pennsylvania during periods of low flow. In the summer of 2011, for example, low flows caused regulators to require industry to stop withdrawing water from 40 locations.[18]

One solution to regulating water withdrawals in the face of varying flow conditions is the use of a *passby flow*, which is an amount of water flow that must be allowed to pass a prescribed point downstream from the point at which a withdrawal for HVHF is occurring.[19] The size of passby flows are determined by the entities that govern withdrawal for each stream or river (see below) from which water will be withdrawn. If weather conditions or amount of water withdrawal cause a stream to fall below its passby flow, withdrawals must cease.

Viewing water requirements for gas drilling as a percentage of water consumption for an entire state can give a very misleading picture of the effects of water withdrawal for drilling. Withdrawals are concentrated in the areas where gas is being extracted, which usually only underlie a fraction of a state (Figure 3.2). They are further concentrated in areas that are within convenient transportation distance to the sites of drilling. This concentration of water withdrawals can strain water resources locally, even while total water requirements for HVHF remain less than 1% or 2% of the total withdrawals for the whole state. In some rural areas in Texas, for example, water withdrawal from groundwater sources for Barnett Shale drilling has reached double-digit percentages of total consumption, although the total use overall for the state remains under 1%.[20] Farther west, water withdrawal for HVHF places even greater demands on already strained resources. In Colorado, 92% of approximately 4,000 wells reported by one study are located in areas classified as having extremely high stress on water resources. In Texas, that number was 47% of the over 11,000 wells included. Pennsylvania had only 2% of 2,000 wells in areas classified as having high stress on water resources, although 70% of its wells are located in areas that have medium to high levels of stress.[21]

The location of water withdrawal along single rivers is also an important factor in determining its effects. As discussed in more detail in Chapter 5, withdrawal of a particular volume of water from the smaller headwaters of a stream or river will have much larger effect than withdrawal of that same volume downstream, where flow is much greater.

WHO CONTROLS WATER WITHDRAWAL?

The location and quantity of water withdrawals are under the auspices of a variety of regulatory agencies and systems, depending upon location.

All of the surface water in New York State occurs in one of 17 major river basins.[22] All of the land that drains into a large river or one of its tributaries is part of that river's basin. A watershed includes all of the land drained by a smaller stream; river basins are composed of watersheds.[23] Nine of the 17 river basins are wholly or partially underlain by the Marcellus Shale (Figure 4.2); five are underlain by the Marcellus

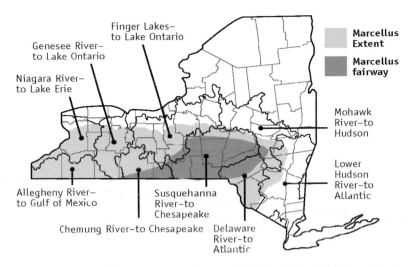

Figure 4.2. *The Marcellus Shale and major river basins in New York. The Marcellus Shale underlies nine river basins in New York State. The Marcellus fairway underlies five basins.*

fairway. The five river basins that contain Marcellus fairway are the Genesee River Basin, the Chemung River Basin, the Seneca-Oneida-Oswego River Basin, the Susquehanna River Basin, and the Delaware River Basin. Although these are counted as separate river basins in New York, the Chemung River Basin is actually part of the Susquehanna River Basin.

Regulations for water withdrawal vary among several of the river basins underlying the Marcellus Shale. This creates the potential for water withdrawal impacts to vary throughout the region as well. Different policies or enforcement standards among the governing entities could cause one or more of these regions to be more severely impacted by water withdrawals than another.

The headwaters of both the Delaware River and the Susquehanna River are in New York, but the majority of the area covered by these river basins is in other states. The Susquehanna River travels through New York, Pennsylvania, and Maryland before emptying into Chesapeake Bay. The Delaware River travels through New York, New Jersey, Pennsylvania, and Delaware before it empties into Delaware Bay. Withdrawals from these river basins are governed not by state environmental agencies, but by multistate regulatory agencies—the Susquehanna River Basin Commission (SRBC) and the Delaware River Basin Commission (DRBC). These organizations govern water withdrawal from their respective river basins in all of the states underlain by the basin. This regulatory structure is designed to treat river basins as entire geological and ecological systems, rather than fragmenting them according to political boundaries.[24] It also allows a single agency to collect flow data in the basin, ensuring that it has adequate knowledge to regulate withdrawals in such a way as to ensure enough flow

69

in the more fragile headwaters as well as downstream, where the cumulative impacts of upstream withdrawals can have serious effects on flow.

The SRBC is responsible for withdrawals of both surface and groundwater within the entire Susquehanna River Basin. In New York, this includes both the Susquehanna and Chemung rivers and their tributaries. Prior to natural gas development in Pennsylvania, withdrawal regulations had required permits only for consumptive withdrawals of over 20,000 gallons per day; since 2008, however, regulations have required a permit for withdrawal of any amount of water from the Susquehanna River Basin, including withdrawals from municipal supplies. The SRBC is responsible for the quantity, although not the quality, of the water; quality is monitored by the individual states.

As of January 2013, the SRBC has approved two sites for surface water withdrawal associated with 13 natural gas wells in New York State. Twelve of the natural gas wells are approved for withdrawals ranging from 100,000 to 150,000 gallons of water, with one approved for 2.1 million gallons.[25] The volume of water required for natural gas development in the Marcellus Shale in New York will obviously increase the amount of water withdrawn and the number of sites approved for withdrawal from river basins to meet the needs of high-volume hydrofracking. The SRBC has developed an interactive map to track the water withdrawal and well sites within the river basin.[26]

The DRBC is responsible for both water quantity and quality within the Delaware River Basin. Proposed revisions to current regulations will require all natural gas water withdrawals to be approved by the DRBC and include rules for siting well pads, access roads, and other activities associated with drilling that must be followed in addition to any state regulations.[27] They have included special provisions for their Special Protection Waters (areas of special ecological or scenic value), which extend from Hancock, New York, to Trenton, New Jersey.

Withdrawals from the Genesee River and Seneca-Oneida-Oswego River basins, which both empty into Lake Ontario, are regulated under the Great Lakes-St. Lawrence River Basin Water Resources Compact. The Finger Lakes, in central New York State, are part of this Compact. A 2011 law requires NYSDEC to approve water withdrawals of over 100,000 gallons in areas, like the Great Lakes-St. Lawrence Basin, that do not fall under a multistate river basin commission.

TRUCKED-IN WATER

Withdrawal sites are not always close to well pads, so water usually must be transported to the various well pads before it can be used for drilling and hydrofracking. This is primarily done via truck. An estimated 500 of the 1,148 truck trips used per well pad (see Chapter 5) are dedicated to water transportation. In some areas, water pipelines have reduced the need for trucks to transport water. This usually occurs when a company has enough pads in an area to construct a large central holding pond to provide water via pipeline to several nearby well pads. Pipes are also sometimes constructed if the water source is particularly close to a well pad. One estimate stated that the number of truck trips to bring water to well pads would be decreased from 500 trips to 60 trips per well pad because of pipeline construction during peak development periods.[28] Extensive truck transport of water adds to the amount of diesel fuel burned, and therefore to increased air pollution caused by natural gas development. It also increases erosion from roads, especially when the roads were not constructed for heavy truck traffic, as is common in much of the Marcellus Shale areas of development. Pipelines, on the other hand, create habitat fragmentation problems similar to those that can be attributed to access roads and natural gas pipelines. These effects are discussed further in Chapter 5.

CHEMICALS ADDED TO HYDROFRACKING WATER

Recall from Chapter 3 that a number of chemicals are mixed with water to create hydrofracking fluid. The overall purpose of these chemicals is to make the fluid able to fracture the rock at depth, deliver proppant to hold open the fractures when the fluid pressure is released, and leave the proppant in the fractures when some of the fluid returns from the well. These chemicals fall into a few broad classes by purpose, as discussed in Chapter 3 (see Table 3.1). Perhaps a dozen or so specific chemicals are used in the hydrofracking of a single well, but hundreds of chemicals have been used in different wells and in different basins.

The total amount of chemicals added to the hydrofracking fluid is small (typically approximately 1%) compared to the total volume of water. But this can add up quickly. In a well using 4.2 million gallons of water for hydrofracking, 1% is 42,000 gallons of added chemicals. Over a 20-year period, the total mass of chemical additives (not including sand proppant) could amount to several hundred tons per day, especially if repeated hydrofracturing is used.[29]

Although some of the chemicals used in hydrofracking—such as guar gum, citrate, and some alcohols—pose no threat to human health, many of the fracture chemicals are harmful, even if only in high concentrations.[30] The identity of these chemicals has been a controversial topic in the debate over HVHF in the Marcellus, in part because companies did not want to release this information, claiming that it was a trade secret. Regulators, emergency responders, health care providers, and residents have therefore not known what exactly was being put into the ground in their areas.[31]

To get some overview of the potential risks posed by these chemicals, we compiled available Material Safety Data Sheets (MSDS) for the individual chemical constituents listed in the 2011 NYSDEC environmental impact statement and the chemicals that were listed as being used in New York in the Endocrine Disruption Exchange (TDEX) database.[32] Between TXEX and the Supplemental Generic Environmental Impact Statement (SGEIS),[33] 334 chemicals were listed (Table 4.3). Of those, MSDS sheets could be located for 187. Most of these MSDSs provide hazard information for the chemicals in much higher concentrations than those likely to be encountered

71

Table 4.3. Analysis of the potential negative human effects of 187 chemicals known to be frequently added to hydrofracking fluid (based on the 2011 rdSGEIS (NYDEC, 2011) and TDEX.

- 88% are eye irritants
- 87% are skin irritants
- 72% are harmful if swallowed
- 68% are respiratory irritants
- 54% are harmful if inhaled
- 50% are harmful if in contact with skin
- 38% can affect the gastrointestinal system
- • 31% have health effects caused by chronic exposure
- 18% affect the brain and nervous system
- 13% cause burns
- 11% affect the kidneys
- 11% affect the liver
- 10% affect the reproductive system
- 10% affect the cardiovascular system
- 9% are mutagens or suspected mutagens
- 9% are carcinogens or suspected carcinogens
- 7% are teratogens or suspected teratogens
- 3% affect the urinary tract
- 1% affect the immune system

as a result of gas drilling operations. Many of them have to be inhaled or come in contact with mucous membranes or eyes before their effects would be felt. The health hazards that they represent are therefore likely to be lower than suggested here, especially any acute effects. That being said, some of the chemicals can be hazardous to humans even at very low concentrations.[34] As one author recently put it, "The mere introduction and usage of hundreds of tons per day, over decades, of such toxic chemical additives in watersheds that provide drinking water to millions of New York City residents, is a significant cause of concern."[35]

WASTEWATER

How much risk these potentially harmful chemicals pose depends in part on what happens to them after drilling and hydrofracking. As discussed in Chapter 3, fluids that come back out of a well after it has been hydrofracked are called *wastewater* (Figure 3.10). Wastewater includes both *flowback fluid,* which comes back out of the well soon after the hydrofracking is complete, and *produced water,* which that flows out of the well later and over the entire lifetime of the well. Flowback fluid and produced water differ in chemical composition. Flowback fluid is similar in composition to, although not exactly the same as, the hydrofracking fluid that is pumped down the well to hydrofrack the rock. In the Marcellus Shale, hydrofracking fluid makes up about 32% of all wastewater produced.[36] Produced water has been in contact with the target formation for much longer than flowback fluid, and therefore contains the salts, heavy metals, and naturally occurring radioactive material present

72

in the shale (see Chapter 2). Produced water makes up the remaining 68% of the wastewater.

The amount of water—both flowback fluid and produced water—that returns to the surface after hydrofracking varies among different formations being drilled, and from well to well within the same formation. This is a result of both the specific characteristics of the target formation and the combination of chemicals used in the fracturing fluid. In Marcellus Shale HVHF drilling, most of the water that is used to stimulate a well will not return to the surface. For example, in Pennsylvania, between 9% and 35% of the hydrofracking fluid returns to the surface over the lifetime of a well, with an average of about 10% returning.[37]

This means that for a 4.2 million gallon well, between 387,000 gallons and 1,505,000 gallons of fluid will return to the surface, an average of approximately 430,000 gallons of wastewater. Typically, approximately 60% of that wastewater will flow out of the well within the first few days after fracturing, before natural gas begins flowing in high volumes. After that, the amount of fluid drops to 2–5% of the total for about two weeks.[38] Wells produce wastewater for longer than this, but the quantities are typically much lower than in this initial period. NYSDEC estimates that after the initial flowback period, between 400 and 3,400 gallons of wastewater will be produced per well per day, depending upon how long the well has been in production.[39]

The ratio of flowback fluid to produced water changes over time as well. The wastewater has a higher percentage of flowback water at first, with its similar chemical

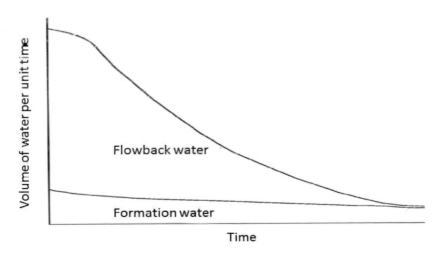

Figure 4.3. The proportion of flowback fluid to produced water over the life of a well. Schematic diagram showing that in the weeks and months after drilling, flowback fluid dominates wastewater. Later in the life of the well, formation water is dominant, thus the chemistry of wastewater changes through time.

composition to hydrofracking fluid. After that, the produced water with its high dissolved solid concentrations dominates (Figure 4.3).

The fracturing fluid that flows back is similar in chemical composition to the fracturing fluid pumped down the well, but it is not identical. This is because chemicals in fracturing fluid can break down, interact with each other, or interact with chemicals in the target formation. These interactions decrease the amount of the original chemicals in the fracture fluid, and also create new chemical compounds not originally present in the fracturing fluid. What specific compounds form in flowback water and how the chemicals interact with the Marcellus are not well understood. Certain chemicals stay in the formation at higher rates than others, thus, relative concentrations in the wastewater change through time.[40]

Water is present to some degree in almost all sedimentary rocks. This water, generally called *formation water*, contains the chemicals naturally present in the rock formation itself. The Marcellus Shale contains heavy metals, certain radionuclides (and is thus naturally occurring radioactive material, NORM), volatile organic compounds (VOCs), and other dissolved solids (primarily salts) (see Chapter 2). Some of the produced water can be formation water that was in the Marcellus Shale before it was drilled and fractured, although experts disagree about how much water is actually present in the Marcellus.[41] If the produced water is not formation water, it is instead hydrofracking fluid that has been in contact with the shale longer than flowback fluid, and has acquired its salt and metal content from the Marcellus Shale. The results for fluid disposal are the same whether or not the produced water is true formation water; the chemical constituents have the potential to harm human health and the environment if they are not disposed of properly (see below).

Marcellus wastewater thus contains heavy metals, naturally occurring radioactive material, volatile organic compounds, and salt, along with the constituents of hydrofracking fluid and the products of their chemical reactions.

HEAVY METALS AND NORM

Marcellus wastewater can contain a number of *heavy metals*, including lead, arsenic, barium, chromium, magnesium, manganese, strontium, and uranium.[42] Heavy metals can harm living things even in low concentrations and can bioaccumulate in organisms and food webs.[43]

Exposure to heavy metals can have various adverse health effects for humans if the exposure exceeds certain thresholds for a long enough period of time. Specific ill effects vary by the type of metal. Lead exposure, for example, can cause brain and nervous system damage, anemia, increased blood pressure, kidney damage, damage to reproductive organs in both men and women, and even death—if the exposure is severe or prolonged enough. The effects of lead are more severe in children than adults.[44] Exposure to arsenic at low levels over a long time can cause skin and nerve damage, gastrointestinal problems, and cancer.[45] Exposure to barium at levels above the Pennsylvania Department of Health (PDOH) and EPA drinking water standards can cause gastrointestinal problems, muscle weakness, and changes in blood pressure.

Chromium exists in several forms and danger from chromium exposure depends upon which form is present. Chromium-3 is an essential element in human health. Chromium-6, on the other hand, is toxic and likely carcinogenic. Manganese is also essential to human health, but too much can harm the nervous system. Strontium is both a heavy metal and a radioactive element (radionuclide). It is absorbed by the body like calcium, and stays in bones, sometimes causing cancers such as leukemia.[46] Uranium is also both a heavy metal and a radionuclide. It can cause kidney damage as well as cancer.[47]

Among all of the radionuclides in Marcellus wastewater, radium is of most concern in wastewater because it is highly soluble. Like strontium, it is also processed by organisms like calcium, and can therefore stay in the body for long periods of time and continue to emit radiation.[48]

VOLATILE ORGANIC COMPOUNDS (VOCS)

Volatile organic compounds (VOCs) are relatively light hydrocarbons (molecules made up of carbon and hydrogen) that readily evaporate. They sometimes persist in drinking water and can be toxic to humans.[49]

BTEX compounds are of particular concern in Marcellus Shale wastewater. As discussed in Chapter 2, these can co-occur with the methane in the parts of the Marcellus Shale that produce wet gas. They are also present in some of the chemical components of hydrofracking fluid. As discussed in Chapter 2, these chemicals also present threats to human health.

TOTAL DISSOLVED SOLIDS (TDS)

As mentioned in Chapter 2, total dissolved solids (TDS) are solids dissolved in water that a normal filter cannot remove. They are mostly salts, which break apart into their constituent ions, for example, table salt (NaCl) breaks down in water into the positively charged sodium ion (Na$^+$) and the negatively charged clorine ion (Cl$^-$). TDS concentrations in wastewater from the Marcellus Shale are very high, and the concentration increases over the life of the well. The median concentration in Marcellus wastewater tested in Pennsylvania, for example, was between two and five times that of seawater; maximum TDS levels from these wells are much higher.[50] This high TDS concentration could negatively impact aquatic ecosystems (see Chapter 5) if allowed to contaminate surficial waters.

The Fate of Drilling Water
Remaining in the Ground

The behavior and fate of the fluids that remain in the ground after drilling are still incompletely understood.[51] As discussed in Chapters 2 and 3, all sedimentary rocks, including those adjacent to the Marcellus Shale, contain naturally-occurring fractures or joints, and it is possible that drilling water remaining in the ground could migrate via these fractures. Hydraulic fracturing in horizontal drilling is only done well below the fresh groundwater table, and at these depths the largest compressional force is vertical (see discussion in Chapter 3). Therefore, only vertical joints or highly inclined fractures will be reactivated or created by HVHF. Theoretically, fluids could leak outside of the intended fracturing zone along pre-existing fractures that cut several units, but if this were to occur, the fluid pressure would dissipate, and so the ability of the fluid to hold open pre-existing fractures would also diminish, inhibiting further migration. This is the main reason that many geologists and engineers think that it is unlikely that hydrofracking can have significant impacts on shallow aquifers or surface waters.[52]

In a study conducted in Pennsylvania, some locations had brine in the groundwater that contained a composition of isotopes, indicating that its likely source of the brine was the Marcellus Shale.[53] These areas were not near gas drilling, however, and the likely cause was not migration due to gas drilling, but rather higher connectivity from natural fractures that connect the deep Marcellus Shale to groundwater sources near the surface. Such fluid migration would have taken many thousands of years through these fractures, and the study did not suggest that it happened recently.[54] The authors argued that this indicated that some areas would be more prone to fluid migration than others, if the natural fractures already connect deep formations to shallow formations.[55]

Nevertheless, different models of fluid migration through fractures underground have produced disparate results. One study claimed that HVHF could reduce the time that it takes for fluid to migrate from the Marcellus Shale to shallower formations to tens or hundreds of years.[56] Based on older data, NYSDEC estimated the risk of fluid contamination from hydraulic fractures places the timeframe in thousands of years, even with pressure from hydrofracking sustained over the entire time. This is likely to be an area of active additional research in the near future.

Wastewater Disposal

What to do with the large quantities of wastewater is a major challenge for operators of HVHF operations, in the Marcellus and elsewhere. In the early years of Marcellus gas development in Pennsylvania, stories were reported (some verified but others not) of companies or individuals working for companies disposing of wastewater illegally, for example dumping it into streams, rivers, or at the surface (see below).

Wastewater from HVHF can be legally disposed of in one of three ways: recycling; treatment in an approved wastewater treatment plant (in or out of state); or treatment in an out-of-state treatment plant, or placement in an underground injection well.[57]

Before disposal, however, wastewater must be stored onsite, at least temporarily. Although other states have allowed drillers to store the wastewater in lined open pits, regulations proposed by NYSDEC require that wastewater be stored in closed tanks instead of pits. Storing water in closed tanks provides a number of environmental benefits over open pits. First, leaks can be more easily detected and fixed in above-ground tanks than they can be in a pit. Second, storage in tanks poses less of a threat to local wildlife and livestock. The USDA has quarantined cows in Pennsylvania, for example, after they might have ingested hay from damp ground contaminated by a leak in a nearby wastewater pit.[58] There have been additional reports of cattle dying in Louisiana and Pennsylvania after ingesting substances near drilling rigs. Although tanks do not eliminate the potential for such contamination at drill sites, they do significantly reduce these risks. Third, storing flowback and produced water in open pits allows VOCs from formation water to escape, even if none of the water itself leaks. VOCs by definition evaporate from liquids under normal ambient temperature and pressure. Such evaporation of VOCs is of concern because they react with other chemicals in the air to produce ground-level *ozone*, an important air quality problem.[59]

Figure 4.4. The Abington Regional Waste Water Treatment Plant in Chinchilla, Pennsylvania, treats primarily sewage and sewage overflow during periods of heavy precipitation. Like most such plants, it does not accept wastewater from HVHF operations. Treated water drains to Leggetts Creek on its way to the Lackawanna and Susquehanna rivers and eventually to Chesapeake Bay.

Wastewater recycling means that well operators use flowback fluid from one well to hydrofrack another well after it has been treated in some way.[60] This treatment can happen in a number of ways. It can mean the simple dilution of flowback water with freshwater, or it can be a more complicated process in which certain chemicals are removed from the flowback water. For example, recycling processes can target chlorides, calcium, suspended solids, oil and other soluble organics, bacteria, barium, carbonates, and sulfates when they treat wastewater for reuse.[61]

Estimates of exactly how much wastewater is being recycled in Pennsylvania vary widely. The SRBC reported that, between June 2008 and June 2011, drillers reused 14.5% of the water withdrawn for Marcellus wells: 311 million gallons of water were recycled of the 2.14 billion withdrawn from the Susquehanna River Basin. One recent estimate from Pennsylvania Department of Environmental Protection (PDEP) suggests that as much as 75% of flowback water is currently being reused in another well.[62] Despite the high percentage of flowback being recycled, it only accounts for 10% of the water used to stimulate wells; the other 90% comes from freshwater withdrawals.[63] Another recent report put the total amount of recycled Marcellus wastewater at 40%.[64]

Factors that influence the amount of water that is recycled include the distance and time to the next hydrofracking treatment, the cost of implementing treatment systems, the amount of local freshwater, how much flowback water is recovered from the well and what is in the flowback water, and the local environment, topography, state regulations, and population density. Wastewater recycling reduces both the amount of freshwater that will need to be withdrawn in a region and the amount of wastewater that must ultimately be disposed of.

Even with intensive recycling, some wastewater must eventually be disposed of, either by treatment in such a way that it can be released safely back into the environment, or permanent removal from the water cycle by injection into a storage well. Proposed NYSDEC regulations will require a formal fluid disposal plan for each drilling site. Such plans must include information on both transportation of the fluid and the method of ultimate disposal.[65]

INJECTION WELLS

Most produced water from oil and gas production in the United States is disposed of in injection wells.[66] To be effective, injection wells should isolate their contents from both groundwater sources and other rock layers. Most injection wells dedicated to oil and gas operations are located in Texas, Oklahoma, Kansas, and California. Creating an injection well in New York would require permitting by NYSDEC and the EPA. The use of injection wells for disposal of brine and industrial waste is more common in the western U.S. than the eastern U.S., both because of differences in regulatory systems and because the geology of the eastern U.S. makes it more difficult to find suitable sites. New York currently has six injection wells, and Pennsylvania has seven.[67] Pennsylvania's injection wells are near capacity, and the wastewater that has already been disposed of in injection wells has gone to wells in Ohio, with a small amount going to wells in West Virginia.[68]

Injection wells are commonly cited by industry as the only disposal option currently available that isolates wastewater completely and permanently, preventing it and its constituent chemicals from ever entering surface or groundwater. Wastewater slated for injection-well disposal, furthermore, requires less treatment than water that is disposed of in other ways. These two factors would seem to be strong advantages to injection wells as a method of wastewater disposal for Marcellus drilling.

There are also, however, notable disadvantages to disposing of wastewater this way. First, induced seismic events have been associated with disposal wells of this type (see Chapter 2 for a discussion on induced seismicity). Second, currently wastewater disposed of in such wells must be transported over long distances to the disposal site, likely by truck. This would increase the risk of spills and leaks, and contribute to diesel emissions associated with drilling. Third, this would remove water from the water cycle permanently. Wastewater treatment has the potential to replace at least some of the freshwater removed for hydrofracking, but disposal in an injection well does not.

WASTEWATER TREATMENT

Of the more than 600 publicly owned treatment works (POTWs) in New York State, 115 are capable of accepting *industrial wastewater*—a prerequisite under proposed regulations for accepting and treating Marcellus Shale wastewater (Figure 4 4)[69] None of these facilities, however, can accept Marcellus Shale wastewater without modification of their permits, which depend upon testing their facilities' capacity to treat the water effectively "without disrupting their current program" (i.e., they might not have the physical capacity to handle it in addition to also all of the waste that they currently treat). Because of this, New York might not have the existing infrastructure at POTWs to handle the chemicals, NORM, and TDS, in volumes of water required for drilling.

NYSDEC estimates the amount of wastewater produced from a well to be between 400 and 3,400 gallons per day. If a high-production year of drilling sees 2,462 wells per year (the highest estimate used by the NYSDEC), between 984,800 and 8,370,800 gallons of wastewater could be produced per day. A rough estimate by NYSDEC puts the maximum amount of water that can be accepted at all current wastewater treatment facilities "within the approximate area of shale development in New York" at 300 million gallons per day. NYSDEC estimates, however, that the total amount of Marcellus wastewater that is treatable with existing infrastructure to be "much less" than 1 million gallons per day.[70]

One of the limiting factors for how much water these facilities can accept is their ability to dilute the concentration of TDS present in their discharge water—the water that is released from the facility after treatment—to 500 ppm, the amount in potable water. Existing wastewater treatment plants might not have the capacity to sufficiently reduce the TDS levels.

Another factor that limits how much water a facility can treat is the amount of radium in the wastewater. NYSDEC proposes to cap the maximum concentration of radium that treatment plants can accept in wastewater at 15 pCi per liter to ensure that wastewater treatment plant sludge does not become too radioactive for disposal.[71] At least some of this wastewater has radium concentrations too high to be treated by these plants.

If in fact current municipal capacity to treat wastewater in New York is insufficient, NYSDEC has left open the possibility of using private wastewater treatment plants. They would be held to the same permitting standards for operation and discharge of treated water. Additionally, NYSDEC proposes to allow wastewater to be shipped to other states, including 11 sites in Pennsylvania and West Virginia. The water would be subject to the receiving states regulations rather than New York's, and it is possible that these treatment facilities would refuse the wastewater.[72]

A series of articles in *The New York Times* in February and March 2011 detailed how Pennsylvania municipal water treatment plants were taking in Marcellus wastewater that they could not fully treat.[73] NORMs were of special concern, because regulations in Pennsylvania allow drinking water plant operators to test for NORM only once every 6–9 years. It was also discovered that some wastewater treatment plants located upstream from drinking water plants were discharging water with levels of NORM and benzene much higher than the acceptable drinking water levels. PDEP asked drilling companies to (voluntarily) stop bringing wastewater to be treated at these plants, and a law was passed by the Pennsylvania legislature later in 2011, ending the practice.[74] PDEP later released the results of water testing for untreated water going into the drinking water plants, which showed that levels of radium and radiation were at or below background levels and below EPA drinking water maximum allowable levels.

POTENTIAL FOR WATER CONTAMINATION

The possibility that ground or surface water could be contaminated as a result of HVHF in the Marcellus Shale is probably the single greatest point of environmental concern, and continues to drive most of the opposition to drilling. Such contamination might occur in any of several ways: (1) fluids remaining in the ground could migrate through fractures; (2) spills at the surface; or (3) methane itself contaminating groundwater by migration.

CONTAMINATION FROM FLUIDS IN THE GROUND

The aquifers that provide potable groundwater to wells in New York and Pennsylvania vary in depth down to roughly 500 feet (150 meters) below the surface. This is far above the shallowest level of the Marcellus Shale, which is the target of HVHF drilling.

Thus, the only ways that drilling and/or hydrofracking fluids could contaminate shallow aquifers would be if either (a) the fractures created by well stimulation could extend far enough above the Marcellus to reach drinking water sources, or (b) fractures created by hydrofracking could connect with existing fracture networks to provide a path for the fluids to travel to drinking water sources.

There are some basic geological reasons for thinking that such contamination is unlikely. As discussed previously, at the depths at which the Marcellus Shale is found, the largest compressional forces are vertical, and therefore only vertical joints or inclined shearing fractures will be reactivated or created. Although it is theoretically possible that such fractures could pass from one layer of rock into another, this would be highly unusual unless the layers had almost identical physical properties. If, however, such a fracture were to occur, and fluids did leak outside of the intended fracturing zone along it, they would likely not go far, because the fluid pressure would decrease as the fluids moved, and so would their ability to hold open the fractures, inhibiting further movement.

Most, if not all, documented reports of groundwater contamination during shale gas drilling are, therefore, likely related to problems of the shallow casing of the wells, rather than to the fractures created by the hydrofracking (see below).

On July 20, 2013, the Department of Energy's National Energy Technology Laboratory (NETL) released a very brief statement on their ongoing study in western Pennsylvania aimed at determining whether hydraulic fracturing actually does contaminate groundwater. According to the statement, preliminary analysis has not found any evidence of contamination. It also noted, however, that the results were preliminary, and that a final report on the results is expected by the end of 2013.[75]

LEAKS AND SPILLS

Water contamination can also result from surface spills or leaks of drilling fluids, hydrofracking fluids, or wastewater. According to data collected by the environmental group Toxics Targeting in 2009, there have been two reported commercial vehicle accidents associated with the natural gas industry leading to spills in New York since 1986.[76] There have also been truck accidents with vehicles carrying Marcellus drilling materials and waste in Pennsylvania, although an exact number is not available. In just three days of heavy enforcement in the summer of 2010, Pennsylvania state police issued 669 citations and 818 written warnings to trucks carrying Marcellus wastewater.[77]

Well pads can also be sites of spills and leaks of drilling and/or hydrofracking fluids. One recent study found that, among 43 highly-publicized accidents, 33% were onsite spills.[78] Such accidents can be caused by improper storage or handling of materials, or unforeseen environmental causes. This number is likely to be an underestimate, however, because it included only incidents reported by the media. Improper storage and handling of materials can also contribute to spills at any step in the process. A Pennsylvania Land Trust analysis of PDEP citations of Marcellus drillers found a total of 1,614 violations of drilling regulations in Pennsylvania Marcellus wells between 2008 and 2010, 1,056 of which were judged likely to impact the environment. These include violations that could contribute to a higher likelihood of spills, including 155 "discharge of industrial waste" violations, which means that drilling waste was released onto the ground or into streams.[79]

A more recent assessment analyzed 1,144 environmental violations issued by PDEP to Marcellus drillers. These represented 845 distinct incidents among 3,533 wells between 2008 and August 2011 that resulted in pollution of the environment. Of these, 9 (1%) were classified as "major land spills," 149 (18%) were classified as "minor land spills," 8 (1%) were classified as "major water contamination events," and 258 (31%) were classified as "minor water contamination events."[80] The study found that the percent of incidents per well decreased over the course of the three years in conjunction with changes in regulation and inspection by PDEP.

In addition to human error, certain environmental conditions can contribute to spills and leaks on well sites. Storms and flooding can wreak havoc on fluid storage systems and cause spills. NYSDEC will require comprehensive site-specific Stormwater Pollution Prevention Plans (SWPPP) for each well site. These would provide plans to prevent stormwater runoff from adversely impacting the environment at all stages in the construction and drilling process.

Spills not only contaminate ground or surface waters and bring humans into contact with the harmful substances found in wastewater; they can also damage local vegetation. A study performed in the Fernow Experimental Forest in West Virginia, for example, found that when untreated hydrofracking fluid was spread over 0.20 hectares (less than 0.001 mi²), almost all ground vegetation died within two days, trees started dropping foliage within ten days, and 56% of the trees in that area were dead after two years.[81] Leaks of hydrofracking fluid can also damage other parts of the ecosystem. For example, freshwater mussel populations, many of which are already seriously reduced as a result of human activity, can be particularly vulnerable. These filter feeders are particularly susceptible to toxins in the water.[82] Besides acute toxicity, changes in pH or salinity from hydrofracking fluid or wastewater can affect other plants, animals, and microorganisms that inhabit streams and other surface waters.[83] (See Chapter 5 for further discussion of the effects of Marcellus natural gas development on ecosystems.)

METHANE MIGRATION

The lands overlying the Appalachian Basin have long been known to have some naturally occurring methane in ground and surface waters. How can this methane be distinguished from methane that might be moving through the rock as a result of natural gas development? As discussed further in Chapter 6, natural gas can be classified into one of two categories, depending upon how it is formed. *Thermogenic gas* is formed by temperature and pressure changes deep beneath Earth's surface that change carbon matter into methane. This is the kind of gas that is found in the Marcellus Shale. *Biogenic gas*, on the other hand, is produced by the metabolic activity or decomposition of organisms close to the Earth's surface. These two kinds of gases differ chemically, and the source can frequently be determined by laboratory tests. Furthermore, thermogenic gases of different ages and origins can sometimes be told apart by their chemical signatures, and the rock formations in which they originated can be determined.

Such studies are made more difficult by the frequent lack of established baseline data on existing methane in groundwater.[84] Such data establishes what "normal" conditions are, which allows future measurements to document changes, such as those that might result from natural gas development. Despite this difficulty, several studies that have examined methane in groundwater in New York and Pennsylvania have concluded that the methane was probably derived from the Marcellus, and in association with shale gas development.[85]

Methane that escapes into the atmosphere poses no risk to groundwater (but see Chapter 6). However, methane that seeps into the shallow subsurface presents an explosion risk if it accumulates in confined areas, such as cavities in rocks or human-made structures. Exactly this kind of explosion occurred in the town of Dimock, in Susquehanna County, Pennsylvania, in 2009 (see below).

BLOWOUTS

Unexpected pockets of gas under high pressure are sometimes encountered while a well is being drilled. This can happen in both conventional and unconventional wells. Whereas the depth of some gas reservoirs can be predicted during drilling, some reservoir rocks could have allowed natural gas to migrate into voids in surrounding rocks. (Indeed, this migration into traps—porous rocks overlain by less permeable rocks—provides exactly the conditions that most conventional vertical wells exploit.) If a concentration of gas is not anticipated, however, it can cause a *blowout*, a sudden uncontrolled release of gas and fluids from the well (Figure 4.5). During a blowout, contaminants can move from the source to nearby surface waters, or through the soil into near-surface groundwater.

To help prevent blowouts, various technologies are used to monitor the pressures in the well as it is drilled. Valves called *blowout preventers* that help regulate erratic pressure changes that can be found while drilling, are installed at all gas wells to help prevent and contain blowouts. Furthermore, in principle, the pressure of the drilling mud (a combination of the density and temperature of the muds, the height in the well, and gravity) counters the increasing pressures in the well until the next section can be cased. If, however, a shallow, unexpected pocket of gas is encountered while drilling, pressure in the well will quickly and dramatically increase. If the pressure provided by the drilling muds is not sufficient to contain the pressure from the gas pocket, the gas can mix with the drilling muds and flow back to the surface. The higher the pressure in the shallow gas pocket, the more gas will be released suddenly. This poses a danger at the surface, because gas is explosive and can be ignited by the machines running above ground (Figure 4.5). It can also contaminate nearby

Figure 4.5. In June 2010, a drilling operation on a gas well in Marshall County, West Virginia, struck an abandoned coal mine triggering a blowout and explosion that injured seven workers (three seriously).

groundwater sources with methane if casing has not yet been installed to separate the fluids in the well bore from the surrounding rock.[86]

Blowouts have occurred in Pennsylvania Marcellus wells. A total of four blowout or venting incidents, all classified as major, occurred in Pennsylvania between 2008 and 2011. In April 2011, a well in Bradford County experienced a blowout that released thousands of gallons of fluid and required the evacuation of homes in the area. In June 2010, a well in Clearfield County had a blowout that resulted in the release of natural gas, flowback fracture fluid, and brine.[87] The amount of damage caused by a well blowout depends upon the pressure of the gas pocket, how fast the well can be contained, and the speed with which appropriate mitigation measures can be implemented.

CASING FAILURES

Well casings can fail or be constructed improperly, creating the potential for groundwater contamination. In the Marcellus Shale, HVHF is carried out along the horizontal leg of the well, thousands of feet below the water table, but well bores must first go through groundwater sources to reach the Marcellus. Recall from Chapter 3 that metal casings and cement are put into place during the drilling process to seal off the well bore from the surrounding rocks. This is done for several reasons: to help prevent methane from escaping the well bore into other, shallower rock units (including aquifers); to help prevent groundwater from entering the well bore and being extracted with the gas (requiring it to be processed back out at the surface); to help prevent hydrofracking fluid from entering formations other than the Marcellus; and to help prevent the collapse of the well bore. A well that is not cased properly can cause some or all of these, in particular the migration of methane into potable groundwater sources.[88]

Improper casing of unconventional gas wells or casing failures have contributed to contamination of groundwater in Pennsylvania, Colorado, and Wyoming. One of the more publicized recent incidents of groundwater contamination occurred in Dimock, Pennsylvania.[89]

Other parts of the country experiencing development of unconventional fossil fuels have also had issues with water contamination. For example, reports of BTEX contamination and attendant health effects have been associated with natural gas drilling in coal bed methane formations in Wyoming, and tight sands in Colorado. In Garfield County, Colorado, contamination was due improper casing of the well. When drillers attempted to fracture a tight sand formation 7,000 feet (2,134 meters) below the surface, the protective well casing failed, and they instead contaminated groundwater 3,500 feet (1,067 meters) away through a shallower fracture system. Benzene was found in some of the samples, but not in the domestic water wells. Along with methane, which they were not able to definitively source from the natural gas wells, they found increased levels of chloride, fluoride, nitrate, selenium, iron, and manganese.[90]

The EPA sampled 39 wells in 2009 in the town of Pavillion, Fremont County, Wyoming—the site of a natural gas field extracting coal bed methane—after complaints from residents. Samples indicated "high levels" of benzene, xylene, and other hydrocarbons like methylcyclohexane, naphthalene, and phenol.[91] Hazardous levels of lead, phthalate (a substance used in hydrofracking fluid), and nitrite were found. EPA resampled in 2010 and confirmed that this was "highly contaminated shallow groundwater occurring in the same aquifer as drinking water wells."[92] At the time of the 2010 report, EPA had not yet determined the source of the contamination, which might have included storage pits from older projects. In Sublette County, Wyoming, home to one of the largest coal bed methane fields in the U.S., benzene levels 1,500 times the acceptable concentration levels were discovered in groundwater.[93]

Chapter 4 Summary

- Water, which mostly comes from surface water withdrawals, is an integral part of the current practice of shale gas extraction. Approximately 3–5 million gallons of water are used per well.

- Compared to other water uses in the Northeast and compared with other sources of energy, the total water requirements for shale gas extraction are not large, but they can still cause significant problems for ecosystems and human water supplies, depending on source and location of the water withdrawal.

- Water is used to both drill and hydrofrack a well, although most of the water is used in the hydrofracking process. A variety of chemicals are mixed with the water to form hydrofracking fluid, and many of these chemicals can cause adverse health and environmental effects.

- An average of 10% of the water used to hydrofrack a well in the Marcellus Shale comes back to the surface. This water can contain high levels of heavy metals, total dissolved solids, volatile organic compounds, and naturally occurring radioactive material, as well as the chemicals added to the hydrofracking fluid.

- Disposal of this wastewater is a challenge It can be disposed of in underground injection wells, or it can be treated, but only in wastewater treatment facilities that have been modified to handle the chemical composition of the water.

- Natural gas extraction can contaminate ground and surface water. Surface spills and leaks, faulty well construction, and erosion can all contaminate local water supplies. It can be difficult to prove that any single instance of contamination was a result of gas drilling, but establishing baseline data for water near proposed natural gas development projects can help.

Figure 5.1. Service trucks gather on a typical Marcellus Shale natural gas well pad in southwestern Pennsylvania. Silica dust clouds the air.

BEYOND WATER: OTHER ENVIRONMENTAL IMPACTS OF MARCELLUS GAS DEVELOPMENT

The land that overlies the Marcellus Shale gas play is largely rural and hilly, a mix of forests and farmland. Developing this play has affected—and could affect—this land in many ways beyond water (Table 5.1). Construction of well pads, access roads, and pipelines contribute to habitat fragmentation, with large effects on ecosystems. The diesel engines that provide much of the power needed for drilling, hydrofracking, and transport of materials, equipment, and people affect air quality. There is solid waste that must be disposed of. Land use changes and increased heavy truck traffic can result in greater erosion and runoff into streams. Transport of materials and equipment from other areas of the country into the Marcellus region carries with

Table 5.1. Major non-water categories of potential environmental damage from large-scale hydrofracking in the Marcellus Shale.

I. Air quality
    A. Smog
    B. Particulates
    C. NO_x
II. Solid waste disposal
    A. Cuttings
    B. Drilling and residue
III. Soil erosion
IV. Water quality (as a habitat for wildlife)
    A. Chemical pollution
    B. Siltation
    C. Reduced flow
V. Habitat damage
    A. Habitat loss
    B. Habitat fragmentation
VI. Noise

it the potential for transport of invasive species. Even the sounds of drilling and hydrofracking, aside from their impact on humans, can affect local wildlife.

When considered well pad by well pad, these changes have relatively small consequences for the environment, which decrease the farther one looks from the area immediately adjacent to drilling. When these changes are considered for thousands of well pads on a regional scale, the consequences to ecosystems can be much larger and much more difficult to repair afterward. Moreover, unlike water contamination—which can be reduced, although not entirely prevented, by keeping human error to a minimum and carefully choosing options for disposal—habitat fragmentation, diesel emissions, erosion, and noise impacts are all unavoidable consequences of drilling operations, and are less likely to be regulated, especially across a region.

In this chapter, we discuss some of the effects that large-scale shale gas drilling operations have on ecosystems, and the potential for minimizing or remediating these effects.

LOCAL AIR QUALITY

Gas drilling affects air quality because various pollutants are emitted during well completion and flowback, and from the diesel engines used to power and supply much of the gas extraction process.[1] Air quality issues have been attributed to natural gas drilling in other parts of the country.[2] The EPA considers the oil and gas industry to be a major source of volatile organic compounds (VOCs), which lead to *smog*, among other negative effects. In Wyoming, for example, drilling has led to the release of ground level ozone (O_3), causing smog that was worse than levels recorded in Los

Angeles. Air quality issues connected to drilling in the Barnett Shale in Texas have also been at the forefront of environmental concerns.

VOCS AND METHANE EMISSIONS

Recall from Chapter 4 that after a well is hydrofracked, but before the gas can be collected, a period of flowback must occur in which some of the water used to hydrofrack the well flows back to the surface. The flowback fluid that returns to the surface usually contains methane, VOCs, and potentially other air pollutants. Technologies do exist that can be used to reduce these emissions. *Green completion* of a well is a term used to refer to the application of such technologies during the flowback period to help prevent gas from escaping into the atmosphere.[3] (See further discussion in Chapter 6.)

VOCs are chemical precursors to ground level ozone. In sunlight, VOCs and NO_x (nitrogen oxides) react with each other to produce ozone, which not only contributes to smog, but can be a human health hazard. If this reaction happens high in the stratosphere, the ozone serves to block harmful ultraviolet radiation from the Earth's surface. If it happens close to the ground, however, it causes smog, and can harm human respiratory systems. It can also seriously damage plants, reducing crop yield and making ecosystems more vulnerable to pests and disease. Ozone creation is seasonal. Because the reaction that creates ozone is dependent upon sunlight, ground-level ozone concentrations rise in the summer, when there is more sunlight.[4]

DIESEL EMISSIONS

Emissions from diesel engines contain NO_x, which combines with VOCs to make ground level *ozone*, and *fine particulate matter*, which can damage respiratory systems with chronic exposure.

Building a well pad and drilling and fracturing wells is a truck-intensive process, and trucks largely use diesel engines. All of the equipment, personnel, proppant, and chemicals must be transported to the site by truck. In the early stages of development in the region, all of the water needed to fracture the well usually must be transported by truck as well. All of the equipment and the waste fluids must also be transported away from the well pad by truck. NYSDEC reports that 1,979 trips would be required at an average well in the early stages of development. As development ramps up and pipelines are put in place for water, this number decreases by approximately 29%, to 1,420 round trips.[5] Subsequent wells on a pad will require somewhat fewer truck trips, as much of the equipment will already be there. Total VOC and NO_x emissions due to increased truck traffic are estimated to increase 0.17% and 0.66% over baseline, respectively.[6]

Other equipment associated with drilling and fracturing includes the drilling equipment to create the well bore and the pumps required to force the water and proppant into the target formation. Power for this equipment also usually comes from diesel engines. A typical drilling rig diesel engine, were it to operate continuously for a year, releases approximately 333.7 tons of NO_x, and a typical diesel-powered hydrofracking pump, if it operated continuously for a year, wiykd produce approximately 144.1 tons of NO_x.[7] Based on these calculations and estimates of the number of wells drilled, NYSDEC estimates that if drilling begins in New York, NO_x emissions from drilling and fracturing activities will be approximately 10.4% over current upstate emissions in peak development years.[8]

Compressor stations, used to transport natural gas in pipelines, also require engines to power them, although natural gas can be used rather than diesel. Natural gas emits NO_x from combustion as well, but not as much as diesel fuel. NYSDEC's estimate for NO_x emissions from a single compressor station engine is 48.3 tons per year.[9] Unlike pumps and drilling equipment, the engine in a compressor station is expected to run continuously. Compressor stations are also a source of methane emissions (see Chapter 6).[10]

SOLID WASTE

Recall from Chapter 3 that drilling mud is fluid used to lubricate the drill bit during drilling and carry cuttings back to the surface. Recall also that compressed air is sometimes used for this purpose. Drilling muds can be recovered, treated, and reused in other wells, especially if getting the mud to and from different well sites is convenient, as on a multiwell pad.[11] Proposed NYSDEC regulations would require that when chemicals are used in drilling muds, they must be part of what is called a *closed loop* drilling system. In such a system, these muds are held in containers at the surface, circulated through the well bore during drilling, then stored in containers when it comes back out of the well bore—it is never supposed to be stored in open pits. Eventually they must be disposed of.

Recall that cuttings are a mixture of coarse rock chips, fine particles, and shavings that are displaced from the well bore while the well is being drilled. If fluid, rather than air, has been used to drill a well, these cuttings are a wet slurry (Figure 2.1). If the well has been drilled using air, they will be drier, although they can contain some formation water. Cuttings from the Marcellus formation itself could represent half or more of the total cuttings, because the lateral well legs within the Marcellus are in some cases longer than the vertical well length to the Marcellus. Marcellus well cuttings contain all of the chemicals present in other Marcellus waste, including radionuclides (see Chapter 2), as well as the mineral pyrite.

As mentioned in Chapter 2, Marcellus drill cuttings show radiation levels similar to natural outcrops at the surface of Marcellus Shale and other dark shales, and have been judged by NYSDEC not to pose a danger of radiation exposure to either workers or the general public.

Pyrite is a mineral that is commonly found in dark shales such as the Marcellus. When exposed to air and water, pyrite breaks down into iron oxides and sulfate.

The sulfate then combines with water, producing sulfuric acid, which can damage certain storage pit liners and contaminate water with acid discharge. At Marcellus well sites in New York, cuttings would be stored either in lined pits or steel tanks if the cuttings are dry. If the well has been drilled with oil-based muds, the cuttings must be contained within tanks and disposed of in an off-site solid waste facility. Dry cuttings could be buried onsite if they are buried with chemicals that neutralize potential acidic discharge from oxidizing of pyrite. If this is not done correctly, the discharge could cause a change in soil or groundwater pH, making them more acidic and potentially damaging local vegetation.[12]

WATER, EROSION, AND ECOSYSTEMS

Marcellus drilling activity has the potential to adversely affect the wildlife and ecosystems of streams and rivers in the area underlain by the formation (Table 5.1, Figure 5.2). Some of these adverse effects could also extend downstream to areas that do not see gas drilling. The Delaware River Basin Commission (DRBC), for example, has determined that the potential threat to the streams of the Delaware River Basin from natural gas development is sufficient for them to regulate drilling in their entire watershed, which includes sections of seven New York counties in the southeastern portion of the state (Figure 3.2).

As discussed in Chapter 3, one major consequence of HVHF is the removal of high volumes of water from streams and rivers. Recall that NYSDEC estimated that the total water required for Marcellus Shale drilling in New York could reach 9 billion gallons in a peak development year. Most of the area underlain by the Marcellus Shale in New York is part of the headwater nter areas of several river basins. Because they are small, headwaters are often the part of the river that is most sensitive to environmental changes, such as water withdrawal. Altered flow in a river can affect specific aspects of ecosystems, such as water temperature, movement of sediment through the stream, and the shape of the channel itself, all of which can alter abundance and diversity of stream biota and how the ecosystem functions.[13]

Other impacts to wildlife come from construction of the well pads, roads, pipelines, and associated infrastructure (Figure 5.2). These include physical disturbance caused by well pad and road construction, loss of forest cover, and increased impermeable surfaces. All of these increase surface water runoff, soil erosion, and temperature, and these in turn can have major impact on both land and stream ecosystems. By one estimate, construction of an average 2.5-acre (1-hectare) well pad in New York might lead to the erosion of 8.5 tons of sediment.[14]

Forest cover influences many aspects of streams, including temperature, levels of dissolved oxygen, erosion rates, and input of nutrients.[15] Under natural conditions, vegetation acts as a natural filter during strong precipitation, slowing the rate at which eroded soil enters surface water. If, however, well pads, access roads, and staging areas are cleared of vegetation, the filtering effects are reduced or eliminated.

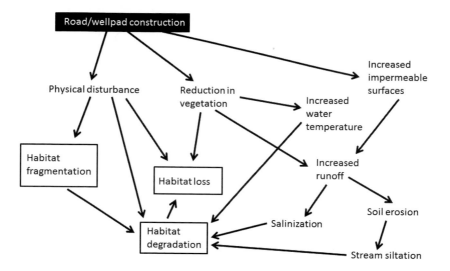

Figure 5.2. Summary of the major environmental impacts resulting from well pad (and other) construction.

The hilly topography of much of the land being developed for natural gas in the Marcellus will exacerbate this problem.

Erosion is an environmental problem for several reasons (Figure 5.2). First, it reduces available topsoil, diminishing land plant growth. Topsoil erosion is a major global environmental problem because it reduces the amount of land available to produce crops. The U.S., for example, is currently losing topsoil ten times faster than it is replenished.[16] Second, all of the eroded topsoil has to go somewhere, and that is usually into local surface water. Increased runoff and sedimentation can be extremely harmful to stream ecosystems. Some of these adverse effects could also extend downstream to areas that do not see gas drilling. Excess sediment in streams can alter habitat and directly harm aquatic organisms.[17] Many stream species depend on hard surfaces at the bottom to successfully complete their life cycles; if stream bottoms are covered with sediment, eggs and/or larvae of fish and aquatic invertebrates (such as insects, crustaceans, and mussels) can be smothered, and adults can have their available habitat reduced or eliminated.[18] Filter feeders, including freshwater mussels (Figure 5.3), can experience effects ranging from reduced feeding ability in waters turbid from excess sediment, to mortality when sediment clogs their gills.[19]

A variety of measures can reduce the effects of these land-use changes. Proposed NYSDEC regulations would require that the edge of well pads not be closer than 150 feet (46 meters) to streams without a site-specific review. Erosion and sedimentation controls, including berms, ditches, sediment traps, sumps, or fencing, can also be constructed around access roads and well pads.[20] Such measures can reduce impacts, but removal of vegetation, combined with creation of new impermeable surfaces (concrete, paving, packed dirt, etc.), will inevitably increase sediment erosion.[21]

INVASIVE SPECIES

All of the truck traffic associated with drilling can also raise the risk of introducing *invasive species*—microorganisms, plants, and animals—into new habitats. Invasive species are already among the most serious threats to ecosystems in the northeastern U.S. and elsewhere, and this could worsen that situation.[22] Ironically, reclamation of well sites can also introduce invasive species, for example by using hearty non-native grass blends, especially in forests.[23] Invasive species are an environmental problem because they can alter and damage local ecosystems, especially if those ecosystems are already disturbed or weakened by other environmental changes (such as from gas drilling). Often invasive species will have left behind the diseases and predators that limit their population, and can out-compete native species and disrupt the normal ecosystem interactions of their new environment. They can also be very difficult to eradicate once established. Pennsylvania and New York State already have numerous invasive species to contend with, both aquatic and terrestrial.[24]

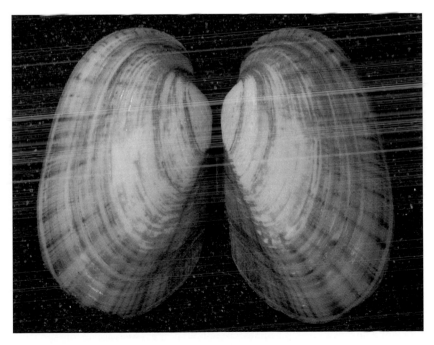

Figure 5.3. Freshwater mussels, like this species from New York, face more environmental threats than perhaps any other animal group. Invasive species (especially Zebra Mussels), physical changes in habitat (e.g., damming), and poor water quality are among the more serious threats to their survival.

HABITAT LOSS AND FRAGMENTATION

Some degree of *habitat loss* and *fragmentation* is an unavoidable result of shale gas development. Habitat loss is the conversion of one kind of habitat to another, dissimilar habitat. In the case of Marcellus Shale drilling in New York, this would mostly involve clearing of forest land for access roads, well pads, and pipelines. Habitat fragmentation occurs when a continuous area of habitat is broken up into smaller pieces, separated by areas of a different type of habitat (Figure 5.4).

The major consequences of habitat fragmentation for native wildlife include reduction in the size of patches of the original habitat, increase in the distance between individual patches of the original habitat, and changes along the margins of fragments (*e.g.*, drying of forests). Habitat fragmentation is also known to have negative effects on the number of species—or *biodiversity*—in an ecosystem. These effects result from barriers to migration between patches (fragments) of the original habitat, as well as the inevitably smaller size of the patches.[25]

Habitat fragmentation can, however, occasionally also have positive effects on particular species with certain kinds of life cycles and habitat preferences. Many species need more than one type of habitat to successfully complete a life cycle. A more fragmented habitat can increase the chances that the different habitats needed are close or adjacent to one another. This is true for certain reptiles and amphibians that inhabit New York State forests.[26]

Fragmentation can also benefit species that prefer edge habitats, which are places where one kind of habitat is adjacent to a different kind of habitat. The number of these kinds of species increases when habitats become more fragmented. Examples of such "edge species" in the northeastern U.S. include White-tailed Deer, Raccoons, Cottontail Rabbits, and Blue Jays. These species are sometimes described as "weedy," because they do well in human-disturbed habitats. The Nature Conservancy and Audubon Pennsylvania have estimated that an average of 21.2 acres (8.6 hectares) of new edge habitat is created per Marcellus well site.[27]

Although habitat fragmentation can increase abundance of certain species and increase total diversity in some locations, significant habitat fragmentation almost always changes the composition (and decreases the diversity) of the species in an ecosystem. One study done on reptiles and amphibians at gas well sites in the Monongahela National Forest in West Virginia suggests that the picture could be complicated. The researchers found that whereas fewer woodland salamanders were present near gas wells than were present in forests, a larger total abundance of amphibians was found in areas with higher road densities. This could be a result of the drainage ditches being used as breeding grounds for species like the American Toad (Figure 5.5). They also found no difference in the number of reptiles near gas wells and in forests farther away from them, and found the small mammal population to be higher near gas wells than farther away from them. But the small mammal species that they found are those characteristic of early successional habitats, that is, those recovering from a recent disturbance, like the kind of habitat provided by a gas well.[28]

Figure 5.4. Access roads for wells and pipelines lead to habitat fragmentation. This aerial photograph shows HVHF wells and a compressor station in Chartiers Township in Washington County, Pennsylvania. The compressor station (white arrow) sits on a buried pipeline with cleared land above that connects to the nearby wells.

Figure 5.5. Some amphibians, such as the American Toad (Bufo americanus, *left*), could benefit from more disturbed habitats that result from Marcellus gas development. Others, such as the Northern Dusky Salamander (Desmognathus fuscus, *right*), could suffer from reduced or degraded habitats.

Studies done in other areas that have seen gas drilling might provide insight into the potential effects of gas drilling in the northeastern U.S. For example, in Alberta, Canada, which has seen intense oil and gas development, over half of the land was originally boreal forest, and approximately 90% of those forests have been fragmented since the early 1900s.[29] Although most of the forest fragmentation is the result of logging, the oil and gas industry is now interacting with the timber industry to alter forests that remain. Changes have been seen in the kinds of species that inhabit areas that have been fragmented. The species that inhabit older forests, continuous forests, and species that avoid humans have decreased, whereas the species that inhabit younger forests, fragmented forests, non-native species, and human-tolerant species have increased. This situation in Alberta also indicates that habitat fragmentation can be greater in areas with more separate gas companies operating, because access roads are frequently built with little coordination among companies.[30]

The southwestern U.S., which has also seen gas drilling, is home to a variety of reptiles with fairly specific habitat needs that could be disrupted by such drilling. In this case, the concern has been that roads would alter the form of blowing sand dunes, thus altering and eliminating the habitat of species living there. One study of six lizard species found no indication that the access roads altered the size or area of the sand dune features. Although higher abundance of all six species was positively correlated with the amount of area, abundance was not correlated with the presence or absence of access roads or drilling activity.[31]

One study done on birds in the grasslands of Alberta showed different results for each of the three species studied. One bird species, known to be more tolerant of humans, showed increased abundance with increased well density. A second showed no correlation with gas well density, and a third species decreased in abundance with an increase in well density.[32]

Animals aren't the only parts of ecosystems that can be affected by habitat fragmentation and well development. A study done on oil wells in Saskatchewan found that lease sites were found to have fewer herbaceous (non-woody) plants, more bare ground, altered soil chemistry, and a higher abundance of undesirable (invasive) grass species than non-lease sites. It was also shown that these impacts could last for 50 years or more, and for up to 82 feet (25 meters) away from the well pad.[33]

Different kinds of development, e.g., urban development, agriculture, and road construction, create different patterns of habitat fragmentation.[34] Natural gas development also breaks up ecosystems in a distinctive way. The footprint of Marcellus drilling consists of well pads and staging areas (where drilling takes place and equipment and materials are stored), access roads to reach the pads, and pipelines to transmit gas once it has been recovered. Additional pipelines could be built to carry the water needed for HVHF to the well pads, in lieu of truck transportation. The individual well pads used for Marcellus drilling will be larger than the well pads that have been built in New York State for vertical gas drilling. More wells being drilled from a single pad and the increased storage requirements for materials and equipment needed for horizontal drilling and hydrofracking contribute to this. The collective footprint of these pads over the region, however, will be smaller. Vertical wells can be drilled with 40-acre (16-hectare) spacing. Proposed Marcellus drilling regulations have the horizontal wells limited to 640-acre (259-hectare) spacing.[35]

NYSDEC proposes to minimize the impact of gas drilling on wildlife by, where possible, requiring multiple wells per pad, designing pads to minimize tree removal and fit the terrain, planting bushes around the site to create "soft" edges, limiting or prohibiting mowing and construction during grassland bird nesting season if the pad is located in grassland, limiting the amount of ground that is disturbed both for well pads and access roads, and requiring reclamation as soon as possible using native species.[36]

The apparent industry trend toward *multiwell pads* could reduce the total footprint of drilling further, but actual trends in Pennsylvania show mixed results. Although the vast majority of pads built for HVHF drilling have the capacity to be multiwell sites, in fact, most have only one, two, or three wells on them, with an average of just slightly over two per pad. This could change later, especially if development is still in the early stages in Pennsylvania.[37]

IMPACT OF NOISE

As with most industrial activities, gas drilling can be noisy. Although drilling and fracturing noise levels are expected to be similar for vertically and horizontally fractured wells, the longer duration of activity at unconventional wells (caused by both the increased length of the wells themselves and the development of multiple wells on a pad) is expected to make noise more of an issue with horizontal drilling (Table 5.2).

Sound intensity is measured in decibels (dBa); a jump in 10 dBa (*e.g.*, from 50 to 60) is a jump of 10 times in intensity. Eighty-five decibels is the minimum level at which damage to human hearing can occur, if exposure to the noise lasts longer than eight hours. According to the U.S. National Institutes of Health, these sounds will range

Table 5.2. The noise level and duration of drilling activities at a distance of 500 feet (152 meters).[38]

Activity type	Composite dBa at 500 ft	Duration (days)	This is like...
Access road construction	69	3–7	A vacuum cleaner or hair dryer
Well pad preparation	64	7–14	Normal conversation
Air well drilling	58	28–35	Typical office noise
Horizontal drilling	56		
Hydraulic fracturing	84	2–5	A lawn mower or food blender

from comfortable to annoying. Rural nighttime background level is around 35 dBa. That is a little louder than a whisper, and a little less loud than a refrigerator's hum.

Humans can be annoyed or harmed by loud or constant noise, and wildlife can also be affected. Noise can interrupt communication among animals, hunting, foraging, or predatory-evasion abilities. It can cause panic reactions that risk injury to the animal itself or its neighbors. It can cause animals to temporarily or permanently abandon certain areas, in favor of marginal habitats with less noise. On the other hand, some species seem to be able to acclimate to noise after repeated exposure, and not all of the disruptions are permanent. In other words, it is difficult to generalize and predict the response of an individual species to certain types of noise.[39]

In a study in the boreal forest of Alberta that compared bird occurrence and density between well pads, which were considered quiet, and compressor stations, which have a constant noise level of 75–90 dBa, birds were found to occur less often overall in the noisier sites. Some of the individual bird species were more affected than others by compressor station noise. In fact, some species showed no significant difference in abundance among the different site types, but none of them occurred more often at the compressor stations than at the well pads.[40]

Chapter 5 Summary

- Increases in certain air pollutants, such as volatile organic compounds and nitrogen oxides, both of which contribute to lower air quality, will happen as a result of engines running drilling and hydrofracking equipment, truck traffic, and venting of natural gas in well completion activities.

- Solid waste from drilling, if not properly disposed of, can leach chemicals into the ground.

- Erosion and habitat fragmentation caused by the build-up of drilling sites pose threats to both terrestrial and aquatic ecosystems and wildlife.

- Even the noise produced by drilling and fracturing wells has the potential to affect populations in the areas near well pads and compressor stations.

- At least some environmental degradation is going to occur in New York if gas drilling proceeds. The issues described here are all by-products of typical gas development activity.

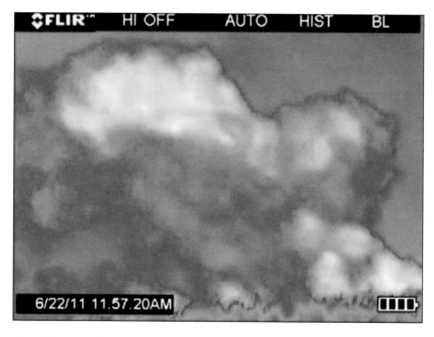

Figure 6.1. A cloud of methane gas emitted into the atmosphere as a result of venting during the completion of a natural gas well in Susquehanna County, Pennsylvania, June 22, 2011. This image is from an enhanced infrared photograph.

CHAPTER 6

LIFE-CYCLE ANALYSIS: SHALE GAS & CLIMATE CHANGE

Natural gas is frequently referred to as an environmentally "cleaner" fuel than coal because burning it does not produce a number of environmentally damaging by-products such as sulfur, mercury, and ash, and because it produces less carbon dioxide (CO_2) per unit of energy than coal.[1] For these reasons, natural gas has been widely considered to be an attractive "bridge" to other sources of energy with less *potential future climate impact* (PFCI), such as renewables like wind and solar. This conclusion has gained in popularity as the supply of natural gas in the U.S. has increased and the price has declined as a result of shale gas exploitation.[2]

Yet the controversy over shale gas has also brought new critical attention on the PFCI of natural gas, specifically on emissions of methane (CH_4)—a powerful greenhouse gas (GHG)—into the atmosphere during all of the stages of natural gas development. Although it might at first glance seem like a straightforward question, figuring out the PFCI of CH_4 emissions associated with natural gas development turns out to be an extremely complicated and difficult problem.[3] It is, however, an extraordinarily important problem, insofar as much of the attractiveness of natural gas as an energy source lies in its reputation as better for the climate than coal.

The question of the PFCI of natural gas is an example of what is frequently called a *life-cycle analysis* (LCA), which seeks to measure the total effect of making,

103

extracting, transporting, using, and disposing of a product or resource by examining the effects of each and every piece of the whole system involved with that particular product.[4]Although they have become increasingly common elements of environmental impact analyses in recent years, LCAs of all but the simplest products are very complex, and their conclusions are frequently subject to high uncertainty.

The task of carrying out an LCA for the PFCI of natural gas might appear relatively simple: measure the emissions of GHGs—mainly CH_4 and CO_2—at each stage of natural gas development, from well to end-user, calculate the *global warming potential* (GWP) of each (expressed in a standard way; Box 6.1); add them all up, and compare this to the total GWP of coal to produce a similar amount of energy. Yet in practice, such an analysis immediately becomes complex. Not only does each step have numerous substeps, but each of these substeps is very complex on its own.[5]

First among these complications is the physics of methane. CH_4 is a much more potent greenhouse gas than CO_2 over relatively short time frames, but its effects over longer intervals are lessened because it stays in the atmosphere for far less time on average than CO_2. GWPs calculated over various time scales will therefore be different (see Box 6.1).

Second is the complexity and difficulty of identifying and measuring accurately CH_4 emissions, and expressing them in appropriate terms. CH_4 is emitted into the atmosphere from both natural and human sources (Figure 6.2).[6] Human (*anthropogenic*) CH_4 emissions, in turn, come mainly from agriculture, waste disposal, and energy development.[7] Within energy, CH_4 emissions come from oil, coal, and natural gas production, and within natural gas, from a variety of sources. Until recently, many of the emissions associated with natural gas development had never even been recognized or measured, and when they have been, it has been surprisingly difficult to decide what any of these measurements really mean. This is hard enough for conventional gas wells; HVHF complicates it still further.

Third, as is true for all projections about future global climate change, assessments about the PFCI of natural gas depend not only on the science and engineering of natural gas, but also on the science of climate change. Although scientists know a great deal about what causes climate to change, and are becoming better making projections, the Earth's climate is an immensely complex system that remains imperfectly understood. We still do not know with perfect certainty what the effect or magnitude of particular factors will be, or when they might occur.[8]

Finally, it's not just about science and engineering. The PFCI of natural gas development not only depends on which and how much GHGs are produced, but also on how long they are produced. If natural gas is really a "*bridge*," we need to know to what it is bridging, when will we get there, and what will happen along the way. Of the technologies that exist, which one or ones will be implemented, how widely, and when? What will they cost? Who will pay for them? Complete answers to these questions cannot be provided by science or technology; they will also depend on policy, politics, and economics.[9]

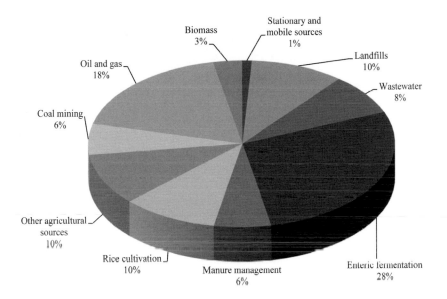

Biomass
3%

Stationary and
mobile sources
1%

Oil and gas
18%

Landfills
10%

Wastewater
8%

Coal mining
6%

Other agricultural
sources
10%

Rice cultivation
10%

Manure management
6%

Enteric fermentation
28%

Figure 6.2. Human-caused (anthropogenic) sources of atmospheric methane emissions. "Enteric fermentation" refers to the digestive processes of livestock.

Each of these complications is large and multifaceted. Most have become clear and the subject of serious investigation only in the last few years. Data for most of the questions needing answers are currently inadequate. And, as is frequently the case with scientific topics that are poorly understood but that have major economic and/or political implications, the process of doing and communicating the science of the potential climate effects of natural gas development has been imperfect and subject to substantial nonscientific influences, such as politics, activism, and the media. Considering all of this, it is perhaps not so surprising that answering the question "What is the potential future climate impact of shale gas?" is difficult and controversial.

In this chapter, we cannot explore all aspects of this topic in detail, but we try to describe the major issues and variables, and review the most current research. This is a rapidly changing field, and new information is becoming available all of the time.[10] Our goal here is not to say whether natural gas has a greater or lesser climate impact than coal. As we will see, despite claims to the contrary, there is currently no unambiguous scientific consensus on an answer to this question, and it could in any case be the wrong question on which to focus.[11] Our goal is therefore to explore why this question is so difficult to answer, so that as new information becomes available, readers can be better able to put it into the correct context.[12]

Box 6.1. Measuring the Climate Impact of Greenhouse Gases

Each greenhouse gas has a different capacity to trap heat in the atmosphere, and this capacity can be estimated and expressed in a variety of ways, which can be confusing. One of the most commonly used is *global warming potential* (GWP).[13]

Nevertheless, the concept of GWP has been widely used as a simple means to establish an approximate comparison of the climate impact of different greenhouse gases. The GWP of a particular gas is defined as the *radiative forcing* that it causes over some *specified interval of time* (20 and 100 years are the most frequently used). (Radiative forcing is the amount of energy per unit area—usually expressed in watts per square meter (W/m^2)—that a certain change in a particular greenhouse gas confers.[14]) To compare the GWPs of different gases, their GWPs are expressed relative to that of CO_2. This is called *carbon dioxide equivalents*. The GWP of methane, for example, can be expressed in units converted to its equivalent in CO_2 emissions, in English units (pounds of CO_2 equivalent for every million BTUs of energy produced ($lbCO_2/MMBTU$), or metric units (grams of CO_2 per million joules, gCO_2/MJ or gCO_2/MWh), or as multiples, as in the table below.[15]

The GWP of a particular gas depends on several factors. First is its "instantaneous impact" on the radiative energy balance of the Earth—or how much infrared radiation it will absorb and emit.[16] This impact can be expressed on a molecule-for-molecule (molar) basis, or by mass. For example, on a molar basis, CH_4 has 37 times the "instantaneous" GWP of CO_2, and 102 times more on a gram-by-gram basis.[17] Second is the amount of time that a gas remains in the atmosphere, usually referred to as its *residence time* or *lifetime*. This is a complex metric, because some gases, notably CO_2, can exist in the atmosphere in *dynamic equilibrium* with other reservoirs, such as the ocean or land biosphere (especially plants). This means that individual molecules come and go in and out of different reservoirs, but without changing their abundance in each reservoir. Thus, the lifetime of a single pulse of gas emitted into the atmosphere can refer to either the average length of time that individual molecules of the gas spend in the atmosphere before they are removed, or the amount of time that it takes until the concentration of that gas in the air recovers substantially toward its original concentration.[18] The latter can be substantially longer than the former.

For example, following the emission of a pulse of CO_2 (e.g., by human burning of fossil fuels), an average CO_2 molecule will remain in the atmosphere for approximately 3–5 years. In most cases, however, when it leaves the atmosphere, it is simply swapping places with one in the surface water of the ocean, and so it does not change the CO_2 concentration in the air. The concentration in the atmosphere only begins to change as CO_2 begins to be transferred from the sea surface to the deep ocean or into land vegetation. Approximately 50% of the pulse is absorbed in this way In the first 50 years after emission, and another 20% in the next 50 years. Absorption slows dramatically after that, with an additional 10% or so being removed over the next 200 years, and the remaining 20% lasting tens, if not hundreds or thousands, of years. The average lifetime of a pulse of CO_2 is probably 30,000 to 35,000 years.[19]

In contrast, methane (CH_4) is more reactive and there are fewer accessible natural reservoirs for it, so the time that an average molecule stays in the atmosphere (approximately 12 years) is close to the time when the concentration will start to decline after emission of a pulse.[20] Methane is removed from the atmosphere mainly by combining with oxygen (oxidation) to form CO_2, H_2O vapor, and ozone (O_3), which are all also greenhouse gases. The GWP of CH_4 therefore also must include the effects of the products of its oxidation, which have their own lifetimes. Furthermore, recent studies suggest that CH_4 increases the concentration of fine particles in the atmosphere (sulfate and nitrate aerosols), adding even more greenhouse effect.[21] (The influence of these CH_4 products is sometimes referred to as indirect effects.[22])

Methane, therefore, always has a higher GWP than CO_2, but this difference declines with time. See table below.

GHG	Instantaneous GWP^MOLAR	Instantaneous GWP^MASS	GWP^MASS 20 years	GWP^MASS 100 yrs	GWP^MASS 100 years (with indirect effects [23])
CO_2	1	1	1	1	1
CH_4	37	102	72	25	33

107

Life-Cycle Analyses of Fossil Fuel Use

The current major uses of natural gas in the U.S. are electricity generation and building heat.[24] The other major source of electricity generation is coal (see Chapter 7), and natural gas from the Marcellus Shale is being used to power electrical plants, displacing coal. At face value, this would appear to be preferable from a GHG perspective: a typical coal power plant emits approximately 0.9 kg of CO_2 per kWh of electricity produced, and a standard natural gas power plant (known as a combined *cycle gas turbine* or CCGT) emits approximately 0.4 kg CO_2/kWh.[25] To determine whether natural gas or coal is preferable from a PCFI perspective, however, an LCA comparing these fuels is required.

Many LCAs have been conducted on conventional natural gas production in North America. Each study has a slightly different set of boundary conditions and makes different assumptions. Only recently, however, have studies begun to examine LCA of greenhouse gases associated with shale gas extraction by hydraulic fracturing, and the consequent PCFI.

A very simplified approach to an LCA of the PFCI of natural gas, conventional and unconventional, is shown in Figure 6.3, and this forms the outline for the discussion below.

Methane Emissions from Natural Gas Development

Natural gas is approximately 80% CH_4, and so it is not surprising that CH_4 is emitted in association with natural gas development. As noted above, CH_4 comes from other sources as well, but emissions from natural gas development are probably the largest single source in the U.S. These emissions—whether from a conventional well or a hydrofracked shale well—can come from numerous sources, which can be grouped into four categories or stages (Figures 6.3–6.4): (1) preproduction—emissions during well drilling and completion (including hydrofracking); (2) production—emissions during production at the well site; (3) processing—emissions while gas is being processed; and (4) transmission—emissions while gas is being transported, stored, and distributed to users. The last three of these four are common to both conventional and unconventional gas wells.

Emissions of CH_4 can be expressed in a number of different ways, which can make comparison of various studies and reports difficult. Emissions can be expressed in the same units as GWP, in CO_2 equivalents (Box 6.1), *i.e.,* pounds of CO_2 equivalent for every million BTUs of energy produced ($lbCO_2$/MMBTU), or grams of CO_2 per million joules (gCO_2/MJ). Emissions can also be expressed as a percentage of all of the gas expected to be produced from one or more wells during their lifetimes (see below),[26] or in CO_2 equivalents per unit electricity generated by each (*e.g.*, $kgCO_2$ / MWh). As noted below, gas is converted to electricity much more efficiently than coal.

One of the most important, and in many ways surprising, aspects of this subject is that careful and long-term measurements of CH_4 emissions in each of these stages are actually relatively few, and consequently the data available are very limited (although this is changing rapidly).[27] Some of these data come from the industry itself, which some critics suggest means that they might not be completely accurate. Other data have been gathered by government agencies (sometimes from industry). The studies that have been done, furthermore, have used different methods, and are difficult to compare directly. They could, for example, span different lengths of time, or include only low and high values, with or without averages or ranges of error or estimates of uncertainty. For all of these reasons, extrapolation, estimation, and inference are common to all of them to a greater or lesser extent, and the conclusions depend to a great extent on assumptions made before or during the analyses.

Each of the categories or stages of CH_4 emissions includes numerous individual potential sources. At all stages, unintentional leaks of gas (frequently referred to as *fugitive emissions*) are potentially among the most significant sources (Figure 6.3). The infrastructure of natural gas development is enormous and complex, so there are lots of places for leaks to occur. A typical well, for example, could have as many as 150 connections to equipment such as heaters, meters, dehydrators, compressors, and vapor-recovery devices.[28] So-called "routine" leaks can occur when valves are opened or closed.[29] Pipelines can extend for hundreds or thousands of miles. Natural gas has been used in the U.S. for more than a century, and many pipelines are more than 50 years old, presumably increasing their likelihood of leaking (see further discussion below).

Emissions can also be intentional, to relieve pressure, or because connecting infrastructure is not in place or functional. Such intentional emissions are called *venting*. Vented gas is frequently intentionally ignited, a procedure called *flaring*. When natural gas is flared, most of the CH_4 is combusted, producing CO_2.

Finally, any type of equipment can fail, and human operators can make errors, small and large, resulting in accidental emissions of various sizes. At the large end are catastrophic incidents called *blowouts*, in which large quantities of gas are suddenly emitted (see Chapter 4). At the smaller end is faulty equipment or human errors (which can quickly add up if numerous). For any given interval of time, only some of the wells or pipes or other equipment leak or fail or are used incorrectly. One study in Texas, for example, found that only 10% of well sites accounted for nearly 70% of CH_4 emissions. Another more recent study of more than 1,500 wells found that only 3% vented CH_4 to the atmosphere.[30] In general, the longer the time period considered in a study or set of data, or the longer a well operates, the higher the probability of emissions.

Not all CH_4 that leaks out escapes into the atmosphere. At least some, in theory, can be captured.[31] Although it might seem obvious that companies producing natural gas would want to capture and sell all that they can, rather than see it escape, this is not so simple.[32] Similarly, it might also seem obvious that producers would not want large quantities of natural gas escaping for safety reasons; CH_4, after all, is combustible

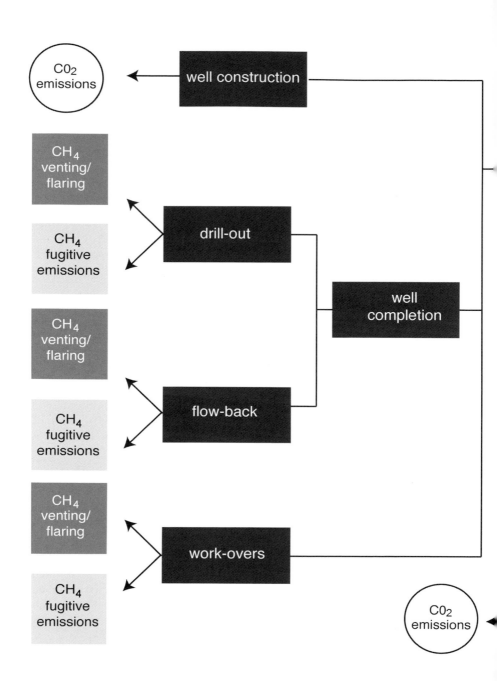

Figure 6.3. Schematic diagram representing the major variables in a life-cycle analysis (LCA) of the total greenhouse gas emissions of natural gas development.

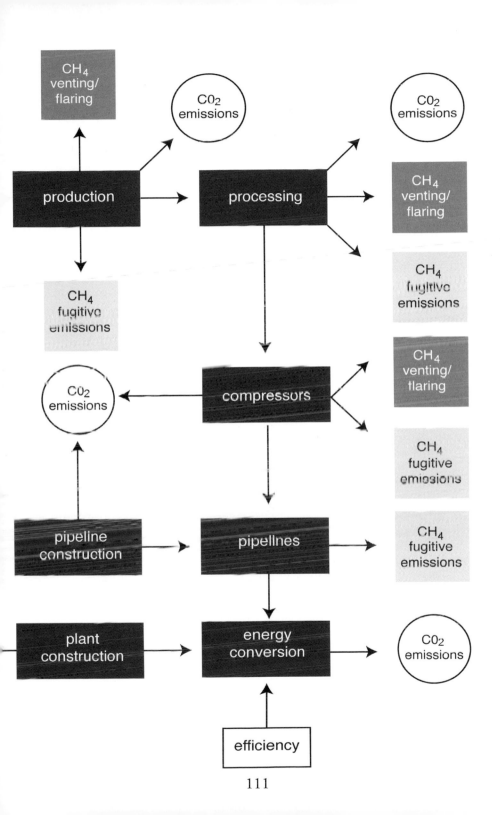

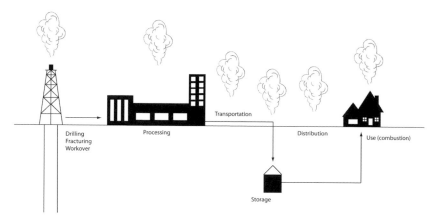

Figure 6.4. Simplified schematic diagram of the major phases of natural gas development in which methane emissions can occur.

and a large cloud of it might explode. Even this, however, is controversial and hard to pin down.[33] In any case, recent EPA regulations require the use of methane-capturing technologies at all new or restimulated gas wells.[34]

EMISSIONS DURING DRILLING AND WELL COMPLETION

The process of getting natural gas out of the ground includes numerous processes (see Chapter 3) during which greenhouse gases can be emitted, including well pad construction, drilling, hydrofracking, flowback, drillout, gas flaring and venting, and removal of liquid from the gas.[35] Non-hydrofracked wells have no flowback or drillout.

Geology also plays an important role. Each gas-bearing rock formation has different geological characteristics, and these can vary considerably, even within a single reservoir. Not all natural gas has the same composition. Thus, the size of the emissions associated with extraction is dependent to some degree on these geological attributes.[36]

Conventional drilling can and does release CH_4, but HVHF has more opportunities for emissions. The process of hydrofracking (see Chapter 4) can release CH_4 mainly through two activities: drillout of the plugs used to hold gas in the ground between hydrofracking episodes, and flowback of wastewater to the surface. Emissions of CH_4 during drillout can vary (0.33–0.62%) for a variety of reasons, and these values do not appear to be controversial.[37]

Emissions during flowback, however, are more disputed. Flowback fluid can contain dissolved CH_4 and can also transport undissolved CH_4 as bubbles. Such a fluid has been described as a "frothy mix."[38] It is not clear how much CH_4 is normally contained in each of these phases. At least in the early stages of flowback, the presence

112

of fluid in the well bore could restrict the upward flow of gas to some degree. As the flow of fluid decreases, however, gas flow can increase. This can be particularly true in the "cleanup" phase of well completion, during liquids unloading.[39] Some of the gas emitted during flowback can be flared, but it is not clear how much.[40]

One reason that it is so difficult to estimate CH_4 emissions is that there are several ways to do it.

- You can directly measure the amount of CH_4 that escapes from a particular point in the production system. This has never been done on a large scale, that is, for many different wells over a long time. Because each individual well is not monitored closely, the usual technique is to take measurements from a few wells and extrapolate to others.

- You can measure the total amount of gas going into a point and the amount coming out, and call the difference the emission. The problem here is that not all of that gas necessarily actually escaped into the atmosphere. For example, you can calculate the total production of a well, and the amount that is put into a pipeline from that well, but some of that difference might have been flared or collected in various ways.

- You can measure the amount of gas going into one end of a pipe and subtract the amount coming out the other end. Yet not all of this *unaccounted-for gas* (UAG) has necessarily leaked into the atmosphere. Some might be due to measurement error or even theft.[41]

When emissions are estimated or reported as a percentage of the total amount of gas that will be produced by a particular well over its lifetime, the value of that production (known as *expected ultimate recovery*, EUR) is of great importance. EUR, however, turns out to be very difficult to estimate consistently. One reason is that gas wells produce at varying rates and for varying lengths of time. The peak rate is called *initial production* (IP). It usually occurs early in a well's lifetime, during the completion phase, after which production declines, but this can occur quickly or slowly. The total lifetime of a particular well can, furthermore, vary from a few years to decades. Both rate and length of production can depend on many factors, from the geology of the reservoir to how the well is managed (*e.g.*, how many times a shale well is refracked or worked over). Conventional gas wells regularly produce for decades. Hydraulically fractured wells, however, have not been around long enough for this to be known by direct observation. All of these complexities add uncertainty to emissions reports: all else being equal, if EUR estimates are too high, CH_4 emissions will appear to be lower than they really are, whereas if EUR estimates are too low, emissions will appear to be higher than they really are.[42]

113

As discussed in Chapter 3, some natural gas, whether from conventional or unconventional wells, emerges "pipeline ready," and can be sent directly to end users. Other gas, however, contains too much water, heavy hydrocarbons, and/or other impurities (such as sulfur) to be put directly into pipelines, and requires some processing before transport. Some of this processing takes place at the well site, and some takes place at processing plants that are remote from the well. Emissions of CH_4 are possible at many points throughout this processing (although the major GHG source during processing appears to be diesel emissions from compressors).[43]

EMISSIONS DURING TRANSPORT, STORAGE, AND DISTRIBUTION

Once extracted and processed, natural gas must be transported to where it will be used. Gas is commonly transported via pipelines, including *gathering pipelines* that take methane from nearby wellheads, *transmission pipeline* networks that transport the gas across the country, and *distribution pipelines* that bring the gas to end users. Although most studies have generally agreed on the magnitude of GHG emissions during transmission, the total range of estimates of CH_4 emissions is large. On one extreme, some studies have suggested that emissions during transport could be as high 1.4-2.5%, or even higher, whereas other estimates are much lower.[44] As mentioned above, leakage from pipelines can be difficult to identify and/or measure because of variation in reporting of "unaccounted-for gas."

Natural gas is also transported across oceans. This process requires that the gas be liquefied and loaded onto a cargo ship. Liquefied natural gas (LNG) is then regasified once it reaches port, put into a pipeline, and distributed to end users. LCA analyses of LNG might or might not include the temporary storage of natural gas in their transportation data, which increases the amount of natural gas lost or unaccounted for. Some of the gas—up to 5%—that is stored in underground storage facilities (such as salt caverns or old oil and gas reservoirs) is never returned to the surface, and so not emitted to the atmosphere.[45] Of course, storing and again extracting the natural gas for further transportation requires additional facility construction and machinery, which increase further GHG emissions.

LCA COMPARISON OF COAL AND NATURAL GAS

So what does all of this mean for determining the PFCI of natural gas (especially shale gas) versus coal? The answer at present appears to hinge on a few major points, each of which remains unclear.

COAL BED METHANE

Like natural gas, coal originated from accumulated organic material (mainly land plants in coastal swamps), and so it is not surprising that coal beds naturally contain methane. This *coal bed methane* is emitted into the atmosphere when the coal is exposed at the surface (or to reduced pressures in mines or fractured rocks above coal seams). Coal bed methane is important as a fuel source, and also as a safety hazard in coal mines.[46] Estimating the amount of CH_4 emitted from coal is a crucial element of any LCA that seeks to compare the potential future climate impact of coal and natural gas.

Underground coal mines worldwide liberate an estimated 29–41 billion cubic meters of CH_4 annually, of which less than 2.3×10^9 cubic meters are used as fuel.[47] The remaining CH_4 is emitted to the atmosphere.[48] Open pit and other "strip" mines are safer to operate than shaft mines in part because they vent all of their CH_4 into the atmosphere.

COAL PARTICULATES AND SO_2

Burning coal produces not only CO_2 (a greenhouse gas), but also *particulates*, which can have a more complex range of effects on climate. Understanding these effects is necessary to fully understand the PFCI of coal burning. Particulates from coal burning include black carbon (BC), which can act like a GHG, absorbing solar radiation and so contributing to global warming. Yet burning coal also produces sulfate (SO_2), which in turn forms sulfate aerosols, and these can reflect solar radiation and so have a cooling effect on the Earth. Determining the net effect of these materials is complex. In addition to absorbing solar radiation, BC also can contribute to cloud formation, which can have a cooling effect. Furthermore, recent technological fixes on coal-fired plants, at least in the U.S., have considerably reduced sulfate aerosol emissions, reducing their cooling potential (and thereby increasing the potential GWP difference between coal and natural gas).[49]

NON-CLIMATE COSTS OF COAL

Although many LCA studies of burning coal have focused mainly on its effects on greenhouse gas emissions, it is clear that most of the total environmental and/or societal and economic costs of coal-fired electricity are not related to climate change.[50] These include thousands of deaths and injuries in mining accidents, the public health costs of air pollution from sulfates, particulates, and the many chemicals that are routinely emitted when coal is burned (including mercury, cadmium, etc.); water contamination due to coal sludge; storage accidents; and land transformation due to strip mining or mountain-top removal. Estimates of these non-climate-related costs range from $62 billion–281 billion per year. The total cost for such damage from the most-polluting, coal-fired, electrical generation plants has been estimated to be seven times as much as the damage from the most-polluting natural gas-fired electrical generation plants. It remains unclear how these costs should be integrated into LCAs that focus mainly on the climate effects of coal versus natural gas.[51]

EFFICIENCY OF FINAL USE

Natural gas is burned by the end user to produce heat. This heat can be used directly for buildings, or for generation of electricity. In theory, this piece of the LCA should be transparent; for example, we know how much natural gas burned to produce electricity, and it is seemingly relatively straightforward to calculate the PFCI arising from the combustion of natural gas (as opposed to processes such as extraction). Even in this case, however, values vary according to the quality of the gas and the efficiency and type of power plant burning it to produce electricity. For example, steam generation units heat water and create steam to turn a turbine; coal is more commonly used in this sort of plant, which has relatively low efficiency (U.S. average 32.7%). Natural gas-fired power plants have much higher efficiency (U.S. average 41.8%). This difference must therefore be taken into account in any LCA of coal versus natural gas.[52]

If natural gas is used for purposes other than electricity generation (*e.g.*, automotive fuel or home heating), the range of PFCI between it and other fossil fuels widens further, because the efficiency of natural gas use in each situation is different. For example, a recent study of compressed natural gas (CNG) vehicles compared to gasoline or diesel vehicles found that increased use of CNG vehicles would have *increased* GWP for 80 or 280 years, respectively, before beginning to produce benefits. CNG vehicles could, however, have lower GWP over all time frames if total CH_4 leakage is low enough.[53]

ESTIMATES OF METHANE EMISSIONS

Prior to 2011, almost no scientific studies had been published on life-cycle CH_4 emissions from natural gas production. In that year, however, a number of such studies were published. Most of these estimated CH_4 emissions in the range of 1–3%.[54] In their study, however, Cornell professor Robert Howarth and colleagues suggested that between 3.6% and 7.9% of the CH_4 from shale gas production escapes to the atmosphere in venting and leaks over the lifetime of a well.[55] Howarth *et al.* not only argued that emissions were high from hydrofracked wells, but also that they were high from "upstream" infrastructure associated with conventional gas production, such as pipelines. Such high emission levels, they argued, make natural gas no better (and perhaps even worse) than coal from a PFCI point of view. These conclusions produced considerable attention in the media and among the general public.[56] Scientific reaction has been mixed: some subsequent peer-reviewed studies have generally supported some of Howarth *et al.*'s conclusions, whereas others have not.[57]

TIME FRAMES

As mentioned above, the time frame over which future GWP is estimated is a very important part of LCA, especially with respect to CH_4, which has a much higher instantaneous GWP but shorter residence or lifetime in the atmosphere than does CO_2. GWPs are traditionally estimated over both 20- and 100-year time frames. Because of the physics of CH_4, its effects will be much larger over the shorter interval, whereas CO_2 will have higher GWP over the longer interval. Which time interval is the "right" one to focus on?[58]

116

Many analyses of global climate change focus on the longer view; for example, what Earth's likely temperature will be in the year 2100, or what the maximum rise in temperature will be under particular scenarios. In these cases, CO_2 is clearly the major causal factor. It is by far more abundant in the atmosphere than CH_4 and remains in the atmosphere many times longer.[59]

Such a long-term focus, however, largely ignores the potential role of *tipping points* in future climate change. A tipping point is a point within the lifetime of a system at which it changes abruptly from one state to another. Several potential tipping points have been identified in the climate system that could lead to an abrupt, qualitative change in its future state, including: loss of Arctic summer sea-ice; irreversible melting of the Greenland ice sheet; disintegration of the West Antarctic ice sheet; reorganization of North Atlantic ocean deep-water circulation; and melting of frozen methane on the ocean floor and Arctic permafrost, among others.[60]

Advocates for a focus on shorter time scales point to increasing evidence that at least some aspects of climate change seem to be occurring more rapidly than expected, and that tipping points can have very large—perhaps even crucial—effects.[61] They argue that CH_4 concentrations should be of particular concern because they are disproportionately likely to affect such tipping points, due to the high short term GWP of CH_4. In support of this point of view are an increasing number of studies that conclude that there are not only a larger number of tipping points, but also that some of them might be reached relatively soon, at much lower temperature increases than previously thought.[62]

NATIONAL AND GLOBAL ENERGY PATTERNS

Total CH_4 emissions from natural gas development might turn out to matter much less than other variables that have little to do with science or engineering. Rather, the PFCI of natural gas usage could end up being determined by the much larger-scale decisions of how long natural gas is used, what replaces it, and when.

For example, the recent increase in the supply of natural gas in the U.S. (produced mostly by HVHF in shale) has reduced the price, which is spurring usage. Yet, even if it is true that natural gas has lower PFCI than coal, and increased use of natural gas could reduce overall PFCI, falling natural gas prices might reduce the cost-effectiveness—and therefore the adoption rates—of "greener" energy sources (such as wind or solar), which have even lower PFCI. In other words, natural gas might become such an attractive "bridge" that it becomes not an intermediate step toward a lower-carbon world, but the new status quo, meaning that global CO_2 might continue to climb rather than eventually decline.[63]

The price of natural gas depends (at least in part) on the demand, and predicting the future demand for natural gas is not straightforward. For example, although recent production in the Barnett Shale in Texas has slowed due to declines in natural gas prices, more recent projections of future electricity demand have encouraged some natural gas investors that demand will rise soon.[64]

Implied in "bridge" scenarios favoring the use of natural gas as a way of moving toward greener energy sources is that this bridge period must be short enough so that GHG emissions do not continue to grow at their present rate. Most studies of the advantages/disadvantages of natural gas, however, have not explicitly studied this. One recent study that did try to consider such a scenario—in which natural gas is eventually phased out completely—concluded that given what it called "fairly ambitious" stabilization objectives (*e.g.*, 450 ppm CO_2), "a natural gas bridge is of limited direct emissions-reducing value, since that bridge must be short," to get to a completely zero-carbon energy system. In such short-term bridge scenarios, coal and gas must both be phased out quickly. In contrast, given "more modest but still stringent" objectives (*e.g.*, 550 ppm CO_2), natural gas could "offer commensurately greater advantages over simply delaying a transition away from coal for a similarly long time."[65]

Such analyses, however, ignore some critical points. First, an increasing number of climate scientists are warning that atmospheric levels of CO_2 above 350 ppm will cause irreversible environmental damage.[66] Second, a still-small but growing number of climate scientists and engineers are arguing that, if it decided to, society could move quickly toward using only renewable energy, and that it would be cost effective to do so.[67]

SO, IS NATURAL GAS "BETTER" THAN COAL?

Few, if any, credible mainstream environmental scientists would not argue today that burning coal for electricity should be reduced as quickly as possible, if only to reduce the public health consequences of coal. At least for now, however, there is still no strong consensus about the size of CH_4 emissions from natural gas development, and therefore no strong consensus about whether, or to what degree, natural gas has a lower PFCI than coal. There appears to be solid (and increasing) data suggesting that CH_4 emissions are higher than previously recognized, possibly high enough to justify serious concern about short-term climate effects. There also, however, appear to be significant questions among a number of qualified scientists about various aspects of this topic. What is needed to break this impasse? More data on actual levels of CH_4 emissions from natural gas infrastructure—published in peer-reviewed scientific papers—is likely the single most important requirement, together with a better understanding of how close various climate tipping points might actually be.

Such a conclusion is frustrating not only to those who hold to one of the alternative points of view, but also to policy makers, for whom a clear and strong consensus one way or the other would be much more helpful. The situation is, however, typical of points in science at which debate is intense, and more data and hypothesis testing are required to increase confidence in one direction or the other.

This uncertainty is not, however, a prescription for complacency. The issues involved here are potentially of enormous consequence, and a current (and, we hope, temporary) lack of strong scientific consensus is not sufficient reason to not worry

118

or take action on them. Scientific conclusions about the way that the world is do not, in and of themselves, dictate what humans should do. This is because human actions are driven as much or more by values than by "facts." If, for example, we place a very high value on something that science tells us has a certain probability of disappearing if we act or don't act in a certain way, then we might choose to change our behavior in the direction of preserving that thing, not just because of science but because of our values. We can always choose to "err on the side of caution." Science might (or might not) be able to tell us what the probability of a particular outcome is, but it certainly cannot tell us what we should do. That, as we discuss in the next two chapters, we must decide in other ways.

Chapter 6 Summary

- Emissions of methane (CH_4) from natural gas production and transport are significant sources of greenhouse gases (GHG) and so of global warming potential (GWP). All credible scientific studies agree that CH_4 emissions should be reduced as quickly as possible to reduce risks of global climate change.

- Measuring CH_4 emissions from gas wells and other infrastructure is difficult and complex, and many more data are needed to reduce uncertainty in current estimates.

- At present, there is still no strong consensus about the size of CH_4 emissions from natural gas development, and therefore no strong consensus about what, whether, or to what degree natural gas has a lower GWP than coal. There appears to be solid (and increasing) data suggesting that CH_4 emissions are higher than previously recognized, possibly high enough to justify serious concern about short-term climate effects. There also, however, appear to be significant questions among a number of qualified scientists about various aspects of this topic.

- The time frame over which GWP is measured is extremely important. Over 100+ years, CO_2 is clearly the most important influence on climate. Focusing only on these longer time scales, however, obscures the importance of climate tipping points, which might turn out to matter more than total long-term GHG levels.

- Regardless of the amount of CH_4 emissions, replacing coal with natural gas could be a bridging step toward slowing global climate change, but only if it is a very short bridge. If cheaper natural gas makes lower-carbon energy sources less attractive, or encourages more fossil fuel use overall, then increased natural gas use would likely increase rather than decrease GHG emissions, accelerating rather than slowing climate change.

Figure 7.1. Hydropower on the Niagara River. The Niagara River boasts substantial generating power. Ontario's Sir Adam Beck Power Plants (there are two), in this photograph, produce almost 2 gigawatts of electricity and sit across the river from New York State's largest power plant—the 2.4 gigawatt Robert Moses Niagara Hydroelectric Power Station in Lewiston, New York.

CHAPTER 7

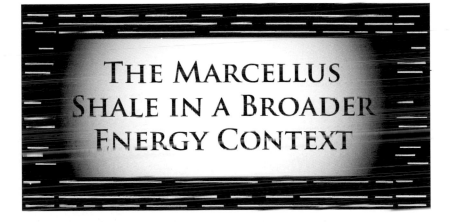

THE MARCELLUS SHALE IN A BROADER ENERGY CONTEXT

Human society was once powered only by biomass—biological material from living, or recently living, organisms: our own muscles (powered by the food we ate), the muscles of animals, or the burning of wood. Over many millennia, humans found other ways to tap into natural energy sources, from water and wind power, fossil biomass (such as oil and gas), geothermal heat from inside the Earth, the sun, and the nucleus of atoms. The transition from brute force and wood-burning to the various industrial sources of energy—and the accompanying adoption of energy-intensive lifestyles—have occurred remarkably quickly, in the course of just a few generations. This has caused changes in virtually every aspect of human life, from economics to war to architecture. As recently as the late 1800s, Pennsylvania's oil wells produced half of the world's supply. Nuclear power has been a commercial source of electricity only since the late 1950s. Electric power has been widely used for just a little more than a century. The U.S. was largely energy self-sufficient until after World War II, when the demand for energy—petroleum in particular—began to outstrip domestic production.

In 2011, petroleum, natural gas, coal, and nuclear power accounted for just over 90% of the energy that Americans use, with various renewable energy sources accounting for the remaining 9%.[1] Energy moves people and goods, produces

123

electricity, heats our homes and businesses, and is used in manufacturing and other industrial processes.

Energy use varies substantially from region to region, and different energy sources are used to fuel different sectors of the economy. The transportation sector is almost completely dependent upon petroleum, whereas the overwhelming majority of both coal and nuclear power is devoted to electricity production. Natural gas use is split nearly into thirds among the industrial, residential and commercial, and electric power generation sectors, and only 3% of the transportation sector's energy comes from natural gas. Because it is a relatively versatile fossil fuel, how much natural gas we use and the ways in which we use it have shifted over time. The impact of developing "unconventional" fossil fuel resources, like the Marcellus Shale as a source of natural gas, cannot be fully understood without first understanding the impacts of modern energy use and production.[2]

No energy resource developed on a commercial scale is environmentally benign, and the growth of both human population and per capita energy consumption in the developing world mean that the impact of even those energy sources that have relatively less environmental effect is increasing. Thus, although conservation and efficiency are essential parts of national and global energy strategies, the practical decisions that need to be made are substantial and not altogether obvious. There are no magic bullets. Understanding and contrasting the different impacts of energy *extraction* (in the case of fossil fuels and uranium), *capture* (in the case of wind, solar, or geothermal), or *harvest* (in the case of biomass) and *use* will help us to make informed choices about future energy development that might occur in or near our communities, and to better understand the impacts of energy development far from home.

Although predictions about changes in the way we procure and use energy in the future must be regarded as uncertain, we can gain some perspective on the way that different energy sources and uses are likely to change in the coming decades. Oil and coal have dominated global energy production and use for generations, although easy-to-access deposits are drying up and the environmental costs of accessing unconventional deposits are becoming clearer. As we develop alternatives to oil and coal, energy development in the future is likely to occur in closer geographic proximity to the end users than it has in recent decades.

Energy sources have a complex range of environmental and economic impacts. This chapter is an overview of where energy comes from: how we use energy, how sources for and uses of energy can change, and the costs and benefits of different energy choices. Energy choices include more than energy sources, but also the decisions about what energy is used to do, the technologies used for extracting or developing energy sources, and the modifications to infrastructure associated with changing energy use, as well as the technologies that depend upon energy. Further, energy choices involve behaviors. How we live determines how much and what kinds of energy we use.

MOST OF THE ENERGY WE USE COMES FROM THE SUN

Excluding nuclear and geothermal, and the influence of gravity in the very small percentage of commercial power captured from ocean tides, the energy sources that power society are ultimately all traceable to the Sun's energy (itself, a nuclear fusion power plant). Biomass energy—from the burning of wood, grass, and other plant matter—releases stored energy that was a product of photosynthesis; fossil fuels are ancient biomass resulting from photosynthetic reactions that occurred millions and millions of years ago. Wind power made global trade possible by powering ships across the sea over a thousand years ago and wind is now providing a small but rapidly growing portion of our electricity. The wind is driven by convection caused by the Sun's uneven heating of Earth's surface. Hydroelectric power (and the waterwheels that preceded it) is made possible by the solar-powered water cycle. Taken together, these fossil and modern Sun-driven sources account for more than 90% of U.S. energy consumption.

Nuclear power is produced by the fission ("splitting") of the nuclei of relatively heavy atoms, such as uranium. Typically, the method for electricity production from nuclear fission is similar to that from fossil fuel power plants—the energy from nuclear reactions (rather than fossil fuels) is used to boil water that produces steam to turn turbines. Nuclear power accounts for about 8% of U.S. energy production. [3] Geothermal energy uses Earth's internal heat either directly for heating or indirectly to produce electricity. Earth's internal heat comes largely from the decay of radioactive elements and from the residual heat left from Earth's formation. Geothermal sources currently account for less than 1% of U.S. energy production.

LOW-COST, HIGH-DENSITY FUELS MADE MODERN SOCIETY

Figure 7.2 shows the sources of the energy that drive our economy and the sectors that use that energy. For most of human history, burning wood and other biomass cooked meals and provided warmth. Fossil fuels (coal, oil, and natural gas) produce much more energy per pound, have been present in huge quantities, and are easier to transport and store. The energy produced by burning wood from clearing a large forest pales in comparison to the energy produced from mining a large coal seam. The Industrial Revolution of the early 19th century was not powered by wood, but was in large part made possible with the advent of new technologies for extracting and burning coal.

In the short term (on the scale of years, decades, or even a century or more), the economic cost per unit of energy from fossil fuels also appeared to be remarkably low. The pairing of high energy density and low short-term cost is behind the structure of energy flows shown in Figure 7.2. Exploitation of these low-cost, "dense" energy sources is fundamental to what makes modern society what it is today. A gallon of petroleum-based fuel can move a typical car 20 miles (32 kilometers) or a ton of freight on a modern locomotive 500 miles (805 kilometers). The convenience

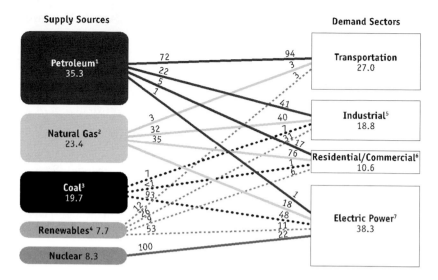

Supply Sources

Petroleum[1]
35.3

Natural Gas[2]
23.4

Coal[3]
19.7

Renewables[4] 7.7

Nuclear 8.3

72
22
5
7
3
32
35
1
<1
93
12
26
9
53
100

Demand Sectors

Transportation
27.0

Industrial[5]
18.8

Residential/Commercial[6]
10.6

Electric Power[7]
38.3

94
3
3
41
40
1
21
17
76
1
6
1
18
48
11
22

Figure 7.2. Primary energy flow by source and sector 2009.

provided by these low costs and high-energy densities, and the infrastructure that we've developed to use and move these fuels, have made it difficult to bring other technologies or economic choices to fruition on a large scale. But, the easy-to-find-and-extract fossil fuels, referred to as "conventional" fossil fuel resources, have become considerably scarcer (especially oil and natural gas) at the same time that their longer-term environmental impacts (especially coal and oil), most notably climate change, have become clear. Costs of these energy sources appear low only when longer-term environmental costs are not included. Understanding this idea is fundamental to understanding transitions in local and global energy sources and uses in the coming decades. Localized environmental impacts of the use of coal, like soot-filled skies, were obvious as fossil fuel use rapidly grew, while other impacts, like climate change and acid rain, were effectively invisible. Only now—years after the Industrial Revolution—are we beginning to more fully understand its unintended consequences for the environment.

A CLOSER LOOK AT ENERGY SOURCES

Our energy comes from petroleum, natural gas, coal, renewable sources, and the nuclear reactions that power some electric plants. That energy is used to meet four different kinds of demands: transportation, industrial processes, residential and commercial buildings, and electric power generation. Production cannot be understood independent of consumption. This section will provide a brief overview of the total energy picture for the U.S., and then describe where certain fuels come from and the history of their use, give selected import and export data, and note changes in use and/or production. Notable environmental impacts of using or extracting different energy sources are described in a later section.

Each energy source might reasonably be considered multiple sources, because there are a variety of reservoirs of each fuel source, those reservoirs can vary substantially in nature, and they can be found in many different parts of the world. For example, oil can come from a conventional land-based well in Texas, Pennsylvania, or Saudi Arabia; from deep below the sea floor in the Gulf of Mexico or the North Sea; from tar sands in Alberta, Canada; or from oil shale from North Dakota, Estonia, or China. These sources all provide oil, but the environmental and economic costs of extraction vary considerably, as does the quality of the oil produced. Such an expanded description could be made for each of the supply sources, and a few of these "sources within sources" will be briefly explored.

We typically measure power in *watts* and energy in *kilowatt hours* (kWh) or British thermal units (BTUs). Light bulbs are labeled with their power usage in watts, with traditional incandescent bulbs ranging from 25–150 watts and compact florescent

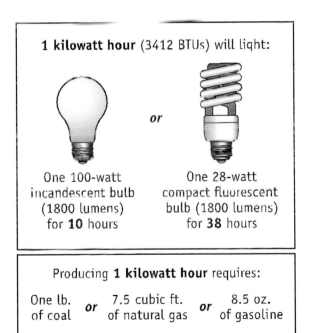

1 kilowatt hour (3412 BTUs) will light:

or

One 100-watt
incandescent bulb
(1800 lumens)
for **10** hours

One 28-watt
compact fluorescent
bulb (1800 lumens)
for **38** hours

Producing **1 kilowatt hour** requires:

One lb.
of coal   *or*   7.5 cubic ft.
of natural gas   *or*   8.5 oz.
of gasoline

Consumption based on traditional thermal power plant production, which loses about 50% of energy as waste heat, plus electrical transmission losses of about 7%.

Figure 7.3. Comparing the energy demand for different light bulb types and fuel sources.

127

bulbs ranging from 5–30 watts to produce a comparable amount of light (Figure 7.3). The largest power plants produce power on the order of hundreds of megawatts (MW) to a few gigawatts (GW). A megawatt is one million watts and a gigawatt is one billion watts. One kilowatt hour (kWh) is the energy required to light a 100-watt light bulb for 10 hours. One BTU is the approximate heat and light energy released in the burning of a standard kitchen match or the amount of energy needed to raise one pound of water one degree Fahrenheit. One kWh is equivalent to 3,412 BTU. A quadrillion BTUs (1,015 BTUs), called a Quad, is equal to 293,000,000,000 kWh.[4]

Steam-driven turbines produce most (but not all) electricity. The trans-portation sector is nearly completely driven by internal combustion engines. Industrial processes are largely heat-driven, and our homes and businesses are mostly warmed through burning natural gas, oil, coal or biomass. That means that the BTU and the Quad are more fundamental units of energy than the kWh. In 2011, 97.3 Quads of energy flowed through the U.S. economy. Figure 7.2 shows U.S. energy flow by source and sector. If all of that energy were converted (with 100% efficiency) to electricity, it would equal 28.5 trillion kWh.

Power plants, however, are never 100% efficient. Typically, about half of the energy content of a fuel is lost as waste heat at the power plant. Newer combined heat and power plants are more efficient, but even these plants lose one third of the energy content of their fuels as waste heat. Roughly another 7% is lost as heat from transmission lines.

Some energy sources tend to be used in specific ways, and some energy needs can be met with more than one kind of fuel. The largest source of energy for the U.S. in 2011 was petroleum at 35.3 Quads, and 71% of the petroleum the country uses is used in the transportation sector. *All* commercially produced nuclear energy and almost all (92%) of the coal burned in the U.S. are used for electricity production.[5] Between 2001 and 2012, coal fell from producing 51% to 37% of U.S. electricity, while natural gas rose from producing 17% to 30%. During this time period, non-hydro renewables more than doubled their percentage of U.S. electricity production— from less than 2% to more than 5%. Both nuclear (approximately 20%) and hydro (approximately 6%) remained relatively flat while petroleum liquids dropped from more than 3% to less than 0.4%. Our energy system is both diverse and changing rapidly (see Figure 7.4).

The decrease in coal's share of electricity production has occurred in tandem with an increase in the contribution of natural gas. Between 1989 and 2012, for example, coal dropped from producing four times as much electricity as natural gas to producing just 23% more. After six decades of steady growth, the use of coal for electricity production began to fall sharply in 2007. During the *six decades* prior to 2007, electricity production from coal increased almost every year. During those sixty years, production never dropped two years in a row, but production has now fallen for four of the last five years.

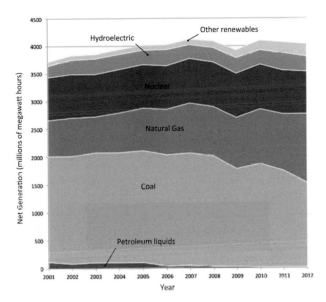

Figure 7.4. U.S. net electric generation by source, 2001–2012.

There are multiple reasons behind the decline in coal use (see discussion below), importantly including the economic recession, so the likelihood of this trend continuing is uncertain. In fact, coal use is expected to increase in 2013, in tandem with a decrease in the use of natural gas for electricity production. In the longer term, however, it seems likely that the share of electricity generated by coal will continue to decline relative to gas.[6]

Petroleum was used as an illuminant, a lubricant, and an ingredient in patent medicines long before it was widely used as a fuel. As mentioned in Chapter 3, the first commercial oil well was drilled in northwestern Pennsylvania in 1859. Petroleum production peaked in the U.S. in the early 1970s, and in 1994, oil imports surpassed domestic production for the first time. Net oil imports generally rose until 2005 when they plateaued for two years and then began to fall. The fall in oil imports coincides with a fall in domestic consumption. In 2009, 9.7 million barrels per day were imported and 7.2 million barrels per day were produced domestically.[7] Since 2009, U.S. oil production has increased, largely due to unconventional production by hydraulic fracturing of oil shales. In 2012, imports accounted for 40% of U.S. petroleum consumption—the lowest since 1991.[8] With less than 5% of the world population, the U.S. consumes approximately 22% of petroleum consumption.[9]

Canada is our largest source of foreign oil. Approximately 40% of crude oil production in Canada is from *tar sands*, naturally occurring mixtures of sand, clay, water, and a very thick kind of oil known as bitumen.[10] Like the Marcellus Shale, tar sands are an unconventional energy source. The process of extracting oil from tar sands is very water and energy intensive. Although the country that is the second

129

largest supplier of foreign oil varies from year to year, the second largest region (after Canada) to supply U.S. oil is the politically unstable Middle East.

Natural gas is often co-produced with oil, and was once simply burned off as waste from oil wells. Most U.S. natural gas is produced and used domestically, with imports dropping to 6% of total gas consumed in 2012. In the first decade of the 21st century, imports averaged 15% of consumption. The decrease in imports is due largely to increases in production from the Marcellus.[11] The overwhelming majority of imports come by pipeline from Canada. Pipeline imports also come from Mexico and some natural gas is exported from the U.S. to both Canada and Mexico.

As mentioned in Chapter 6, Liquefied Natural Gas (LNG) is natural gas that has been cooled into a liquid state so that it takes up only 1/600th of the volume of natural gas. LNG is imported from a variety of countries. Trinidad and Tobago is the lead exporter to the U.S. LNG's small portion of U.S. domestic use grew rapidly early in the last decade, but the U.S. Energy Information Administration projects that it will remain minimal through 2035.[12] The development of shale gas increases the likelihood of gas exports and decreases the likelihood of further imports.

Coal was used as a fuel long before the other fossil fuels—as early as 1100 BCE. Widespread use began in the Middle Ages, when the invention of fire bricks in the 1400s made chimneys cheap and practical. Britain was a coal exporter, including to the colonies of North America, in the 1700s. Although the U.S. burned some coal early in its history, more wood than coal was burned here until the late 1800s.[13]

Between 2008 and 2012, coal consumption fell in the U.S. by 21%. The majority of the drop in usage is attributed to reduction in use for electric power generation. The absolute decrease was 231,000 short tons.[14] The drop in coal production is a result

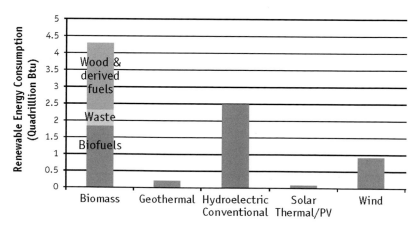

Figure 7.5. U.S. renewable energy consumption by energy source, 2010.

130

of two primary factors—new gas-fired power plants coming online in the last decade, and diminished demand due to the struggling economy.

Almost all coal used in the U.S. is mined here, and some of it is exported. In 2009, production fell considerably (8.3%) to 1,075 million short tons with exports of 59.1 million short tons and imports of 22.6 million short tons. The quality of coal varies substantially in BTU production and amount of particulates and other pollutants that are emitted by burning (Table 7.1).

Nuclear power has only been a commercial source of electricity since 1957 and its substantial growth stopped (or paused) in the United States in the late 1970s as a result of a combination of prohibitive economic cost and environmental concerns, highlighted by the 1979 accident at Pennsylvania's Three Mile Island nuclear generating station, and the long-term handling of nuclear waste. Unlike the later accidents at Chernobyl and Fukushima, there were no documented deaths associated with U.S.'s best-known nuclear accident.

In 2009, the U.S. imported 58.9 million pounds (26.7 million kilograms) of uranium and produced another 4.1 million pounds (1.9 million kilograms) domestically. The U.S. is the largest producer of electricity from nuclear power in the world, but the much smaller population of France gets 74% of its total electricity from nuclear power.[15] In 2009, nuclear power accounted for 8.3% of all U.S. energy production and 22% of its electricity.[16]

RENEWABLE ENERGY

Renewable energy is energy that comes from sources that are naturally replenished. It accounted for 8% of U.S. energy consumption in 2010 and comes in many forms (Figure 7.5). *Biomass* has thousands (if not millions) of years of history as an energy source and it is still the largest renewable source of energy. Wood and wood products still account for just over half of U.S. commercial biomass energy production, but it is now nearly equaled by biofuels (ethanol and biodiesel). This does not include much of the home heating provided by wood burning. Energy from waste, including landfill gas, is also included as biomass. Landfill gas is a mixture of methane and other gases produced by microorganisms breaking down biomass within a landfill.

Table 7.1. Coal classification by type.[17]

Coal type	Percent of U.S. Production (2008)	Range of Heating values (thousand BTU/lb)
Lignite	6.9	4.0–8.3
Sub-bituminous coal	46.3	8.3–13.0
Bituminous coal	46.9	11.0–15.0
Anthracite coal	< 0.1	> 15.0

131

Hydropower is the longest established renewable energy source used for electricity production, and still accounts for the largest portion of renewable electric generation in the U.S. The world's first commercial-scale power plant began operation at Niagara Falls, New York, in 1881. Hydropower accounts for about 7% of U.S. electricity use, and because most substantial river systems have already been dammed for electricity use or their damming has been deemed too environmentally costly to pursue, there is little likelihood that the U.S. can obtain much more energy from traditional hydropower.[18]

U.S. *wind power* generation grew from 4.5 GW in 1999 to 73.9 GW in 2009 and wind power led all other sources of electric power in terms of *new* capacity in 2008 and 2009. *Geothermal* both provides direct heat and generates electricity, using Earth's internal heat as an energy source. It has long been used on a small scale for heating where the heat release is high—at hot springs, for example. In recent decades, capturing Earth's heat for power production has grown substantially, but it remains a small part of the global energy portfolio. Such deep geothermal energy systems sometimes use hydraulic fracturing to increase the flow of water through the rock, which regulates heat and controls energy production. Also in the last few decades, small-scale, relatively shallow (less than 300 feet, or 91 meters) geothermal heat pumps have been effectively used to preheat air in winter or cool it in summer, thus reducing HVAC costs in homes and other buildings. These systems take advantage of nearly constant temperature (approximately 50–60°F) below the surface and do not require fracturing bedrock. Globally, geothermal electricity production has grown 20% since 2005, but its total contribution is still comparatively small at 11 GW of installed electric generating capacity.[19]

In addition to photosynthesis (what green plants do to convert solar energy to biomass), two processes convert the Sun's rays to power for our life and work: *solar thermal* uses the Sun for heat; and *photovoltaic cells* (PV) convert light into electric current. Solar power offers examples of sources within a source as there is not only solar thermal and PV, but many different technologies used for both of these subtypes of energy production. Both are growing rapidly, with global PV generating capacity more than doubling between 2008 and 2010 (from 16 to 40 GW). Both solar thermal and PV systems can range in scale from very small household systems to very large power plants. Global solar thermal capacity, excluding systems to heat swimming pools, grew 16% in 2010, to 185 GW.[20] Solar energy production (thermal + PV) in the U.S. increased 60% between 2006 and 2010.[21] Further, passive solar building design coupled with good insulation and control of airflow can eliminate or practically eliminate the need for heating systems.

Possible future sources of energy include nuclear fusion, cellulosic ethanol, hydrogen fuel cells, tidally driven turbines, and many others. Efficiency, conservation, and lifestyle changes also have the potential to greatly lower energy demand. But lifestyle changes and economic development—and in addition, population growth—also have the potential to increase energy demand.

ALL LARGE-SCALE ENERGY SOURCES HAVE NEGATIVE ENVIRONMENTAL IMPACTS

It has become common knowledge that the extraction and use of fossil fuels damages the environment in a number of ways. Environmental impacts are associated with *any* type of large-scale energy development, although the type and scale of impact vary widely among them.

Coal is frequently mined in ways that risk human life and dramatically alter the landscape, for example, by removing entire mountaintops.[22] Its use contributes to acid rain and has history of yielding huge spills of coal slurry that decimate landscapes. Coal can be surface mined or mined from below ground. When burned, coal has a range of impacts. In recent years, attention has been given to climate impacts, but coal has historically blackened cities and released mercury and pollutants that yield acid rain. In addition, black lung disease and coalmining accidents have killed thousands around the globe every year. Coal mining and accidents also contaminate streams and rivers. The Martin County, Kentucky, coal sludge spill of 2000 sent an estimated 300 million gallons of sludge into two tributaries of the Tug Fork River.[23]

Oil can spill during extraction, shipment, or end use. Oil and natural gas extraction are also hazardous. Less than a month after the 2010 disaster at the Upper Big Branch Mine that killed 29 people came the explosion of the Deepwater Horizon Drilling Platform, and with it the death of 11 crewmembers and the beginning of the worst oil spill in the nation's history. In July 2013, an oil train derailed and exploded, killing an estimated 47 people and decimating a small town in Quebec. More locally, the impacts of Marcellus Shale gas drilling have been reported from numerous regions in Pennsylvania, and traffic accidents are anecdotally on the rise. Natural gas lines can blow and leak. Other environmental, public safety, and public health issues related to shale gas development are detailed throughout this book.

There remain huge reserves of fossil fuels in the world, but these reserves are increasingly difficult and expensive to recover, are generally more water- and energy-intensive than previous extraction, and hold substantial environmental risks. Although substantial reserves remain, fossil fuels are a finite resource. Fossil fuel extraction methods are distinct and each has a suite of overlapping environmental concerns.

Negative environmental impacts are not, however, limited to fossil fuels. The burning of biomass, like fossil fuels, yields carbon dioxide and often other emissions, although carbon emissions are cancelled out if the rate or regrowth of the same or similar biomass equals the rate of harvest. Wind development industrializes rural landscapes in some ways that parallel shale gas development. There is initial heavy construction and the building of access roads in formerly wild places, with similar storm-water pollution and habitat-fragmentation issues. It involves substantial truck traffic for the delivery and pouring of massive amounts of concrete for the turbine towers (and cement production is a large contributor to carbon dioxide emissions). Further, the physics and economy of wind turbines favors the construction of large diameter blades. This brings permanent structures to rural landscapes that are scores to hundreds of feet high. Although impacts upon bird populations appear smaller than initially believed, current designs of turbines could have substantial impacts on bat populations. Turbines also make noise and cast flickering shadows that can impact sensitive residents' well-being.

Solar energy produces no emissions once systems are installed, but there are concerns about the manufacture and disposal of photovoltaic solar cells, and related to the mining practices, particularly outside the U.S., of rare earth metals used in PV and battery production. Whether a commercial-scale solar energy installation generates heat or electricity, it must cover and industrialize considerably more physical area compared to other kinds of power plants that generate the same amount of energy, although smaller-scale solar energy systems can be roof-mounted, reducing these concerns.

There are very serious concerns about nuclear power, especially related to accidents and the long-term management of highly toxic waste material. Accidents in the nuclear industry are uncommon but when they do happen, they appear devastating in scale. However, power production driven by fossil fuels has led to many times more documented fatalities than nuclear power production. Technological advances have drastically cut the amount of radioactive waste used by newly designed nuclear power plants, but cost and environmental concern for accidents remain. Commercial scale hydropower appears unlikely to expand substantially in the U.S. using current technology because the flooding of gorges or valleys typically required for such generation destroys human and wildlife habitat. Indeed, many hydropower plants have been removed in recent decades because of their impact on wildlife, particularly fish migration.[24] There are also concerns related to copper mining, and copper is central to the distribution of electric power. The world's largest human-made hole is Utah's Bingham Canyon Copper Mine, which experienced a massive landslide in 2013.[25]

Consider that one large nuclear plant produces the same amount of electricity as 3,000 large wind turbines or 50 square miles (130 square kilometers) of photovoltaic cells. It is not a simple question to determine the most environmentally benign energy source, and the answer can vary depending on local contexts. There is no such thing as a free megawatt, with the possible exception of the one that is not consumed in the first place. The environmental impact of an energy source is a complicated issue, and although it is clear that some energy sources are more environmentally friendly than others, *all commercial energy production has negative environmental impacts*. For any energy source, there is a wide range of factors to consider, and those factors should be considered in contrast to current energy practices.

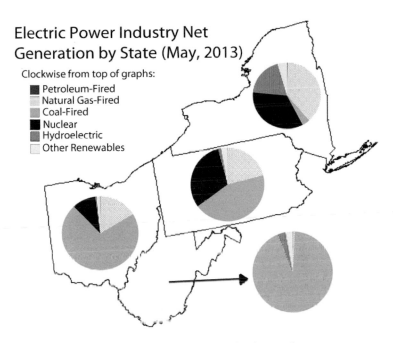

Electric Power Industry Net Generation by State (May, 2013)

Clockwise from top of graphs:
- ■ Petroleum-Fired
- ▨ Natural Gas-Fired
- ▨ Coal-Fired
- ■ Nuclear
- ▨ Hydroelectric
- □ Other Renewables

Figure 7.6. Electric power industry net generation by state within the Marcellus region.

ENERGY PRODUCTION AND USE VARIES CONSIDERABLY BY REGION AND OVER TIME

The four states within the Marcellus region have substantially different energy portfolios (Figure 7.6). West Virginia, which has substantial coal fields, is especially dependent upon coal for both its economy and its energy with 98% of electricity generated by coal. West Virginia leads the nation in net interstate electricity exports. In contrast, 2011 statistics show that coal accounts for only 6% of New York State electricity production. Although this is the smallest percentage in many decades, the percentage of New York electricity that comes from coal has not reached 20% since 1993. Natural gas and nuclear each produce roughly one third of New York State's electricity.[26] Hydropower, mostly from Niagara Falls, accounts for 21% of generation. Thus, the energy status quo depends greatly upon what energy sources exist near where you live.

The diversity of New York's electricity portfolio is unusual for the region. The four largest electric power plants in New York State are powered by four different sources (from larger to smaller: hydroelectric, natural gas, nuclear, and petroleum). The 2,353-mW Robert Moses Niagara plant, harnessing power from the Niagara River, is one of the largest hydroelectric facilities in the world and is the largest single power plant in New York State (Figure 7.1). The Ravenswood Generating Station in Queens is a very close second. Ravenswood burns primarily natural gas, but can also burn petroleum. Four of the plants rounding out the top ten are powered by natural gas and none of the ten biggest power plants in New York State are coal-fired. In both Ohio and West Virginia, nine of the ten largest power plants are coal-fired. In fact, the eight largest plants in both states are coal-fired. The largest power plants in Pennsylvania, Ohio, and West Virginia are all coal-fired and are all larger producers than Niagara Falls' Robert Moses hydroelectric plant. All three of these states also have active commercial coal mines, whereas New York does not.[27]

The energy portfolio also varies substantially over time (Figure 7.7). In 1990, more New York State electricity was produced from petroleum than from any other source. Since then, hydroelectric, natural gas, and nuclear have all taken turns as the leading source of electricity generation in the state. Since 1994, either nuclear (for seven of those years) or natural gas (for nine of those years) has led production.[28] Energy costs vary over time and by source, and power plants are built, retrofitted to use different fuel sources, and are temporarily taken offline for maintenance or repairs.

WHAT DO WE USE ENERGY FOR?
ENERGY DEMAND SECTORS

Different energy sources tend to be used to power different things. Consider lifting a satellite into orbit, powering that satellite, powering the GPS unit that depends upon the satellite, and powering the vehicle with the GPS unit inside it that takes you to your heated or cooled home. Each step requires a different energy source, although the GPS functions through the vehicle's transformation of one energy source into another.

The Energy Information Administration describes energy use as falling into one of four demand sectors: transportation, industrial, residential and commercial, and electric power. We will discuss the two largest sectors: electric power and transportation.

ELECTRIC POWER

North America's electricity grid is the world's largest machine. Electric power is the largest energy demand sector. Electricity is also the largest source of U.S. greenhouse gas emissions, accounting for 33% of all U.S. emissions according to the EPA.[29] Due to its dominance in both use and emissions, and due to its complexity, electricity receives more attention in this document than the other demand sectors. The electrical system is also tremendously inefficient—the majority of the energy input into the system is lost, primarily as waste heat. For 2012, Lawrence Livermore Lab estimates that 25.7 of the 38.1 Quads consumed for electricity generation—two-thirds of the energy for the sector—is rejected as waste heat.[30] So, the electrical system is the biggest machine, the biggest source of greenhouse gas emissions, and one of the biggest sources of wasted energy.

Spinning coiled wires in a magnetic field generates electricity. Most electric power is generated in this way, converting mechanical energy into electrical energy through

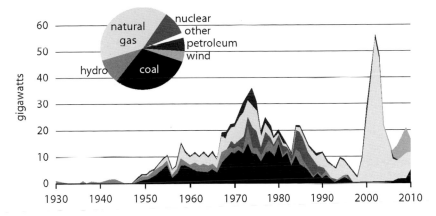

Figure 7.7. U.S. energy capacity by energy type, 2010. Data for 2010 are preliminary. Generators with online dates earlier than 1930 are predominantly hydroelectric. Data include non-retired plants existing as of year-end 2010. This chart shows the most recent (summer) capacity data for each generator. This number changes over time as generators undergo an increase or decrease in generating capacity

the use of a turbine. Power plants heat water to generate steam to turn turbines. The most common sources of that heat are coal and natural gas, with dependence on coal decreasing and natural gas increasing in recent years. Coal and natural gas plants and plants powered by biomass or waste burn fuel to produce heat. Wind and hydro use the movement of air or water, instead of steam, to turn turbines. Photovoltaic (PV) solar cells involve a fundamentally different process than turbines, in which light strikes a semiconductor and this moves electrons from the surface of the semiconductor or between different bands within the material, thus generating electricity.

The heat in fuel-burning plants does not all go to drive the turbines. Traditionally, some heat has been exhausted as waste, but an increasing number of plants now use it for other purposes. These are referred to as *cogeneration* or *combined-heat-and-power* (CHP) facilities and are substantially more efficient in the conversion of fuel to usable energy. As Figure 7.7 shows, most of generating capacity that came online in the last decade was natural gas-fired. Most of this new generation, and most (65%) of the natural gas plants that have come online since 1980, are CHP plants.[31]

In 2009, electric power generation dropped 4.1%.[32] Most of the drop in generation was from coal-fired power plants. Nuclear power generation also dropped by 0.9%, whereas production from natural gas, hydro, petroleum and renewables all increased.[33] The decline in demand is primarily a result of two factors—the economic recession and improvements in appliance efficiency. That the drop in electric production primarily was a drop in electric production from coal is a result of substantial increases in electric production from wind and natural gas.

137

In the first half of the 20th century, coal—used to fuel trains—was the dominant fuel for transportation. Coal was an important transportation fuel through the 1940s but its use in this sector fell rapidly in the 1950s. Now, with the widespread use of cars and trucks, 94% of the sector's power comes from petroleum. The remaining 6% of the sector's energy is split nearly evenly between renewables and natural gas.[34] Most of the renewable contribution to the sector is in the form of biofuels (see Figure 7.1).

As in the electric generation sector, most of energy input into the transportation sector is lost as waste heat. Indeed, transportation is the least efficient energy sector —of the 26.7 Quads of energy consumed by the sector, just 5.6 Quads (only 21%) is used to provide energy services.[35]

California vehicle regulations have a history of influencing energy in the transportation sector. A change went into effect in the summer of 2011 that limits single occupant riders in California's High Occupancy Vehicle (HOV) lanes to pure zero-emission vehicles (100% battery electric and hydrogen fuel cell) and compressed natural gas (CNG) vehicles. Prior to July 1, 2011, certain gasoline-electric hybrid vehicles were allowed in HOV lanes. This change in regulation, along with federal tax incentives, is rapidly bringing new demand for the production of electric and CNG vehicles. The BNSF Railway Company, one of the largest haulers of rail freight in the U.S., is pilot-testing locomotives powered by liquefied natural gas (LNG)[36] and, because many landfills produce natural gas, many refuse truck fleets are switching to compressed natural gas (CNG).[37]

PREDICTING FUTURE ENERGY USE AND AVAILABILITY IS CHALLENGING

In 1954, the Chairman of the U.S. Atomic Energy Commission predicted, "Our children will enjoy in their homes electrical energy too cheap to meter..."[38] Predictions about a topic as complex as energy are bound to sometimes widely miss the mark, and therefore should be read with a skeptical eye. The Energy Information Administration makes predictions about future energy use and development in their *Annual Energy Outlook*. These projections look decades into the future and typically include a range of likely outcomes based on things like the potential for technological advances, political will, global economic situations, and past use. Looking back to *Annual Energy Outlook 2001* with *Projections to 2020*[39] shows some discussion of the development of natural gas from onshore unconventional sources and substantial growth in supply from this source. Natural gas production was projected to rise just above 20 tcf per year for the lower 48 states and this is exactly what happened, however, the rise in production was not as linear as projected. That same report placed the high renewables case projection for wind development at approximately 8 GW for 2010. The actual value for the year was more than three times higher than the highest projection—in excess of 34 GW.

Chapter 7 Summary

- Our energy system is ever-changing and differs widely across regions. New technologies and societal wants and needs will bring continuous change to where we get our energy from and how we use it. Sweeping and difficult-to-predict changes will doubtless happen repeatedly, while other parts of the system will change remarkably slowly.

- There are many different energy sources, but fossil fuels produce most of our useable energy. Energy use falls into four sectors: transportation, industrial, residential/commercial, and electric power. Some energy sources are used primarily within one sector.

- Comparison of environmental impacts of different energy sources is challenging due to the fundamentally different nature of impacts from different sources. These comparisons can be challenging even when the fuel is the same. Gas procured through HVHF has different impacts than gas extracted by conventional means.

- Any change in the energy system impacts both the environment and the economy. Most increases in energy production and use will damage the environment, and need to be considered in the context of current energy practices. By better understanding the components and their interconnections, and how these have changed in the past, we can make more informed decisions about our energy future.

- Because use of any large-scale energy source has substantial environmental and economic impacts that ripple through the connected systems of our environment and society, the most direct way to reduce negative environmental impacts from energy use is to use less energy.

Figure 8.1. "Grand ball given by the whales in honor of the discovery of oil wells in Pennsylvania," Vanity Fair, *1861.*

CHAPTER 8

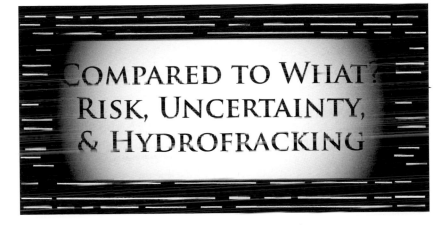

COMPARED TO WHAT? RISK, UNCERTAINTY, & HYDROFRACKING

Contaminated groundwater, lowered air quality, boom and bust economic cycles, global climate change, fragmentation or destruction of ecosystems, diminished landscape aesthetics and quality of life are among the many factors to consider in weighing the risks of natural gas development in the Marcellus Shale. These are risks associated with HVHF, but, as discussed in Chapter 7, there are risks associated with all large-scale energy production and use. We care about these risks because we care about human health and the health of ecosystems, economies, and communities. The fundamental question for a particular large-scale energy source is therefore not, "Is this bad for the environment?" because the answer is invariably "Yes." The fundamental question is, "Is this less bad for the environment than the other ways that we get energy now or might get energy in the near future?"

Managing risks involves both reducing current risk and avoiding future risks while also evaluating the benefits that are associated with the practices and materials in question. Changes in the energy system often involve changes in the nature, scale, and location of risk factors. For example, will an energy change reduce global risk, for climate change for example, while increasing local risks to water and air quality? How and by whom is it determined if such tradeoffs are appropriate?

This chapter will provide no easy answers, but rather try to reveal some of the complexities to help the reader better determine which factors are most important from his or her perspective. It also hints at an important question related to the reality that all large-scale energy production involves substantial risks to human health and the environment: *Can we make a huge reduction in energy demands?* The most direct path to reduce risks associated with energy use is to use less energy. The greater the reduction in energy consumption, the greater the reduction in associated risks. Eliminating one energy source without decreasing the demand for overall energy use means that the risks of energy production are still out there—perhaps externalized to another country, state or community, but still impacting human health, the environment, and the economy somewhere.

This is not to imply that equivalent amounts of energy produced by different means have equally negative impacts, only that they all have negative impacts. The nature of those impacts varies substantially from source to source. Investigating risks associated with energy production is akin to rubbing one's nose in the energy system—and in some sense, it all stinks.

The major risks associated with hydraulic fracturing in the Marcellus Shale have been discussed in the preceding chapters. This chapter will focus on how and why people judge risk, and why that judging is challenging work. From the outset, it is very important to note that whereas scientific literacy is necessary for the evaluation of risk, scientific literacy alone, at least in the traditional sense, is not sufficient.

The chapter addresses three key questions:

- What are the significant anticipated risks associated with HVHF in the context of our energy options?

- What characterizes and bedevils effective risk analysis?[1]

- What can be done to reduce current risks and prevent future risks?

The issue in question is not simply the hydraulic fracturing of rock, but HVHF contextualized in a series of connected processes and systems associated with natural gas extraction. "Hydrofracking" is often used as an abbreviated label for the full suite of activities; slickwater horizontal high-volume hydraulic fracturing (and its partial acronym HVHF) is awkward to read, but is more descriptive of the associated risks.

CONSIDERING RISK

All energy choices have environmental, economic, and cultural consequences. Choosing to develop an energy resource will have consequences at the point of extraction or harvest, along the transportation process, at the point of use, and for the global environment. Choosing not to develop a resource will mean continued dependence on other existing sources, the development of alternatives, or reduction of energy consumption. Many of these consequences pose risk, which can be defined as exposure of something or someone to danger, harm, or loss. Four issues to consider in the evaluation of risk:[2]

1. Probability: "What are the chances of…?"

2. Consequences: "What is the severity of the possible outcome?"

3. Hazard: "If the material or process is hazardous, in what way and to what degree?"

4. Exposure: "How can we decrease or eliminate exposure, and thus harm?"

This provides useful guidance on weighing risk, but is not explicit about the purpose of risk management. In the case that is the subject of this book, we can identify five perspectives that inform public health responses (in the broadest sense) to global warming to the question of hydrofracking:[3]

1. Prevention: "What actions can be taken to avoid harm in the future and reduce existing impacts?"

2. Risk management: "How can risk be systematically be identified, assessed and reduced?"

3. Co-benefits: "What actions will yield benefits in multiple arenas?"

4. Economic impacts: "How can the public be protected at the lowest possible cost?"

5. Ethical issues: "How can issues for future generations, vulnerable populations, and ecosystems be democratically and justly addressed?"

The first issue in the first of these two lists—probability—is a confounding factor for all that follows in both lists. Understanding probability is fundamental to predicting likely consequences, and to determining the appropriateness of preventative action, for two examples. Uncertainty about the impacts of HVHF raises questions about how and whether it can be appropriately managed. That HVHF has only been used on a widespread scale for a short time means that there is little peer-reviewed research on the nature and extent of the impacts on health, environment, and economies.[4] Moreover, impacts past a decade might be estimated, but cannot yet be measured.

Some risks to consider

The different risks associated with large-scale energy production and use number at least in the dozens. Because they are delineated elsewhere in the book, only a selection will be mentioned here. Many of the most serious concerns—including groundwater and surface water contamination, water treatment, concerns about the amount of water used, and NORMs—are described in Chapter 4. Chapter 5 addresses additional concerns, including habitat fragmentation and loss, air quality, noise, truck traffic, and the industrialization of rural landscapes. Chapter 6 addresses what is perhaps the most serious issue that we face in the 21st century: global climate change. This list is not intended to be exhaustive, but rather to generate ideas about potential impacts.

These concerns generally connect to concerns about effects on human health. Because widespread use of HVHF is still relatively new, there is little peer-reviewed literature on the health effects of the technology. In May 2012, the federal Centers for Disease Control and Prevention (CDC) and the Agency for Toxic Substances and Disease Registry (ATSDR) issued a joint statement noting that they "do not have enough information to say with certainty whether natural gas extraction and production activities including hydraulic fracturing pose a threat to public health. We believe that further study is warranted to fully understand potential public health impacts."[5] Also in May 2012, the *Journal of the American Medical Association* published an editorial entitled, "Rigorous Evidence Slim for Determining Health Risks From Natural Gas Fracking" that raised a wide range of health concerns related to HVHF, but, as the title noted, rigorous evidence on health effects are limited.[6]

Some impacts, however, are apparent, especially those related to worker health. Silicosis is a lung disease in which inhaled silica particles become trapped in lung tissue, reducing the lungs' ability to take in oxygen. It can be fatal. Silica dust can also lead to lung cancer, tuberculosis, chronic obstructive pulmonary disease, and kidney and autoimmune disease. Airborne silica dust is common during hydraulic fracturing (see Figure 5.1). The Occupational Health and Safety Administration (OSHA) and the National Institute for Occupational Safety and Health (NIOSH) issued a Hazard Alert addressing worker safety related to silica exposure at HVHF sites after field-testing showed that 31% of 116 full-shift air samples collected from eleven HVHF sites in five states exceeded NIOSH's recommended exposure limit by more than ten times; 47% of workers in the study were exposed to levels of silica dust above the permissible exposure limit.[7] Although silicosis is not curable, it is preventable through reduction of exposure to silica dust.

Health effects related to water contamination from HVHF activities remain a serious concern, but have not been verified on a large scale. Contaminated water wells near HVHF gas wells warrant testing and monitoring. In the spring of 2013, during CDC testimony before the Subcommittees on Energy and Environment of the Committee on Science, Space and Technology in the U.S. House of Representatives, concerns were noted related to possible contamination from HVHF activities on groundwater wells in five states as well as health concerns related to air quality near compressor stations.[8]

RISK COMPARISON: WHAT IS LESS BAD?

Taken together, the two numbered lists above offer guidance in how and why to reduce and prevent risk. In evaluating any energy source, these issues should be considered, and they should be considered in the context of the larger energy system. Part of what that means is that, in addition to considering these issues related to HVHF (the focus of this book), we must also consider these factors for the energy sources that will be used in place of natural gas from HVHF if HVHF does not occur. Alternatively (or perhaps simultaneously), we must consider the impacts of using less energy. Evaluating only the risks directly associated with a single energy source assures unintended consequences by neglecting the larger system effects.

There is no doubt that HVHF uses millions of gallons of water and contaminates that water to a greater or lesser extent; that the development of the infrastructure required to extract gas and move it to market industrializes rural landscapes and communities and alters ecosystems; that it leaks some amount—perhaps a lot—of methane along the way from the well to the burner; and that burning natural gas produces carbon dioxide. All of that is beyond dispute, but without comparing these impacts with the impacts of other energy sources, knowing about these issues is insufficient for large scale decision-making about energy systems.

Because all energy sources have both risks and benefits, evaluating the risks of HVHF should compare the risks and benefits of different energy sources, determine weightings for different factors, and ultimately pursue the question of which energy sources are "less bad," and what combination of energy sources best balances risks and benefits with respect to health, the environment, and the economy. There is no simple, clear answer: different people weigh factors differently. In considering some of these character weightings here, it is not our intent to develop any kind of precise weighting scheme. That is a matter for communities and policy makers to decide. Rather, we will lay out considerations in the hope of informing that decision-making.

Box 8.1 lists selected risks that could increase with HVHF and selected risks that might be diminished. Most of the prospective benefits will only apply if HVHF offsets other energy development. This indicates that the global benefits accrue only if the more risky energy resources are not simply exported, externalizing local risks and compounding global ones. Energy demand has declined (in total and per-capita) within the U.S. in the last several years, but not globally. For example, although coal exports have increased in the last few years, they have not increased to match the overall drop in U.S. demand, so less U.S. coal is being used now both within the U.S. and beyond than was the case in 2008.[9] U.S. greenhouse gas emissions in 2009 were 6.9% lower than 2005 levels and equivalent to emissions in the mid 1990s.[10]

Risk issues directly associated with HVHF are importantly different than recent environmental catastrophes, such as the 2011 Fukushima Daiichi nuclear plant explosions/tsunami disaster in Japan; the Deepwater Horizon oil-well blowout in the Gulf of Mexico in 2010; the Upper Big Branch Mine disaster in West Virginia, also in 2010; or the oil train derailment in Lac-Megantic, Quebec, that killed 47 in 2013. Although it is very important to compare these catastrophes in terms of the scale of injury, death, and damage, the rapidity with which these incidents occurred are not likely to be matched by an accident related to HVHF. A more appropriate analogy might be a disaster that plays out over a much longer timeframe, like Bangladesh's epidemic of arsenic poisoning due to contaminated groundwater. In that case, the scale of the disaster in terms of human lives lost or directly affected was far greater than the other catastrophes listed here.[11]

Box 8.2 lists a series of questions to consider when making energy decisions, beginning with questions focused on natural gas use and development. Note that questions related to environmental impact are generally also closely related to questions of public health.

Table 8.1 delineates estimates of deaths per trillion kWh for different energy sources. The estimates in the table draw from several sources and are historical in nature. In addition to consideration of data from the past, catastrophic potential, "...the ability to take the lives of hundreds of people in one blow, or to shorten or cripple the lives of thousands or millions more"[12] is taken into consideration. In other words, it is not as simple as evaluating how many have been killed or injured in the past to determine the risk of such catastrophes. One must also consider the worst that could go wrong or is likely to go wrong. Nevertheless, historical data matters.

ENERGY TRANSITIONS REDUCE SOME RISKS BUT INCREASE OTHERS

Throughout human history, there has been a repeated pattern of discovering and developing an energy source, harvesting or extracting that energy source until it becomes scarce, increasingly expensive, and/or environmentally damaging to procure, developing an alternative(s) to the now scarce and expensive energy source, and repeating the process. Each time this has happened, it has involved a tradeoff from one set of costs and benefits for another.

The political cartoon in Figure 8.1 highlights one of these transitions—the transition from whale oil to petroleum in the 1860s. To take another example, in the 1600s, Holland rose to become a world power, powered in large part by new technologies for extracting and burning peat. Gradually, peat became scarcer, more expensive and more environmentally damaging to procure; while this fuel source was being depleted, Great Britain was developing ways to more efficiently extract and burn coal.[13] In the United States at the turn of the last century, much of the eastern forests had been nearly completely cleared to power rising industry. The risks that accompanied the burning tons of whale oil, peat, coal, or wood were (and still are) legion.

146

Table 8.1. Estimated deaths per trillion kWh.[14]

Energy source	Mortality rate (deaths/ trillion kWh)	Portion of energy use
Coal (global average)	170,000	50% global electricity
Coal (China)	280,000	75% China's electricity
Coal (U.S.)	15,000	44% U.S. electricity
Oil	36,000	36% of energy, 8% of electricity
Natural gas	4,000	20% global electricity
Biofuel/biomass	24,000	21% global energy
Solar (rooftop)	440	< 1% global electricity
Wind	150	~ 1% global electricity
Hydro (global average)	1,400	15% global electricity
Nuclear (global average)	90	17% global electricity

A century later, the process is again repeating itself, with conventional sources of fossil fuels being supplanted by unconventional fossil fuel sources and so-called alternative energies. "So-called" because, as each energy source emerged throughout history, it was an alternative to some other energy source that had been in place.

Of course, there are differences in how this plays out. The forests of the eastern U.S. have largely returned (although not in the same form) in just a few generations. Nonrenewable energy sources can in fact renew, but likely only on a time frame that is many times that of the existence of humans as a species. It will, for example, take thousands or millions of generations for fossil fuels to re-form.

Renewable energy sources developed on large scales have high environmental costs as well. One of the largest photovoltaic (PV) arrays in New York State is the University of Buffalo's quarter-mile-long 740-kilowatt Solar Strand. It sits approximately 120 miles (193 kilometers) from one of the largest nuclear power plants in the world—Ontario's 4.6-gigawatt Bruce Nuclear Generating Station. If UB's Solar Strand maintained its current width and its length was extended to match the capacity of Bruce, it would need to extend from Buffalo to Denver. Although some environmental impacts could be reduced by mounting the PVs on rooftops, the energy and resources for production are simply huge. The largest human-made hole in Earth's surface is Utah's Bingham Canyon Copper Mine. Producing electricity from renewable sources still requires plenty of copper and we have no renewable alternative to it.

147

Box 8.1. Considerations for assessing the environmental impact of high volume hydraulic fracturing. Note that many benefits only accrue if energy from HVHF offsets the energy use from other sources.

Prospective Liabilities	Prospective Benefits
1. Industrial infrastructure degradation of rural landscape • Loss of recreational tourism and resulting local and state revenue • Fragmentation of wildlife habitat by roads and pipelines • Truck traffic in rural areas with its associated risks, including diesel fumes, traffic accidents, road damage, and noise **2. Uncertainty of effect on global GHG emissions reduction efforts** • Fugitive emissions could result in increased global warming potential • Development of durable infrastructure for natural gas could prolong fossil fuel dependence **3. Local pollution of air by VOCs/ ozone precursors** • Long-term health effects on local populations • Reduction of regional air quality, especially through increases in ground level ozone and smog	**1. Substitution of natural gas for coal and petroleum** • Less particulate, sulfur dioxide, and heavy metals emissions, leading to lower health impacts • Enabled phase-out of coal and petroleum, reducing climate impacts • Reduction of mountaintop removal for coal mining • Comparatively better worker safety • Reduced water contamination through spills from oil pipelines or failure of dams retaining coal slurry • Reduction in accidents like the Deepwater Horizon or Upper Big Branch Mine Disasters **2. Transition fuel to carbon-constrained economy** • Lower natural gas prices to speed rather than slow closing obsolete coal power plants • Enhanced baseload electrical generation capability substituting for intermittent sources (*e.g.*, wind, solar)

Box 8.1 (continued).

Prospective Liabilities (cont.)	Prospective Benefits (cont.)
4. Local pollution and depletion of streams and groundwater • Long-term health effects on local populations and workforce • Ecological impact of increased pollution on local wildlife • Long term increase in chronic contamination of water supply, requiring increased storage, health degradation of residents **5. Community and economic transitions** • Boom-bust economic cycles • Increased income gaps • Changing community dynamics • Worker safety issues, including increased silicosis risk and exposure to NORMs	**3. Proximity of energy source for electrical generation to the urban centers of the NE United States** • Avoidance of natural gas supply bottleneck due to imports and long-distance transportation costs • Reduced transportation risks • Lowered costs for locally-produced gas, electricity **4. Local economic investment in shale gas regions** • Employment year-round, in contrast to current seasonal tourism • Per-capita revenue for local landowners from mineral leasing • Poverty-associated health risks through economic improvement within the region • Water quality improvements due to increased monitoring • Changing community dynamics

Box 8.2. Questions to Consider Regarding Risks for Different Energy Choices

Note that questions related to environmental issues are typically also questions of public health. The term "costs" generally refers to health and environmental costs as well as economic ones.

Many Americans heat their homes and the hot water within their homes with natural gas. A growing portion of our electricity also comes from natural gas.

- Where should that gas come from?

- Or, should we stop heating our air and water and generating electricity with natural gas?

- If we do stop these practices, what should we doinstead?

- Who is paying the health and environmental costs for our current energy habits?

- What health, environmental, and economic costs will come due at a later date?

Questions to consider for any energy source:

- Who would pay the health, economic, and environmental costs if a new resource is developed?

- What are the health and environmental costs and benefits of the energy status quo?

- What happens to the environment at the point of extraction?

- What wastes are generated and disposed of away from the point of extraction?

- What happens to public health and the environment as a result of use?

Box 8.2 (continued).

- Per unit of energy generated, how do these impacts compare for the different energy sources being considered? (This might be a comparison of a proposed or new source to the status quo.)

- Which is greater, the cost of development or the cost of efficiency measures? Stated another way, in the consideration of developing a source that produces 45 megawatts, would it be more beneficial (or more costly) to reduce consumption by 45 megawatts instead?

These questions generally frame the issue as a choice between developing a new energy source and maintaining the energy status quo. *There are more than two choices.*

- What other options exist?

- Are they being seriously considered?

- Are they practical? Why or why not?

More pointed questions to consider for any energy source:

- Are accidents known to kill or injure people? Consider extraction, transit, and use.

- Does standard use alter the environment in ways known to kill or injure people or to make people ill?

- How does the death and injury rate compare to other sources per unit of energy?

- Are there political costs or benefits associated with this energy source?

PLANNING (AND REGULATION) CAN REDUCE RISK

If HVHF is to come to a region, local public health agencies should receive adequate resources and training to support education, outreach, surveillance and monitoring, needs assessment, and prevention activities. The Center for Disease Control and Prevention in Atlanta, Georgia, defines ten essential services for public health, shown in Box 8.3. The first of these—monitoring health status—in the case of HVHF, logically begins with baseline data beginning prior to any drilling. Such practices offer the co-benefit of identifying and correcting sources of waterborne illness that might have gone undetected for years. If fully enacted, many of these essential services offer substantial co-benefits.

Uncertainties abound in the rapidly changing science, engineering, economics, and community dynamics associated with HVHF. However, uncertainties can be anticipated and managed to some degree. Frumkin asserts, "Policies that anticipate potential public health threats, use a precautionary approach in the face of uncertainty, provide for monitoring, and promote adaptation as understanding increases may significantly reduce the negative public health impacts of this approach to natural gas extraction."[15]

EXTERNALIZED RISK

All around the country, nontraditional energy sources are being developed or considered, each of which has particular environmental consequences. In many places, the environmental costs of power source development have been externalized—for example, the environmental costs of coal extraction have often not been close to where the energy from coal is consumed. Figure 8.2A shows energy consumption for New York State in 2011, by energy source; Figure 8.2B shows New York State energy production for the same year. The state's largest energy source—natural gas—accounted for nearly twice as much energy use as the second largest source (gasoline).

Natural gas production in New York yielded 37 trillion BTUs in 2011 while 1,246.9 trillion BTUs of energy were consumed from natural gas, meaning that in-state production yielded 2.5% of demand. Texas is the largest producer of natural gas in the U.S. Pennsylvania is expected to supplant Louisiana in 2013 as the second largest producer. No gasoline—the second largest piece of the state's energy usage—is produced in New York State. The largest source of energy produced in New York is nuclear power (ranking third in terms of consumption) and that is produced using uranium mined outside the state. Thus, the overwhelming majority of the environmental impacts of the extraction of energy resources to power the state are borne by those outside of the state.[16]

Although conventional gas drilling still accounts for most of the natural gas production in the U.S. and the world, HVHF is a very rapidly growing segment of production. Its use has risen as a result of decreased cost and because conventional

Box 8.3. Ten Essential Services for Public Health[17]

1. Monitor health status to identify and solve community health problems.

2. Diagnose and investigate health problems and health hazards in the community.

3. Inform, educate, and empower people about health issues.

4. Mobilize community partnerships and action to identify and solve health problems.

5. Develop policies and plans that support individual and community health efforts.

6. Enforce laws and regulations that protect health and ensure safety.

7. Link people to needed personal health services and assure the provision of health care when otherwise unavailable.

8. Assure competent public and personal health care workforce.

9. Evaluate effectiveness, accessibility, and quality of personal and population-based health services.

10. Conduct research for new insights and innovative solutions to health problems.

drilling has extracted extensively from known reserves, increasing the scarcity of natural gas from these traditional reserves. As was the case for peat in Holland and whales in our oceans, the easy-to-access resources have been extracted. Natural gas is a very large source of our energy and the environmental costs, which have always been significant, are increasing.

That others bear so much of the risk of New Yorkers' energy use raises questions of ethics, values, of NIMBY ("not-in-my-backyard")-ism, and of what is known as the

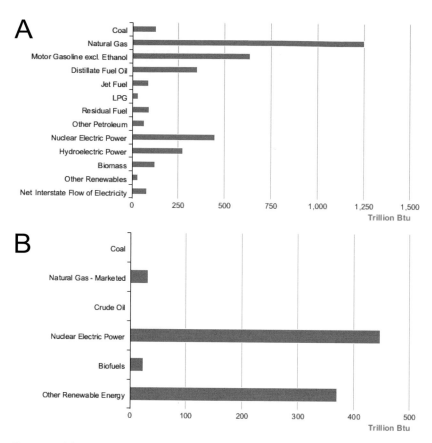

Figure 8.2. (A) New York State energy consumption estimates in trillions of BTUs. (B) New York State energy production estimates in trillions of BTUs. Note the very large difference in scale between (A) and (B). New York State uses more energy from the natural gas that it imports from other states than it produces from all "in state" energy sources combined.

"status quo bias."[18] Preventing risks in one's community is an understandable goal, but if the activities that create the risk are merely moved outside of the community and not ended, then the solution is problematic.

RISK PERCEPTION AND SCIENTIFIC LITERACY

Figure 8.3 is excerpted from work by Professor Dan Kahan and the Cultural Cognition Project at Yale Law School.[19] The trend for the general public in the nationally representative sample of 2,000 people in a poll taken in the spring of 2013 shows no strong relationship between level of scientific literacy and the assessment of risk for either global warming or HVHF. When the sample is divided according to worldviews, however, increasing science literacy increases the polarization of the

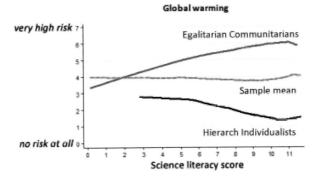

"How much risk do you believe each of the following poses
to human health, safety, or prosperity?"

Global warming

very high risk 7
6
5
4
3
2
1
no risk at all 0

Egalitarian Communitarians

Sample mean

Hierarch Individualists

0 1 2 3 4 5 6 7 8 9 10 11
Science literacy score

"Fracking" (extraction of natural gas by hydraulic fracturing)

very high risk 7
6
5
4
3
2
1
no risk at all 0

Egalitarian Communitarians

Sample mean

Hierarch Individualists

0 1 2 3 4 5 6 7 8 9 10 11
Science literacy score

Figure 8.3. The relationship between science literacy and cultural polarization.

population according to perceptions of risk. That is, deeper scientific understandings alleviate concerns regarding risk for some and deepen those concerns for others.

This and associated issues of how to define and build "Marcellus Shale Literacy" are discussed further in Chapter 9. This includes issues of cultural cognition, loss aversion, motivated reasoning, and cognitive bias. All of these issues are associated with difficulties of understanding risk.

Chapter 8 Summary

- Real, substantial risks are associated with HVHF, but because they are different in nature from those associated with other energy sources, it is difficult to universally evaluate whether HVHF risks are lesser or greater than those associated with other energy choices.

- Successful risk management involves diminishing existing risk, preventing future risk, evaluating co-benefits, and making economic/ethical decisions.[20]

- Preparation and regulation can ameliorate risk. If HVHF is coming to a region, local public health agencies should receive adequate resources and training to support education, outreach, monitoring, needs assessment, and prevention activities.

- It is not possible to maintain current energy systems indefinitely, and the current system has substantial risks. Risks for any single method of generating energy on a large scale are also substantial.

- Transitioning from one energy source to another typically means transitioning from one set of risks and benefits to another. The fundamentally different nature of different energy sources makes comparisons of risks challenging.

- Substantial risks associated with New York State's energy system in 2013 are externalized; that is, the risks are borne by people, ecosystems, and economies outside of New York State.

- Uncertainty confounds risk preparedness, but effective risk management across a range of issues provides valuable lessons. Monitoring, adapting, and using a precautionary approach that anticipates potential changes in public health, economies and ecosystems can reduce, but never eliminate, risk.

- Because all large-scale energy production methods have substantial risks, the most direct approach to lowering risks to public health, ecosystems, economies, and communities is to use less energy.

Figure 9.1. A piece of the Marcellus Shale from a quarry in Seneca County, New York.

CHAPTER 9

TEACHING ABOUT THE MARCELLUS SHALE

Suddenly people are interested in where their energy comes from. The interest that many people are taking in the Marcellus Shale has created a "teachable moment." This is an opportunity to help build understanding about the risks and benefits of HVHF, but it is more than that. Indeed, one of the greatest challenges of offering education about the Marcellus Shale is helping people to understand that some of the most important things to understand are not directly about hydrofracking, but about the larger energy system. Educational initiatives should therefore reach beyond simply teaching about the risks and benefits for human health, the environment, and the economy directly associated with extracting natural gas from the Marcellus Shale, but to larger Earth system science issues, and, perhaps most importantly, a broader understanding of energy and climate.

This chapter is intended to serve as a gateway to a range of resources that can support teaching about the Marcellus Shale and the larger energy system. Before simply listing these resources, however, we provide some background about the types of knowledge needed to effectively teach this kind of content. The chapter begins with an overview of those ideas, and concludes with a list of resources for building that knowledge. It is heavy with links to online resources; many others are included in the book's endnotes and references.

Special knowledge and skills needed to teach

Effective teaching, of course, requires an understanding of the subject matter at hand, but subject matter knowledge alone is not sufficient for someone to become an effective educator. Almost anyone with a college degree has sat through enough classes to have experienced at least one smart teacher or professor who knew the content well yet was simply a poor teacher. Most have experience with this before leaving high school.

To be an effective teacher, one has to know how to teach. To put it in the language of the discipline of education, understanding pedagogy is required, and, one can't deeply understand pedagogy in a way that stands apart from the content to be taught. The skills and knowledge that a math teacher needs to be effective are different from the skills and knowledge that an English teacher needs, and that difference is more than a difference in content knowledge. In the language of education, this is Pedagogical Content Knowledge.[1]

Neither an English teacher nor an engineer needs to understand the variety of approaches to solve particular kinds of mathematical problems (even if they have to occasionally solve such problems), but a math teacher does. A medical researcher does not need to know common misconceptions related to the understanding of evolution, or how to address controversial issues in the classroom, but a biology teacher certainly does. These are examples of PCK.

Understandings needed to teach about the Marcellus Shale

It would be ideal if there was a consensus definition of what it meant to be "Marcellus Shale literate" before determining what specialized skills and knowledge are needed to teach toward such a goal. The information in this book and the other materials and resources that we have produced for Marcellus Shale outreach serve as a good introduction to the science related to the Marcellus Shale. However, waiting for a scientific consensus regarding the environmental impacts of HVHF before defining Marcellus Shale Literacy is not really an option. Part of Marcellus Shale PCK therefore includes knowledge about teaching uncertainty and the process of science. Although scientific understandings are never fully settled, consensuses emerge regarding many ideas in science—and some areas of science are more settled than others. The nature of the impacts for human health, the economy, and the environment associated with HVHF in the Marcellus Shale is an area of science that contains numerous areas of active study not yet settled.

Some people will disagree regarding the degree to which there is a consensus, and what that consensus is. If we can take as "givens," however, that some questions of environmental impact are unsettled, and that it is necessary to help people understand the science as best we can anyway, where do we begin?

One key piece of this answer is that the Marcellus Shale cannot be understood independently of its context. So, resources are needed to help us understand the Marcellus in the context of the energy system, the environment, the geological context in which it formed, and other contexts as well.

For the sake of simplicity, here is a list of topics and kinds of understanding that are needed to teach about the Marcellus:

- Systems and system effect
- Geology
- Technology (of extraction)
- Hydrology
- Toxicology and human health
- Climate and climate change
- Ecology
- Economics
- Energy systems
- Cultural issues
- Government/civics
- Risk analysis
- Pedagogy
- Psychology
- Technology (for teaching and learning)

In such a short list, important categories have surely been omitted, and an exhaustive list would be very long indeed. Read the list, weight the importance of the categories included, and consider what might be more important that was not included. The last bullet might seem redundant, but is significant enough to deserve a bit of additional attention. The technologies for teaching and learning are important and changing rapidly.[2] Each of the bullets above can be broken down into supporting topics or ideas, and this will be addressed to some degree in what follows.

The genesis for this list was work with a group of experienced educators who generally needed neither introductory content material for their discipline, nor beginners' readings on teaching. The remainder of the chapter will include a few resources for those who are unfamiliar with what educational research says about best practices, but it primarily focuses upon the needs of the educators with some familiarity with this body of educational research.

TEACHING CONTROVERSIAL SUBJECTS

In this book and in the associated educational outreach done at the Paleontological Research Institution, our outreach goal has been: (1) providing more in-depth, easier-to-read information about the science aspects of HVHF, based on available data and literature, than is generally available elsewhere; and (2) using a point of view and language that is impartial regarding particular policies for or against HVHF.

Our materials have been externally reviewed by specialists on the respective topics, regardless of their point of view for or against drilling, and we try to be especially clear about points on which competent researchers disagree and why. A number of other organizations and individuals have taken a similar approach, and each educator must consider how and where to draw the line between helping their audience to understand a topic to make informed decisions about their actions and persuading the audience to take a particular actions.[3]

Like many other science educators, PRI educators have substantial experience in addressing other controversial issues, particularly evolution and climate change, and in helping other educators to do so. Each science topic that involves public controversy has its own unique aspects, depending on the degree of disagreement among experts in the field and particular societal decisions and risks associated with the topic. HVHF is importantly different from evolution and climate change in that for both climate change and evolution, there is scientific consensus about the issues of general concern. The overwhelming majority of scientists who study climate agree that the climate is changing and that humans are contributing to the change. Likewise, the overwhelming majority of biologists agree that life has evolved over billions of years of Earth history.

For the question of whether HVHF does more or less harm to the environment than other practical ways of producing energy at very large scales, there is currently little in the way of scientific consensus. The issue is not one of simple scientific literacy, although that is an essential component. If it was simple scientific literacy, then those who are scientifically literate would all agree, and that is not the case. We can look to the scientific literature being written right now about these issues, or, for some of us, to our own circles of friends to find highly scientifically literate people who profoundly disagree on the nature of the environmental threats posed by HVHF. This is similar to other controversial issues—people who disagree with the scientific consensus often have extensive technical knowledge related to the science in question, but that knowledge is often not contextualized with the broader related science, and other situational factors.[4]

As we have emphasized throughout this book, the issues surrounding HVHF, energy, and the Marcellus Shale are profoundly complex. Educators often strive to *simplify the seemingly complex*, and that clearly has its place. The world, however, is indeed a complex system of systems, and the desire to simplify too much can become an obstacle to effective teaching. At such times, educators need to *complexify the seemingly simple*. Some specific strategies for helping learners explore the complexities follow.

EDUCATIVE ASSESSMENT OF BASIC ENERGY LITERACY

Many of the programs on the Marcellus Shale offered by Paleontological Research Institution for the general public and educators begin with a simple question: *"What are the two largest energy sources for electricity produced in New York State?"* Participants are shown an alphabetical list of the largest energy sources for electric generation for both New York State and the United States:

- Coal
- Hydro and pumped storage
- Natural Gas
- Nuclear
- Other Gases
- Other Renewables
- Petroleum

As the list is read, participants are asked to raise their hands twice, once for each of what they think are the largest sources. The largest sources since 1998 have been natural gas and nuclear power, with natural gas as the largest source for New York State electricity since 2010. As of August 2013, the question has been asked of at least 1,500 participants, and fewer than 5% have correctly identified the two largest sources.

There are a number of reasons to ask and discuss the question. First, it draws attention to the problem of making informed decisions about changes to the energy system when some of the most basic information is not widely known. Asking the question and discussing its implications also helps learners connect their existing conceptions about the content to factual information that might refute those conceptions. Without making such connections, learners are likely to maintain their initial conception rather than integrate the factual information into their understandings.[5] In the ensuing discussion, it is noted that when the entirety of New York energy use is considered, nearly twice as much energy is produced from natural gas than from the second largest source (gasoline) and that, although there are thousands of gas wells within the state, they provide less than 3% of the natural gas consumed within the state.

The question is intended not simply to assess what the audience knows, but also to serve as a hook (as a result of its unexpected answer) to engage them in new learning that refutes their current conception. Simply providing correct information, however, even if the audience is hooked, is unlikely to substantially change understanding.[6]

TEACHING SCALE

Understanding HVHF and its impacts on human health, the environment, and the economy requires understanding scale, often using sizes, volumes, and other numbers that are well outside of most people's experiences. For example, the Marcellus Shale is estimated to contain trillions of cubic feet of undiscovered, technically recoverable, natural gas. The typical hydrofracked Marcellus well is on the order of a mile deep, whereas drinking water wells are typically on the order of a few hundred feet. Millions of gallons of water are used to fracture a well, as well as thousands of gallons of chemicals. A gigawatt is 1,000 megawatts and a megawatt is 1,000 kilowatts. The

Marcellus Shale is hundreds of millions of years old. We are concerned that carbon dioxide concentrations in the atmosphere have reached 400 parts per million.

Understanding *scale* is fundamental to understanding Earth system science, energy, and the Marcellus Shale. The range of scales relevant to these issues is astronomical and requires abstract thinking that is a challenge to most learners. There are helpful approaches. Put zero on one end of blackboard or piece of paper, and a trillion on the other; ask people to place a thousand, a million, and a billion in between the end points. Typically, the points will be far more spread out than the "to scale" reality of placing all of the listed values in a space equal to one thousandth of the distance between endpoints.[7] This activity and its subsequent discussion is, like the question on New York State's electricity production, a form of educative assessment.

Another strategy for teaching scale is to connect the abstraction of very large and very small numbers to familiar examples. The Reflecting Pool on the National Mall in Washington (Figure 4.1) holds approximately 4 million gallons—roughly the equivalent of the amount of water required to fracture a typical Marcellus gas well. A backyard swimming pool holds about 30,000 gallons—on the order of the volume of required chemical additives. A kilowatt lights ten 100-watt light bulbs (although 100-watt light bulbs are far less common now than they were a few years ago; see Figure 7.3 for more on the energy required to light a light bulb), and a kilowatt-hour (kWh) will light those light bulbs for one hour. A megawatt-hour is one thousand kWh, and a little more electricity than the average U.S. home uses in a month. Eight gallons of gasoline provides about one million btu (MMbtu) of energy. The energy equivalent of one person's physical labor for an eight-hour workday is approximately three tablespoons of petroleum. (See Chapter 7 for further discussion of energy density.)

Resources to support teaching about the Marcellus Shale

Many learners seek evidence-based information that is relevant to the Marcellus Shale, but a few critics on both sides of the issue might express frustration if they perceive that the information provided does not always support their own positions. (Indeed, reviewers of drafts of this book aligned at both poles of this issue commented that the book was biased against their positions *when referring to the same chapters*.) Readers of this book, like the participants in our programming, are expected to reach their own, hopefully informed, decisions about whether to support or oppose drilling in the Marcellus Shale and how to participate in discussions of regulations and monitoring.

The close study of the energy system required for doing this work deepens the understanding of one core idea: we must use far, far less energy than we presently do if we wish to maintain healthy ecosystems. As U.S. Senator (and founder of Earth Day) Gaylord Nelson noted, "The economy is a wholly owned subsidiary of the environment, not the other way around."[8] Maintaining our way of life depends upon using less energy.

Of course, this list is just a start—one doesn't develop the skills and knowledge to be a master teacher by reading a book, or even following up on the resources described within this chapter. All one can do is scratch the surface, but hopefully it will be a useful scratch. Although the list proposed here might seem long, it is only the beginning of such a task. Most of the bullets above could stand alone as worthy chapters on their own, or entire books, or more.

The types of included resources vary. All are intended to be grounded in research that's relevant to the particular area of interest, and some are peer-reviewed research articles. Most are one degree removed from the primary source and are hopefully more accessible to the general public than reports of research tend to be. Some of the resources were written by researchers for a general audience, whereas others were written by educators or journalists.

BIG AREAS: GENERAL RESOURCES, SCIENCE CONTENT, PEDAGOGY, & A BIT ABOUT SYSTEMS

GENERAL MARCELLUS SHALE RESOURCES

- *The Science beneath the Surface: A Very Short Guide to the Marcellus Shale* (the book that you are reading right now)

- *The End of Country* by Seamus McGraw[9]
  Here's a blurb that describes McGraw's book well: "Deeply personal, sometimes moving, sometimes funny, *The End of Country* lays out the promises and the perils faced not just by the people of one small Pennsylvania town but by our whole nation."—Robert F. Kennedy, Jr.

- *Under the Surface: Fracking, Fortunes, and the Fate of the Marcellus Shale* by Tom Wilber.[10] Wilber also maintains the blog "Shale Gas Review."[11]

- Links from the Resources page of Paleontological Research Institution's Marcellus Outreach site:[12]
  ¤ Cornell Cooperative Extension Natural Gas Resource Center[13]
  ¤ Cornell's Water Resources Institute[14]
  ¤ Penn State University's Natural Gas Resources[15]

- "There's no such thing as a free megawatt: The Marcellus Shale as a Gateway Drug to Energy Literacy" is a detailed but still introductory presentation on the Marcellus Shale and the broader energy system that we have assembled for use in our programming.[16]

- *A Research Guide to the Marcellus and Utica Shales*, a project of Carnegie Mellon and the Pennsylvania State Association of Boroughs. This website includes over 1,200 resources, mostly in the form of articles in both the popular and scientific press.[17]

- The *WSKG Marcellus Resource Page* has information on recent news items on shale gas both in the Marcellus region and nationally.[18]

- *The Marcellus Shale Information Clearinghouse* at The Institute for Energy and Environmental Research for Northeastern Pennsylvania at Wilkes University has reports and links to a variety of resources, focused especially on Pennsylvania.[19]

- *The Science of the Marcellus Shale* is PRI's project name to help build public understanding of the scientific issues surrounding the Marcellus Shale, of which this book is a part. From PRI's Marcellus Shale website,[20] you can follow the links to a range of resources.

THE SCIENCE OF HOW PEOPLE LEARN

There is a huge number of books and articles written about how to teach well. To understand how to teach, it is essential to understand how people learn, so that's where we suggest starting. Many good teachers seem to understand this intuitively, but every teacher can benefit from looking more closely at what research says about cognitive science. The National Research Council's Committee on How People Learn has produced a few reports, and we especially recommend two of them—one short and one long, with the introduction to the longer one providing a mid-range choice. Both are available as free pdfs from the National Academies Press, where hard copies of the books can also be purchased. You need to register to download the free pdfs, but it's free, quick, and easy (see the links in the endnotes).

- *How People Learn: Bridging Research and Practice.*[21] This is the short one, and the Key Findings can stand alone, for the shortest overview.

- *How Students Learn History, Mathematics, and Science in the Classroom.*[22] This is book length, and you can pick and choose relevant chapters to meet your particular goals. The summary, which you can download without registering, is

166

a little heftier version of the Key Findings of the book above, with richer descriptions.

Although the two above resources are useful for understanding learners in any setting, they are more tailored to the school setting. The National Academies Press also has resources for informal educators. *Surrounded by Science: Learning in Informal Environments*[23] is focused on learning *science* out of school settings, and understanding the Marcellus Shale goes beyond understanding the science. Hopefully some of the resources below will be helpful in rounding out the omission.

The above are more targeted toward learning than teaching, but teaching tends to go better when the nature and needs for learning are considerd before, during, and after engaging in teaching. Educators should also give good thought *before they start* about where they wish to end up. That is, before teaching, think carefully about what the goals are in terms of what the learners should know and are able to do as a result of the experience. Wiggins & McTighe's *Understanding by Design*[24] provides guidance on how to engage in backward planning. There are many resources to support what is laid out in the book, but we suggest starting with the book.

A BIT ABOUT SYSTEMS

Systems thinking warrants much more attention than space allows. A systems perspective involves seeing the relationships of the parts of a system as the focus of study as much as the parts themselves. Such a perspective is necessary to understand the multitude of ways that HVHF has affected the environment, communities, and economies. Those who already see the world from a systems perspective see the interconnections among everything here. If you don't, then...

> *What happens is that when you breach a holistic structure, and you say, or do it without saying it, ... 'I am only going to attend to this end of the relationship. I am going to study the role of the doctor.' ... Now a role is a half-assed relationship, you know. It's one end of a relationship. And you cannot study one end of a relationship and make any sense. What you will make is disaster.* —Gregory Bateson[25]

Like considering a doctor's effectiveness without considering the healthcare system in which she operates, if one considers the Marcellus independently of the larger energy system, and the systems to which the energy system is connected (that is, everything), one will simply miss too much. For example, simply consider sitting at one's computer, browsing information about energy. Where does the energy for the computer come from: which power plant(s), and what is the source of energy for that power plant? Is it local, or from another state (or country)? Where do the parts for the computer come from, and where did the energy come from to produce those parts? How were the materials for the parts mined, transported, manufactured, and transported again, and where did the energy for those processes come from? Which environments were impacted, and how were humans impacted in those places? What are the benefits, on the other hand, of having access to information and education about energy via that computer. Do those involved in, or impacted by, extraction of the materials and energy that make computer use possible also have access to computers, education, and information? One can easily add examples of such interconnections *ad infinitum*. Bringing the example back around to HVHF, where HVHF is or is not used (in the Marcellus Shale or another shale gas deposit), what energy source might be used instead, and what would be the difference in environmental and human impacts?

The last paragraph is more of an example of how systems thinking is relevant to the matter at hand than it is about the nature of systems. *Thinking in Systems: A Primer* is an excellent introduction to the topic.[26]

THE REALLY BIG PICTURE: WHAT SHOULD EVERYONE UNDERSTAND ABOUT THE EARTH SYSTEM?

NATIONAL SCIENCE STANDARDS

The Next Generation Science Standards (NGSS)[27] were released in April 2013, built upon *A Framework for K-12 Science Education*[28] and intended to replace the 1996 *National Science Education Standards*[29] now in use. Among the fundamental changes in NGSS is a shift in focus to so-called "Core Ideas," "Cross-Cutting Concepts," and, "Science and Engineering Practices," all of which include much more attention to systems approaches than the 1996 standards. Each of these documents offer a vision of the scientific knowledge and skills that every high school graduate should have.

EARTH SYSTEMS SCIENCE LITERACY INITIATIVES

In 2004, oceanographers and marine science educators came together to craft *The Ocean Literacy Framework*.[30] Scientists in other Earth science disciplines followed suit, each crafting their own sets of "literacy principles." As a result, there are now many different sets of literacy principles for different Earth systems science disciplines. These are helpful resources because they describe consensus views that scientists and educators think are important within each of these disciplines.

Although the consensus of scientists and educators within the different Earth science disciplines (oceanography, climate science, atmospheric science, geology, and energy) is helpful, the process also created an unwieldy set of expectations for practical use in classroom—38 "Essential Principles" and 247 "Fundamental Concepts," all related to the Earth sciences and all written at the commencement (12th grade) level. Where high school Earth science is offered in the United States, Earth science is almost always a single one-year course (also typically including astronomy). One-hundred-and-eighty days of instruction in the typical school year makes it unlikely that all of these principles and concepts will be successfully taught.

We have compared and synthesized these principles into a set of five Bigger Ideas and two Overarching Questions that, when taken together, address all of the different literacy initiatives.[31]

Overarching questions:

- How do we know what we know?
- How does what we know inform our decision making?

Earth system science Bigger Ideas:

- The Earth is a system of systems.
- The flow of energy drives the cycling of matter.
- Life, including human life, influences and is influenced by the environment.
- Physical and chemical principles are unchanging and drive both gradual and rapid changes in the Earth system.
- To understand (deep) time and the scale of space, models and maps are necessary.

THE ENERGY SYSTEM

This chapter's introduction notes that the Marcellus Shale must be understood in the context of the larger energy system, so a key part of the science of the Marcellus is the science of energy, and the status of our energy system. This is highlighted in Chapter 7.

A great deal of information about the energy system is available from the Energy Information Administration website.[32] There you can find information about power production and energy use, primarily focused upon the U.S., but also with information from around the world. The geography tab allows users to explore state-level data and a user friendly interactive map of the United States' energy infrastructure and resources. Every commercial-scale power plant is on the map, as are coal mines, pipelines, major power lines, oil and gas basins, and more. Clicking on a power plant's icon on the map reveals production data for that plant.

CLIMATE CHANGE

Our energy system has produced changes in the climate system, and climate issues are extremely relevant to the Marcellus Shale. Natural gas is a fossil fuel that when burned releases carbon dioxide, and when natural gas (which is primarily methane) leaks, the warming effects are greater still. The simple combustion reaction of natural gas releases less carbon dioxide per unit of energy produced than the burning of coal or oil, but if the energy system leaks gas, this advantage could be lost.[33]

References on climate change are abundant. A few include:

- The National Oceanic and Atmospheric Administration (NOAA) website[34]

- NOAA's National Climatic Data Center (NCDC) has excellent resources documenting climate through time globally and nationally[35]

- The Intergovernmental Panel on Climate Change has a wide variety of highly regarded technical information on climate change gathered by an international team of experts.[36]

- The Climate Literacy and Energy Awareness Network hosts an extensive collection of materials for learning and teaching about climate and energy. Each included resource has been through a rigorous review process involving both content and pedagogical experts.[37]

RISK

Understanding risk and how to teach about risk is central to teaching about energy and climate. Chapter 8 provides an overview on risk, and two other resources for teaching about risk include the following:

- In *Risk: A Practical Guide for Deciding What's Really Safe and What's Really Dangerous in the World Around You*, the authors Ropeik and Gray[38] describe issues to consider in the evaluation of risk.

- "Risk School," by Michael Bond,[39] is a short article from the journal *Nature* on whether or not we can teach people to understand risk.

RESOURCES FOR TEACHING CONTROVERSIAL ISSUES

Polarizing issues, such as HVHF and the Marcellus Shale, are also emotional issues. Those emotions are connected to controversy, and these resources address teaching controversial issues.

- *The Debunking Handbook.* This short publication offers valuable insights into how to avoid your advocacy backfiring. You might be familiar with the feeling more entrenched in your beliefs after a debate. Chances are

fairly good that the person you debated also feels his or
her beliefs more strongly.[40]

- Motivated avoidance is the practice of avoiding learning
  more about issues one knows little about to prevent
  unpleasant realizations. Irfan briefly describes the practice
  in a news story on the study by Shepherd and Kay.[41]

Understanding cognitive biases, including the status quo bias and confirmation bias,
is also fundamental to effectively teaching controversial issues. This is addressed to
some degree in all three of the above resources, but it warrants further mention.
We're all victims of confirmation bias—the tendency to favor information that
confirms our preconceptions. It's natural to try and fortify your position, but that
natural tendency can be a serious impediment to understanding. Likewise, people
tend to favor the status quo, even if change can bring reduced risk and additional
benefits. Change is scary and unfamiliar, even if current practice has substantial
known risks. Daniel Kahneman's *Thinking Fast and Slow*[42] deeply explores cognitive
biases and strategies to move from gut reactions to more analytical approaches to
thinking things through.

COMMUNITY IMPACTS

HVHF, even the idea of HVHF, can bring sweeping changes to communities.
Dynamics change with the infusion of money, workers, trucks, and more.

- Community impacts are well described in *The End of
  Country*,[43] described above. The book includes both
  positive and negative impacts, focused on the author's
  hometown in rural Pennsylvania.

- "With Gas Drilling Next Door, County in New York
  Gets an Economic Lift," is a *New York Times* article on
  economic impacts for Elmira, New York.[44]

171

Chapter 9 Summary

- Teaching well requires knowledge of content, learners, and pedagogical approaches that are typically specifically related to the content you wish to teach. This approach recognizes that the educational system is a complex system, in which relationships among the system's parts are at least as important to understand and study as the parts themselves.

- The Marcellus Shale, high volume hydraulic fracturing, and the broader energy system are each better understood in relation to one another. They too, in other words, are best understood from a systems perspective.

- The nature of controversial issues, the teaching of scale, and common biases provide substantial challenges to teaching about the energy system, but can be overcome with careful planning and reflection.

- To teach about the Marcellus Shale and associated environmental impacts of drilling, it is helpful to tap into the wide array of resources that exist on both content and teaching strategies.

CHAPTER 10

SO WHAT?

As we stated in the Introduction, the purpose of this book is not to provide policy or regulatory recommendations about what decisions need to be made on high-volume hydraulic fracturing in the Marcellus Shale. Rather, our goal is to review and summarize in an accessible way, and in as impartial manner as we are able, the sort of scientific information and analysis that one might reasonably expect should be considered in making such decisions. Science isn't policy. It does not tell us what we should do. However, it should surely inform policy, and we should surely look to it for rational analysis of the possible consequences of what we choose to do. And science does—frequently but not always—reach conclusions that are recognized by a large enough proportion of knowledgeable experts to be codified as "what we know." The short summary below attempts to summarize the *current* state of what science "knows" (*i.e.,* has reached a reasonable consensus on) about natural gas in the Marcellus Shale. As discussed in the preceding chapters, there is ample reason to believe that many aspects of this tentative consensus might change in the near future as research proceeds.

The geologic history of the Marcellus Shale explains the occurrence and behavior of natural gas in the formation, and also informs many aspects of the processes of extracting that natural gas and the environmental concerns associated with that extraction. The Marcellus Shale was deposited approximately 390 million years ago in a warm, shallow sea with little bottom oxygen. Organic matter accumulated on the sea floor as microscopic organisms that lived near the surface of the water died and were buried without decomposing. Over time and with great heat and pressure, the organic matter was transformed into natural gas. Today, gas-bearing portions of the Marcellus Shale underlie parts of Pennsylvania, New York, West Virginia, and Ohio. The Marcellus contains a very large amount of recoverable natural gas.

The formation of the gas in the rock combined with tectonic activity to create natural fractures (joints) in the Marcellus Shale. These fractures increase the ability of gas to flow through an otherwise relatively impermeable rock. Artificial fracturing of the rock, however, increases the potential amount of gas that can be extracted. The process of fracturing the rock—by pumping large quantities of water, sand, and chemicals into drilled bore holes—is called high-volume, slickwater hydraulic fracturing (HVHF), or hydrofracking.

Natural gas has been known to exist in the Appalachian Basin (which includes New York and Pennsylvania) for hundreds of years. New York was home to the nation's first natural gas well, and has been producing gas commercially since the 19th century. Hydrofracking was developed in other shale gas basins, and has been used in its current form since the 1960s. What is new in recent years is the combination of hydrofracking with horizontal directional drilling, which was first used in the 1980s. The novelty of these combined technologies is the reason that natural gas drilling in the Marcellus Shale is referred to as "unconventional."

The purpose of hydrofracking is to increase the permeability of the shale to allow more natural gas to flow into the well bore and up to the surface. This is accomplished by fracturing the rock using a mixture of water and chemicals at high pressure to expand existing fractures and create new ones. Another material, usually sand, is then delivered to the fractures to keep them open so that natural gas can flow out of the shale.

Hydrofracking horizontal wells requires very large volumes of freshwater. The sourcing of this water, and its ultimate fate—both in the ground and after it is pumped back out of the wells—are major environmental challenges for large-scale, high-volume hydrofracking. Because of its geological history, the Marcellus Shale contains naturally occurring radioactive material, as well as high levels of salts, volatile organic compounds, and heavy metals. Some of these materials can threaten human health and the environment. Some of the chemicals added to the water pumped into hydrofracked wells are also potentially harmful to human health and the environment.

As with all large-scale energy development, negative effects to the environment are unavoidable in large-scale hydrofracking. There is no question that natural gas extraction (conventional and unconventional) can and has at least occasionally contaminated ground and surface water, although it can be difficult to prove that any single instance of contamination was a result of a particular gas well. Surface spills and leaks, faulty well construction, and erosion can all also contaminate local water supplies. Increases in certain air pollutants, such as volatile organic compounds and nitrogen oxides, both of which contribute to lower air quality, are also associated with Marcellus gas development, as the result of engines running drilling and hydrofracking equipment, truck traffic, and venting of natural gas in well-completion activities. Solid waste from drilling, much of it containing toxic materials, can leach chemicals into the ground if not properly disposed of. Soil erosion and habitat fragmentation caused by the build-up of drilling sites pose threats to both terrestrial and aquatic ecosystems and wildlife. Noise produced by drilling and fracturing activity has the potential to affect both wildlife and human populations in the areas near well pads and compressor stations.

Although current data suggest that hydrofracking itself does not cause significant seismic events (earthquakes), such events have resulted from disposal of drilling wastewater into the ground. The natural hydraulic fractures in the Marcellus Shale might or might not be likely to allow fluid or gas migration from the Marcellus Shale to major underwater sources of drinking water; it is highly unlikely, although possible, that fractures caused by hydrofracking allow additional large-scale migration and resulting contamination of drinking water.

All significant energy development has negative environmental consequences, and different forms of energy differ in the type and scale of consequences. Assuming that global energy needs stay constant or increase (which seems likely for the foreseeable future), the principal question for society is therefore one of choices. For example, from a global perspective, might the unavoidable negative consequences of natural gas extraction in the form of high volume hydrofracturing (in the Marcellus and elsewhere) be "worth it," if the expanded use of natural gas (*e.g.*, at the expense of coal) could reasonably be expected to reduce the potentially much larger risks of global warming due to the buildup of greenhouse gases in the atmosphere and the array of other harmful effects of coal mining and use?

Unfortunately, despite a great deal of heated debate, there is currently no clear scientific consensus on the answer to this very important question. Emissions of methane (CH_4) from natural gas production and transport are significant sources of greenhouse gases (GHG) and so of global warming potential (GWP). Measuring CH_4 emissions from gas wells and other infrastructure is difficult and complex, and many more data are needed to reduce uncertainty in current estimates. Such studies have only recently begun. Although it remains unclear exactly how much CH_4 is emitted from natural gas development, all credible scientific studies agree that such emissions are serious contributors to global climate change and should be reduced as quickly as possible.

At least for now, the majority of studies appear to agree that GHG emissions associated with shale gas production are roughly the same as those for conventional gas production, and that natural gas in total has a lower potential future climate impact (PFCI) than coal over the 100-year time frame. This must, however, be seen as a tentative conclusion and, given the current rapid pace of research on this topic, will clearly be subject to increasingly rigorous tests in the months and years ahead.

The time frame over which GWP is measured sounds arcane, but is extremely important for understanding PFCI. Over 100+ years, carbon dioxide (CO_2) is clearly the most important influence on global climate. Focusing only on these longer time scales, however, obscures the potential importance of more abrupt changes—so-called "tipping points"—which might turn out to matter more for the future of Earth's climate than long-term GHG levels. The larger the effect of such tipping points are, and the sooner they might be reached, the more dangerous the shorter-term GWP of CH_4 becomes.

The current balance of scientific evidence suggests that replacing coal with natural gas in generating electricity currently could be a helpful "bridging" step toward slowing global climate change, but *only if it is a very short bridge* (*i.e.*, 20–30 years). If, however, cheaper natural gas makes even lower-carbon energy sources (such as wind or solar) less attractive, or encourages more fossil fuel use overall, then an increase in natural gas use could increase, rather than decrease, GHG emissions, accelerating rather than slowing global climate change. *In this case, there would appear to be little environmental justification for expanding use of natural gas, and the net scientific judgment of overall risk would likely be that the risks of large-scale hydrofracking outweigh the benefits.*

Throughout human history, changes in our overall energy sources and uses have changed both slowly and very rapidly. These changes—and their consequences—have usually been unforeseen and in retrospect would have been difficult or impossible to predict. Frequently, one part of the system changes gradually while another is quickly transformed. For example, almost all of the nuclear power plants in the U.S. were built in the course of 20 years, and almost all of the wind generated electrical capacity in the world has come online in the last few years. Our transportation system moved from domination by animal power to coal to petroleum over a century, but in steps that each took only a few decades, each occurring after a new technology appeared and showed a clear advantage.

In the present, much more crowded, connected, and faster-changing world, there is widespread need for better forecasting and planning of our energy future, rather than just "letting it happen." If, as many scientists suggest, the already degraded global environment is rapidly approaching multiple tipping points, past which dangerous or even catastrophic environmental changes cannot be avoided, then the stakes for more accurate projections are even higher.

Such predictions remain extremely difficult, however, because energy choices are not just about science and engineering, but also about politics, economics, and society at local, regional, and global scales. This complexity, and the uncertainty that it creates, is not an excuse for inaction, but *must* be recognized if any lasting progress is to be achieved. HVHF in the Marcellus Shale has caused, and will continue to cause, environmental damage. Most of this damage has so far been limited to local or regional scales. The longer-term effects of present and future gas development in the Marcellus, or any other gas shale deposit, however, will depend less on what happens in New York or Pennsylvania than on decisions about national and global energy use and development.

Real and substantial environmental and other risks are associated with large-scale hydraulic fracturing in the Marcellus Shale. Deciding whether these risks are lesser or greater than the risks associated with other energy choices is not just a question about the Marcellus. Successful risk management involves diminishing existing risk, preventing future risk, evaluating benefits, assessing cumulative impacts over decades, and making economic, social, and ethical decisions, none of which can be made with total certainty.

For New York State in particular, where development of the Marcellus has not (at the time of this writing) started and in which it has been so controversial, substantial risks associated with the regional energy system are borne by people, ecosystems, and economies outside of New York State. Although New York residents and businesses get almost twice as much energy from natural gas than any other source, only a tiny amount of the gas used within the state comes from gas wells within the state.

Transitioning from one energy source to another has almost always meant transitioning from one set of risks and benefits to another. The fundamentally different nature of different energy sources makes comparisons of risks challenging. Because all large-scale energy production methods have substantial risks, the most direct—although not necessarily the simplest or least expensive—approach to lowering risks to public health, ecosystems, economies, and communities is to use less energy.

Abbreviations & Acronyms

API—American Petroleum Institute
BC—black carbon
BTEX—benzene, toluene, ethylbenzene, and xylene
BTU—British Thermal Unit
CAS#—Chemical Abstract Service Number
CBM—coal bed methane
CCGT—combined cycle gas turbine
CHP—combined-heat-and-power
CNG—compressed natural gas
dBa—decibel
DOE—U.S. Department of Energy
DRBC—Delaware River Basin Commission
EIA—U.S. Energy Information Administration
EIS—environmental impact statement
EOR—enhanced oil recovery
EPA—U.S. Environmental Protection Agency
EUR—expected ultimate recovery
GDP—gross domestic product
GHG—greenhouse gas
GW—gigawatt
GWP—global warming potential
HOV—high occupancy vehicle
HVAC—heating, ventilation, and air conditioning
HVHF—slickwater horizontal high-volume hydraulic fracturing
IP—initial production
kWh—kilowatt hour
LCA—life-cycle analysis
LNG—liquefied natural gas
mcf—thousand cubic feet
MJ—million joules
MMBTU—million British Thermal Units

MMS—moment magnitude scale
MWH—megawatt-hour
mrem—milirem
MSDS—Material Safety Data Sheet
NORM—naturally occurring radioactive materials
NO$_x$—nitrogen oxides NO and NO$_2$
NYSDEC—New York State Department of Environmental Conservation
pCi/g—picocurie per gram
pCi/L—picocurie per liter
PDEP—Pennsylvania Department of Environmental Protection
PFCI—potential future climate impact
POTW—publicly owned treatment works
ppm—parts per million
PV—photovoltaic
rdSGEIS—revised draft of the Supplemental Generic Environmental Impact Statement (NYSDEC, 2011)
REC—reduced emission completion
SGEIS—Supplemental Generic Environmental Impact Statement
SRBC—Susquehanna River Basin Commission
SWPPP—Stormwater Pollution Prevention Plan
tcf—trillion cubic feet
TDS—total dissolved solids
TENORM—technologically enhanced NORM
TOC—total organic carbon
UAG—unaccounted-for gas
USDA—United States Department of Agriculture
USGS—United States Geological Survey
VOCs—volatile organic compounds

GLOSSARY

Acadian mountain range—mountain range formed in the Devonian Period that rose to the east of the basin in which the Marcellus Shale was deposited.

aerosol—very small particles of liquid or solid material suspended in a gas, *e.g.,* air.

Alleghanian Orogeny—mountain-building event occurring between the Carboniferous Period and the Permian Period that helped form the Alleghanian and Appalachian Mountains and helped to shape the jointing patterns in the Marcellus Shale.

annulus—the space between the casing and the rock on the outside of the well bore.

Anthropocene—a name recently proposed by Earth scientists for the time interval since humanity became such a powerful force of change, roughly the last 200 years.

Appalachian Basin—structural depression formed by tectonic forces associated with the formation of the Appalachian Mountains and located along what is now the western edge of those mountains, from New York State to Tennessee.

basin—structural depression in the Earth's crust.

benzene—organic chemical compound with the chemical formula C_6H_6; part of a collection of volatile organic compounds abbreviated as BTEX that are of concern to human health.

biocide—chemical added to hydrofracking fluid that prevents the growth of bacteria and other microorganisms in the well bore and fractures.

biogenic—produced from the metabolic processes of organisms, usually forming at or near Earth's surface.

blowout—uncontrolled release of natural gas from a well after pressure control systems have failed.

booster—chemical added to hydrofracking fluid that increases the effectiveness of the corrosion inhibitors at high temperature and pressure.

bridge fuel—fuel serving as a transition from a higher-carbon energy source to a lower or no-carbon source.

brine—highly salty water; see also **produced water**.

British Thermal Unit (BTU)—unit of energy equal to the amount of energy required to heat one pound of water by 1°F.

butane—gas with the chemical formula C_4H_{10}, which can co-occur with methane in natural gas resources.

carbon dioxide—greenhouse gas with the chemical formula CO_2, which occurs at trace levels in the atmosphere, and is a byproduct of many metabolic processes of organisms as well as human industrial processes.

carbon dioxide equivalent—unit of global warming potential of a greenhouse gas, expressed relative to the global warming potential of carbon dioxide.

casing—metal tube surrounded by cement that lines the well bore.

casing program—multiple stages used to drill and case a well.

cement—substance that binds other materials together; in hydrofracking, a special cement designed to withstand the temperature and pressure of wells is used to hold the metal casing in place in the well bore and seal any open space between the metal casing and the surrounding rock.

clay—fine-grained sediment that makes up a large part of the Marcellus Shale.

clay stabilizer—salts added to the hydrofracking fluid that prevent clay in the target formation from swelling, migrating, and blocking fractures.

cleanup—collective term for the processes used to remove liquids from a gas well to increase the flow of gas. See also **liquids unloading**.

coal bed methane—naturally-occurring methane released from coal beds during mining.

cold venting—see **venting**.

combined cycle gas turbine (CCGT)—type of power plant that runs on natural gas.

completion—steps used to bring a well into production once drilling operations have ended.

conventional—in reference to oil and natural gas deposits, trapped under an impermeable rock layer in voids or pore spaces; also the drilling technology whereby such deposits are extracted, usually involving vertically drilled wells; see also **unconventional**.

corrosion inhibitor—chemical added to hydrofracking fluid that reduces the damage to steel casing and other equipment that would be caused by the acid used in hydrofracking.

cracking—breakdown of larger molecules into smaller molecules by heat and pressure; also the breakdown of organic matter into hydrocarbons.

cross-linker—chemical added to hydrofracking fluid that maintains fracture fluid viscosity at high heat and pressure found at depth.

curie—unit of radioactivity that describes the number of decay events per second in a substance, based on the radioactivity of one gram of radium.

Devonian—period of time in the geological past, before the Carboniferous Period and after the Silurian Period, extending from approximately 419 to 359 million years ago.

development well—well intended to produce gas that will go directly into pipelines for sale.

directional drilling—in oil and gas exploitation, the drilling of a borehole in any orientation other than vertical with respect to the ground surface; see also **horizontal drilling**.

distribution pipeline—pipeline that delivers natural gas to end users.

downstream—beyond the point of reference, *e.g.,* beyond the point at which natural gas enters a pipeline at the well; see also **upstream**.

drillout—stage in developing an unconventional gas well in which the plugs set to separate fracturing stages are drilled out to release gas for production.

drilling mud—fluids used to lubricate the drill bit and help regulate pressure in the well bore, making the drilling process easier.

earthquake swarm—large number of very small earthquakes in a restricted geographic area.

emission—release of a substance during a process; here, most often referring to the release of a gas into the atmosphere as a byproduct of natural gas extraction.

environmental impact statement (EIS)—document required by federal or state regulations that describes the possible immediate and cumulative effects of a proposed project on the environment; here, referring to the document created by NYSDEC specifically to examine the effects of slickwater high-volume hydraulic fracturing.

epicenter—point on the Earth's surface directly above the origin of an earthquake.

epicontinental sea—sea that forms when the ocean covers part of a continent.

ethane—gas with the chemical formula C_2H_6, which can co-occur with methane in natural gas resources.

ethylbenzene—organic chemical compound with the chemical formula $C_6H_5CH_2CH_3$.

expected ultimate recovery (EUR)—amount of saleable gas expected to be recovered from a well, reservoir, or field by the end of its productive life.

exploration well—natural gas well drilled (at least initially) mainly to search for natural gas, rather than primarily for production.

extraction—removal of a fossil fuel from its source or reservoir.

fairway—area in a natural gas play that is expected to be most profitable.

flare—intentional burning of methane venting to the atmosphere, usually from a gas or oil well site.

flowback—in hydrofracking, the treatment fluid, natural gas, sand, and other debris that returns to the surface upon release of pressure on the well bore, or the process by which these materials return, immediately after fracturing and before well completion.

flowback fluid—fluid that comes back out of a well soon after hydrofracking is complete and the plugs are drilled out.

formation—rock layer made up of a distinctive set of rock compositions (lithologies), formed in a particular area and interval of time, which can be recognized over an area of tens to thousands of square miles.

formation water—fluid that originated from the rock formation itself, and that can have elevated levels of substances such as dissolved solids and radionuclides.

fossil fuel—energy source (*e.g.,* coal, oil, natural gas) that originated from the organic remains of ancient organisms and formed by heat and pressure under Earth's surface.

fracking—see **hydraulic fracturing**.

fracking fluid—see **hydrofracking fluid**.

fracture—crack in a rock layer, or the process that created the crack.

friction reducer—chemical added to hydrofracking fluid that reduces the internal friction of the fluid, to lower the amount of pressure that needs to be exerted at the surface to fracture the well.

fugitive emission—any unintentional emission of gas (usually methane) into the atmosphere from a well or associated drilling, fracturing, production, or transportation equipment or activity; a leak.

geotextile—tough fabric used to line well pads.

global warming potential (GWP)—a relative measure of how much heat that a greenhouse gas traps in the atmosphere; see also **greenhouse gas footprint**.

green completion—technology that captures gas that would otherwise be lost (emitted) at a wellhead; also called reduced emission completion.

greenhouse gas (GHG)—gas that increases the ability of Earth's atmosphere to trap heat.

greenhouse gas footprint—total GHG emissions from developing and using a particular fuel source, expressed as carbon dioxide equivalents, per unit of energy obtained during combustion.

horizontal drilling—type of directional drilling that begins with a vertical well bore that is then angled underground until it is oriented horizontally; the horizontal portion can sometimes continue for thousands of feet.

high-volume hydraulic fracturing (HVHF)—hydraulic fracturing using large volumes (generally millions of gallons) of water, used to hydrofrack horizontal wells.

hydraulic fracturing—process of injecting a fluid into a well at high pressure to create or expand fractures in a source rock formation and thus increase the productivity (release of fossil fuel) of a well.

hydrocarbon chemical compound that contains only carbon and hydrogen atoms, including the constituent molecules of natural gas; the lightest hydrocarbons are methane, ethane, and propane, with only 1, 2, and 3 carbon atoms, respectively.

hydrofracking—see **hydraulic fracturing**.

hydrofracking fluid—the mix of water, sand, and chemicals used to create and expand fractures in a well by hydraulic pressure.

induced seismicity—earthquake or series of earthquakes triggered by human activity.

initial production (IP)—peak rate at which natural gas is produced from a well, usually during the completion phase.

injection well—well (sometimes a depleted oil and gas well) used to inject large quantities of gases or liquids underground within deep geological formations.

isotopes—versions of the same chemical element that contain varying numbers of neutrons in their nuclei.

joint—fracture in a rock formation.

joule—unit of energy, defined as the work required to produce one watt of power for one second, or one watt-second.

kickoff point—in a horizontal well, the depth at which a special drill bit is used to begin to angle the well bore in a horizontal direction.

kilowatt hour (kWh)—unit of energy equal to 1,000 watts, commonly used in billing by utility companies.

lease—contractual agreement calling for the lessee (user) to pay the lessor (owner) for use of an asset; here, an agreement between a company wishing to extract natural gas and the owner of the land below which the gas is located, usually detailing the rights and responsibilities of the extraction company and the compensation due to the landowner.

life-cycle analysis (LCA)—analysis of an aspect (*e.g.*, climate impact) of a process (here, natural gas production, distribution, and use) throughout the entire process, from beginning to end.

lifetime—entire time of productivity of a well; also, mean persistence or **residence time** of a gas in the atmosphere.

liquefied natural gas (LNG)—natural gas that has been cooled into a liquid state (usually for transport) so that it occupies only 1/600 of the volume of natural gas in its gaseous phase.

liquids unloading—process of removing liquids (*e.g.*, water, liquid hydrocarbons) from the well bore that would otherwise slow gas production in a mature well.

lithologies—different kinds of rock layers.

low carbon—with minimal output of greenhouse gas emissions (especially CO_2) into the atmosphere.

Marcellus—town in Onondaga County, New York (2010 population 6,210); also, the Marcellus Shale rock unit.

Marcellus Shale—rock layer, variously referred to as a formation or subgroup at the base of the Hamilton Group, extending from central upstate New York to eastern Ohio, most of Pennsylvania, and eastern West Virginia. The Marcellus was formed by the deposition of fine sediment in a shallow sea during the Devonian Period.

methane—gas with the chemical formula CH_4, the main component of natural gas.

microseismic event—small seismic event, often used to learn about the properties of underground rock formations.

milliDarcy—unit of permeability, equal to 0.001 cm^3/second.

moment magnitude scale—numerical scale that describes the relative sizes of earthquakes based on the size of recorded seismic waves.

natural gas—mixture of light hydrocarbons, mostly methane, which is used as an energy source.

naturally occurring radioactive material (NORM)—material (*e.g.*, black shales) that naturally contains radioactive elements in higher concentrations than surrounding materials.

no-carbon—with no output of greenhouse gas emissions (especially CO_2) into the atmosphere.

oil—see **petroleum**.

overmature—in the thermogenic formation of natural gas, the point at which gas begins to disappear due to increased heat and pressure.

ozone—gas with the chemical formula O_3. High in the atmosphere, ozone protects Earth from some of the Sun's ultraviolet rays, but at ground level, it is a form of pollution caused by the interaction of certain chemicals and sunlight, and can cause respiratory diseases.

Pangea—supercontinent on the Earth that formed approximately 300–250 million years ago, which began to break up approximately 250–200 million years ago.

perforation gun (perf gun)—device that delivers shaped explosive charges in the bottom of the well bore to perforate the casing and annulus and allow the fluid through to fracture the target formation.

permeability—potential for a fluid trapped in a sedimentary rock to flow between pores in the rock.

petroleum—mixture of heavy hydrocarbons that are liquid at room temperature; a fuel also called oil.

play—part of a rock formation targeted for natural gas extraction that is expected to produce natural gas; also, the part of the formation that is drilled for natural gas.

porosity—amount of open space between grains within a sedimentary rock.

processing—phase of natural gas extraction in which water, heavy hydrocarbons, and/or other impurities, such as sulfur, are removed from the natural gas before it is marketed.

produced water—fluid that returns to the surface after flowback fluid; this water is saltier and includes some of the chemicals found in the Marcellus Shale pore fluids; also called brine.

production—all of the steps involved in removing natural gas from the ground and into transportation toward final users.

propane—gas with the chemical formula C_3H_8, which can co-occur with methane in natural gas.

proppant—variously sized grains of sand, sometimes with other materials, that hold open fractures created by hydrofracking after the fluid pressure is released.

pyrite—mineral with the chemical formula FeS_2, which is present in many dark shales; also called iron sulfide or "fool's gold."

radiative forcing—amount of energy per unit area, expressed in watts per square meter (W/m^2), which a certain change in a particular greenhouse gas confers upon the Earth.

radioactivity—particles and energy emitted when an atom spontaneously decays.

radionuclide see **radioisotope**.

radioisotope—isotope of an element that is unstable, meaning that it will spontaneously decay and emit radiation.

reduced emission completion (REC)—see **green completion**.

reservoir—underground source from which fossil fuel can be extracted.

residence time—see **lifetime**.

Richter Scale—numeric scale that expresses the relative size of earthquakes, now replaced by the **moment magnitude scale**.

scale—mineral deposit (*e.g.*, calcium carbonate) that precipitates out of water and adheres to the inside of pipes, heaters, and other equipment.

sedimentary rock—type of rock formed from accumulated particles of clay, silt, sand, gravel, and/or remains of organisms.

shale—type of sedimentary rock formed from fine particles of clay and silt.

shale gas—natural gas formed by thermogenic processes within a shale.

shaped charges—small explosive projectiles shot from a performation gun.

slickwater—particular formulation of hydrofracking fluid that emphasizes friction reducers, and which is used in shale gas extraction.

source rock—rock formation in which fossil fuel forms.

stratum (pl. strata)—rock layer.

stimulation—process of hydrofracking a well.

surfactant—chemical added to hydrofracking fluid that reduces the surface tension of the fluid and increases the amount of water that comes back out of the well.

target formation—rock layer from which natural gas will be extracted.

tectonics—movement of the Earth's plates, creating mountains, basins, earthquakes, etc.

thermogenic—produced from the exertion of heat and pressure on organic matter.

tight sand—relatively impermeable sandstone or limestone formation that contains commercially extractible natural gas or oil.

tight shale—relatively impermeable shale formation that contains commercially extractable natural gas or oil.

tipping point—point within the lifetime of a system at which it changes abruptly from one state to another.

toluene—organic chemical compound with the chemical formula C_7H_8.

transportation—processes by which natural gas moves from the well head to consumers.

unconventional—in reference to oil or natural gas deposits, a source that cannot be extracted through conventional vertical wells; also, new technology to access such deposits, such as high-volume hydraulic fracturing; see also **conventional**.

upstream—prior to the point of reference, *e.g.,* all stages in the production of natural gas before the gas enters a pipeline at the well; see also **downstream**.

venting—intentional, controlled release of gas (*e.g.,* methane) into the atmosphere.

volatile organic compounds (VOCs)—light hydrocarbons that readily evaporate at room temperature and pressure.

water zones—rock layers that are saturated with water.

watt—unit of rate of energy conversion or transfer, defined as one joule per second.

well—human-made cylindrical hole in the Earth to extract some resource, and its associated structures and apparatuses both at the surface and below ground.

well bore—cylindrical hole drilled from the surface, through which hydraulic fracturing fluid travels to the target formation and natural gas or oil and wastewater flows to the surface.

well pad—area at the surface, surrounding the well bore, whichthat is used to conduct drilling and hydrofracking activities.

well site—area at the surface where a well is located, including but not confined to the well pad itself.

wellhead—place at the well where natural gas leaves the well and begins transportation to market, often via pipeline.

workover—replacing parts in a well, or re-hydrofracking, to increase production.

xylene—organic chemical compound with the chemical formula C_8H_{10}.

ENDNOTES

PREFACE

[1] See, *e.g.*, Allmon (2009); Allmon *et al.* (2010).

[2] PRI was founded in 1932 by Gilbert Harris (1865–1952), a professor of geology at Cornell. Although primarily known as a distinguished paleontologist, Harris was also one of the first true petroleum geologists, and frequently a consultant to oil companies. A number of his graduate students went on to have successful careers in the oil business, and several gave or left in their estates significant financial support for PRI (see Allmon, 2007). By an interesting coincidence, one of Harris' students, Pearl Sheldon, was the first to recognize the distinctive joints in the Devonian rocks of central New York, which facilitate extraction of natural gas from the Marcellus Shale (see Wilber, 2012: 5). More recently, PRI has received financial support from the petroleum industry for various research and educational projects, the largest of which was "The World of Oil," a website explaining the role of geology and paleontology in searching for petroleum, set up in 1998 (see http://www.museumoftheearth.org/outreach.php?page=Edu_Prog/earth101/world_of_oil). Paleontology as a scientific field has a long history with the petroleum industry, and as recently as 25 years ago, a substantial proportion of the professional paleontologists in the nation and the world worked for or with the industry in some way. Since then, however, both paleontology and the oil business have changed significantly. Fossils are no longer as important as they once were for dating rock layers, and paleontology as a whole has moved much closer to biology, and therefore inevitably toward a greater focus on topics related to the environment and conservation. There is even now a new subfield within paleontology called "Conservation Paleobiology," the development of which has been led by researchers at PRI (see, *e.g.*, Flessa, 2002; Dietl & Flessa, 2009; Dietl *et al.*, 2012). Since 1992, PRI has offered public educational programs in the Earth and life sciences, including major efforts on environmental topics such as biodiversity and climate change. In 2013, PRI formally took over the nearby Cayuga Nature Center, thereby expanding its base for providing environmental education across central New York State (see Allmon & Ross, 2011).

[3] Statement of PRI's Approach to Educational Outreach on Energy and Environment with Respect to Marcellus Shale Drilling (first posted in 2010): http://www.museumoftheearth.org/outreach.php?page=Edu_Prog/92387/723372.

INTRODUCTION

[1] See, *e.g.*, Zalasiewicz *et al.* (2008, 2010) and Ruddiman (2013).

[2] Although "hydrofracking" or simply "fracking" are the most commonly used shorthand for *slickwater horizontal high-volume hydraulic fracturing*, some literature (*e.g.*, NYSDEC, 2011) uses the acronym HVHF, which is more precise (HVHHF is also used; see, *e.g.*, Kiviat, 2013). Both hydraulic fracturing and and horizontal drilling are common procedures on conventional gas wells. It is *high-volume* hydrofracking associated with long, horizontal lateral wells that makes Marcellus and other similar wells distinctive. Further, "hydrofracking" implies using water for the hydraulic fracturing, which is nearly always the case at present, but wasn't

always the case in the past and might not be in the future if other fluids (such as gelled propane) are used. "Fraking," with the same pronunciation but different spelling, is also vulgar slang popularized in the science fiction television series *Battlestar Galactica* (2004– 2009). The term was used as a way to avoid fines from the U.S. Federal Communications Commission. Wordplay that touches on this is not uncommon (see image on p. 174), but we avoid it in this work. See http://www.urbandictionary.com/define.php?term=fraking.

[3] A few documents that attempt to fill this need include, *e.g.,* Andrews *et al.* (2009), Sweeney *et al.* (2009), and a number of websites (see Chapter 9).

[4] *The Marcellus Papers* were the centerpiece of a multipart educational outreach effort on the geology of the Marcellus Shale undertaken by staff at the Paleontological Research Institution, starting in early 2010. For more information on this effort, see http://www.museumoftheearth.org/outreach.php?page=Edu_Prog/92387.

[5] These are also enormous, and still underinvestigated, topics. For some useful introductory perspectives, see *e.g.,* Kargbo *et al.* (2010), Brasier *et al.* (2011), Kinnaman (2011), Mitchell & Casman (2011), Stedman *et al.* (2012), and Eaton (2013).

CHAPTER 1

[1] Geologists traditionally divide sedimentary rocks into *formations*, which are rocks with sets of lithologies that can be recognized over a geographic area of at least approximately 50 square miles (130 square kilometers). Formations are usually gathered together into *groups*, and can be divided into *members*. The Marcellus has usually been considered to be a formation within the Hamilton Group. More recently, however, geologists have proposed that, because the Marcellus contains within it a major widespread limestone unit, the Cherry Valley, it should be subdivided into two separate formations, a lower Union Springs Formation and an upper Oatka Creek Formation. In this scheme, the term Marcellus would be used as a "subgroup," to refer to both of these formations. See Brett *et al.* (2011) for further discussion and references.

[2] For additional discussion of the Devonian geology of New York, see Whiteley *et al.* (2002), Brett *et al.* (2011), and Ver Straeten *et al.* (2011).

[3] Ver Straeten *et al.* (2011).

[4] Sageman *et al.* (2003).

[5] This is because most of the bacteria responsible for decomposition require oxygen. Decomposition still occurs under low- or no-oxygen conditions through the activity of bacteria that do not require oxygen (anaerobic bacteria). Such decomposition, however, happens much more slowly.

[6] Ver Straeten *et al.* (2011).

[7] Engelder et al. (2009).

[8] Engelder et al. (2009).

[9] Engelder & Lash (2008); USGS Marcellus Shale Assessment Team (2011); EIA (2012). For a discussion of the some of the events leading to these estimates, see Wilber (2012: 95–97).

[10] http://www.eia.gov/dnav/ng/ng_cons_sum_dcu_nus_a.htm.

CHAPTER 2

[1] Permeability is the ability of a fluid trapped in a rock to flow through that rock. Permeability is a function of porosity, which is the amount of open space available in the form of fractures and pore spaces between grains, and the connections among those spaces. The Marcellus has relatively low porosity (0–18%) and very low permeability, ranging between 0.2×10^{-8} to 5.5×10^{-8} millidarcys. A substance with a permeability of 1 darcy permits a flow of 1 cm^3/second of a fluid with viscosity of 1 centipoise (1 cp = 0.001 kg/m/second) under a pressure gradient of 1 atm/cm acting across an area of 1 cm^2. A millidarcy (mD) is equal to 0.001 darcy, and a microdarcy [μD] equals 0.000001 darcy. Values of sediment permeability range as high as 100,000 darcys for gravel, to less than 0.01 microdarcy for granite. Sand has a permeability of about 1 darcy (Lichtner *et al.*, 1996: 5). Even with the most sophisticated hydrofracking technology currently available, if rock permeability is much below 10^{-9} millidarcys, its gas cannot be economically extracted (Hill *et al.*, 2002).

[2] "Unconventional" is an umbrella term for oil and natural gas that is produced by means that

190

do not meet the criteria for conventional production. Resources that have qualified as "unconventional" have differed over time. Application of the term is a function of resource characteristics, available exploration and production technologies, economic environment, and the scale, frequency and duration of production from the resource. The term is currently most frequently used to refer to oil and gas resources for which porosity, permeability, fluid trapping mechanism, or other characteristics differ from conventional reservoirs (mostly in sandstones and limestones). In addition to fractured tight gas shales and sands, coal bed methane and gas hydrates (frozen methane on the seafloor or in permafrost) are considered unconventional resources (http://www.glossary.oilfield.slb.com/en/Terms. aspx?LookIn=term%20name&filter=unconventional).

[3] Engelder et al. (2009).

[4] See Wang & Carr (2012: 159).

[5] Adams & Weaver (1958).

[6] Schmoker (1981).

[7] The New York State Department of Environmental Conservation (NYSDEC) issued its most recent report on HVHF in the Marcellus Shale in 2011. This document is known as the "revised draft SGEIS" and is referred to hereafter in the endnotes as "NYSDEC, 2011." It lays out only recommendations, not a set of legal regulations. As of this writing (September 2013), NYSDEC has not issued any formal regulations on Marcellus drilling. New York State has had in effect an official moratorium on all gas development via HVHF since 2000.

[8] Iyengar (1984).

[9] The basis for the curie is the radioactivity of one gram of the element radium. Radium decays at a rate of about 2.2 trillion disintegrations (2.2×10^{12}) per minute. A picocurie is one trillionth of a curie. Thus, one picocurie represents 2.2 disintegrations per minute; see http://www. firstapmaywound.com/factsheet/pico.htm.

[10] Rowan & Kraemer (2012).

[11] These materials can be referred to as technologically enhanced NORM, or TENORM. Here we use the term NORM to encompass both NORM and TENORM. (Occasionally authors use NORM to refer to the radionuclides themselves rather than to the material containing radionuclides.)

[12] NYSDEC (2011).

[13] Resnikoff et al. (2010).

[14] NYSDEC found that radioactivity of Marcellus cuttings was not significantly higher than other "background" radiation sources; see http://www.dec.ny.gov/docs/materials_minerals_pdf/rdsgeisch50911.pdf.

[15] NYSDEC (2011).

[16] White (2012).

[17] Rowan et al. (2011). The EPA sets a maximum level of ^{226}Ra and ^{228}Ra (combined) in drinking water to 5 pCi/L, and the maximum amount allowed in industrial effluent is 60 pCi/L. For standards for drinking water, see: http://water.epa.gov/drink/contaminants/index.cfm" \l "List and http://water.epa.gov/drink/contaminants/index.cfm#List. For standards for industrial effluent, see: http://www.nrc.gov/reading-rm/doc-collections/cfr/part020/appb/Radium-226.html and http://www.nrc.gov/reading-rm/doc-collections/cfr/part020/appb/Radium-228.html.

[18] NYSDEC (2011).

[19] U.S. Geological Survey, Toxic Substances Hydrology Program, http://toxics.usgs.gov.

[20] U.S. Environmental Protection Agency, http://water.epa.gov/drink/contaminants/basicinformation/benzene.cfm.

[21] Rowan et al. (2011).

[22] The "Glossary of Salt Water" published by the Water Quality Association (http://www.wqa.org/) classifies water with dissolved salts as follows (ppm = parts per million; TDS = total dissolved solids):
Fresh = less than 1,000 ppm TDS
Brackish = 1,000–5,000 ppm TDS
Highly brackish = 5,000–15,000 ppm TDS
Saline = 15,000–30,000 ppm TDS

Sea water = 30,000–40,000 ppm TDS
Brine = greater than 40,000 ppm TDS

[23] NYSDEC (2011); Rowan *et al.* (2011).

[24] Rowan *et al.* (2011).

[25] Among scientists, the Richter scale has largely been replaced by the moment magnitude scale (MMS), but earthquake measurements under the MMS are still routinely (but erroneously) referred to as being quoted on the Richter scale. Seismic events of magnitude 2–2.9 occur more than a million times per year globally. They are felt slightly by some people, but do not generally damage buildings. Events of magnitude 3–3.9 occur approximately 100,000 times per year. They are usually felt by people, but very rarely cause damage. See http://earthquake.usgs.gov/earthquakes/eqarchives/year/eqstats.php.

[26] It also roughly corresponds to a 30-fold increase in the amount of energy released. Thus, the amount of energy released during a magnitude 3.0 earthquake is approximately 1,000 times more than the amount of energy released during a magnitude 1.0 earthquake.

[27] BC Oil and Gas Commission (2012).

[28] Injection wells that hold fluid related to oil and gas are called "Class II" wells.

[29] NRC (2012).

[30] NRC (2012).

[31] Frolich (2012).

[32] Ohio Department of Natural Resources (2012a).

CHAPTER 3

[1] NYSERDA (2007); Lash & Lash (2011).

[2] NYSERDA (2007).

[3] U.S. Department of Energy, Energy Information Administration (EIA), http://www.eia.gov/state/.

[4] U.S. Department of Energy, Energy Information Administration, Natural Gas Data, http://www.eia.gov/naturalgas/data.cfm.

[5] The Marcellus Shale Gas Play: Geology, Development, and Water-Resource Impact Mitigation, available at http://ny.water.usgs.gov/projectsummaries/CP30/Marcellus_Presentation_Williams.pdf.

[6] Fisher (2010).

[7] King & Morehouse (1993).

[8] Wrightstone (2009).

[9] NYSDEC (2011).

[10] Susquehanna River Basin Commission, Frequently Asked Questions, http://www.srbc.net/programs/natural_gas_development_faq.htm.

[11] NYSDEC (2011); Arthur *et al.* (2008a, b, c); Coburn *et al.* (2011); Bishop (2011); Geology.com, *Hydraulic Fracturing Fluids—Composition and Additives,* http://geology.com/energy/hydraulic-fracturing-fluids/.

[12] Kelso (2012); see also Ladlee & Jaquet (2011).

[13] Pennsylvania Department of Environmental Protection, Department of Environmental Protection, Bureau of Oil and Gas Management, *Wells Drilled,* available at http://files.dep.state.pa.us/OilGas/BOGM/BOGMPortalFiles/OilGasReports/2012/2012Wellspermitted-drilled.pdf.

[14] Ohio Department of Natural Resources (2012a).

[15] Johnson (2010).

[16] For an excellent description of the leasing process, mostly from the point of view of landowners, see Wilber (2012).

[17] Johnson (2010).

[18] NYSDEC (2011).

[19] The Drake Well, in Venango County, Pennsylvania, is usually referred to as the "first commercial oil well." Before it, oil-producing wells were wells drilled for salt brine, and produced oil and gas only as accidental by-products. See Brice (2009).

[20] NYSDEC (2011).

[21] Hyne (2001).

[22] NYSDEC (2011).

[23] NYSDEC (2011).

[24] King & Morehouse (1993).

[25] Lee et al. (2011).

[26] Hyne (2001).

[27] Lee et al. (2011).

[28] Lee et al. (2011).

[29] NYSDEC (2011); Arthur et al. (2008b, c); Coburn et al. (2011); Bishop (2011).

[30] Caenn et al. (2011: 3).

[31] NYSDEC (2011); Khodja et al. (2010); Schlumberger Ltd., Potassium Mud, Schlumberger Oilfield Glossary, http://www.glossary.oilfield.slb.com/en/Terms.aspx?LookIn=term%20 name&filter-potassium%20mud.

[32] Caenn et al. (2011); NYSDEC (2011).

[33] Caenn et al. (2011). The SGEIS (NYSDEC, 2011) states that the horizontal portion of the drill bore, "may be drilled with a mud that may be (i) water-based, (ii) potassium chloride/polymer-based with a mineral oil lubricant, or (iii) synthetic oil-based. Synthetic oil-based muds are described as "food-grade" or "environmentally friendly."

[34] Hyne (2001).

[35] Conner O'Laughlin, pers. comm. 2011; Arthur et al. (2008a, b, c).

[36] Arthur et al. (2008a).

[37] Arthur et al. (2008a).

[38] NYSDEC (2011).

[39] NYSDEC (2011).

[40] Struchtemeyer et al. (2012); Geology.com, Hydraulic Fracturing Fluids — Composition and Additives, http://geology.com/energy/hydraulic-fracturing-fluids/.

[41] Coburn et al. (2011).

[42] Hyne (2001).

[43] Arthur et al. (2008a).

[44] NYSDEC (2011).

[45] Capillary action results from the molecular attraction between water molecules and the molecules in the shale, which in the tiny fractures can be stronger than other pressures acting on the water. Therefore, clay can also "trap" the fracturing fluids because clay grains can absorb water, swell, and decrease permeability. Many of the inorganic sediments that make up the Marcellus Shale are clay grains.

[46] U.S. Environmental Protection Agency, Coalbed Methane Extraction (CBM), available at http://water.epa.gov/scitech/wastetech/guide/cbm_index.cfm.

[47] U.S. Environmental Protection Agency, 2004, Hydraulic Fracturing White Paper, EPA 816-R-04-003, Appendix A in: Evaluation of Impacts to Underground Sources of Drinking Water by Hydraulic Fracturing of Coalbed Methane Reservoirs, 23 pp. Available at http://water.epa.gov/type/groundwater/uic/class2/hydraulicfracturing/wells_coalbedmethanestudy.cfm.

[48] For general discussion of the structural geology of the Marcellus Shale, see Engelder (1985) and Moniz et al. (2011).

[49] NRC (2010a); Carter et al. (2000); Jenkins et al. (2009).

[50] Chipperfield (2008). Well logs are descriptions of the rock layers based on data collected by devices lowered into wires into drilled wells. Sonic logs are similar in principle to seismic tests, but use sonic waves instead of sound waves. Gamma ray logs are used to measure natural radioactivity in rocks (see Figure 2.2A), as well as physical features of sedimentary layers, such as grain size. Gamma ray logs are especially helpful for determine thickness and depth of the target rock in the region. Resistivity logs use electrical properties of fluid-filled rocks to measure porosity and fluid content of rock layers.

[51] Digital Energy Journal, 2011, CGG Veritas Real Time Microseismic Monitoring, http://www.digitalenergyjournal.com/n/CGG_Veritas_real_time_microseismic_monitoring/892015e8.aspx.

[52] Hill et al. (2002); Raymond & Leffler (2006).

[53] Cathles et al. (2012b).

[54] Considine et al. (2012).

[55] Pennsylvania Department of Environmental Protection, 2013, Oil and gas well drilling and production in Pennsylvania, 3 pp, available at http://www.elibrary.dep.state.pa.us/dsweb/Get/Document-94407/8000-FS-DEP2018.pdf.

[56] Lee *et al.* (2011).

[57] NYSDEC (2011); Lavelle (2010).

[58] Considine *et al.* (2012).

[59] Halliburton, Data Sheet: CleanStim Hydraulic Fracturing Fluid System, available at http://www.halliburton.com/public/pe/contents/Data_Sheets/web/H/H07550.pdf.

[60] Halliburton, CleanSuite Technologies, available at http://www.halliburton.com/public/projects/pubsdata/Hydraulic_Fracturing/CleanSuite_Technologies.html#.

[61] Chesapeake Energy, Green Frac Program, available at http://www.askchesapeake.com/Pages/Green-Frac.aspx; Gies (2012).

[62] GasFrac Energy Services Inc., http://www.gasfrac.com/.

[63] Halliburton, SandCastleTM PS-2500 Vertical Storage, available at http://www.halliburton.com/en-US/ps/stimulation/fracturing/frac-of-the-future/sandcastle-ps-2500.page.

CHAPTER 4

[1] Chesapeake Energy, 2011, Water use in Marcellus deep shale gas exploration, available at http://www.chk.com/media/educationallibrary/fact-sheets/corporate/water_use_fact_sheet.pdf; Groundwater Protection Council and ALL Consulting, for the U.S. Department of Energy Office of Fossil Energy and the National Energy Technology Laboratory (2009).

[2] Kenny, J. F., N. L. Barber, S. S. Hutson, K. S. Linsey, J. K. Lovelace, & M. A. Maupin. 2009. *Estimated Use of Water in the United States in 2005*. U.S. Geological Survey, Reston, Virginia. Available at http://pubs.usgs.gov/circ/1344/.

[3] Susquehanna River Basin Commission, Frequently Asked Questions, http://www.srbc.net/programs/natural_gas_development_faq.htm.

[4] NYSDEC (2011).

[5] Engelder *et al.* (2009).

[6] Chesapeake Energy, 2011, Water use in Marcellus deep shale gas exploration, available at http://www.chk.com/media/educationallibrary/fact-sheets/corporate/water_use_fact_sheet.pdf.

[7] Charles *et al.* (2012); Susquehanna River Basin Commission, Frequently Asked Questions, http://www.srbc.net/programs/natural_gas_development_faq.htm.

[8] Ladlee & Jaquet (2011).

[9] NYSDEC (2011).

[10] NYSDEC (2011). SRBC estimates 4.2 million gallons are required for the average well, equivalent to approximately 10.3 billion gallons of water per year.

[11] Susquehanna River Basin Commission, Frequently Asked Questions, http://www.srbc.net/programs/natural_gas_development_faq.htm. In Pennsylvania, approximately 93% of the total water consumption is from surface water, and approximately 7% from groundwater. New York currently takes 94% of its water annually for all uses from direct surface water withdrawals. The other 6% comes from groundwater. (New York Department of Environmental Conservation, *Water Use in New York*, available at http://www.dec.ny.gov/lands/67073.html.)

[12] Chesapeake Energy, 2011, Water use in Marcellus deep shale gas exploration, available at http://www.chk.com/media/educationallibrary/fact-sheets/corporate/water_use_fact_sheet.pdf.

[13] Data from Mielke *et al.* (2010); U.S. Department of Energy (2006).

[14] Rahm & Riha (2012).

[15] See Eaton (2013), and references therein.

[16] U.S. Geological Survey, USGS Real-Time Water Data for the Nation, available at http://waterdata.usgs.gov/nwis/rt.

[17] Susquehanna River Basin Commission, 2008, Consumptive use mitigation plan, publication no. 253, available at http://www.srbc.net/programs/docs/CUMP.pdf.

[18] Charles *et al.* (2012).

[19] NYSDEC (2011).

[20] Galbraith (2013).

[21] Freyman & Salmon (2013).

[22] NYSDEC, Watersheds, Lakes, Rivers, http://www.dec.ny.gov/lands/26561.html.

[23] North Carolina Department of Environment and Natural Resources, River Basins, http://www.ee.enr.state.nc.us/public/ecoaddress/riverbasinsmain.htm.

[24] Pennsylvania State College of Agricultural Sciences Cooperative Extension, 2010, *River Basin Approaches to Water Management in the Mid-Atlantic States*, http://pubs.cas.psu.edu/FreePubs/pdfs/ua466.pdf.

[25] Mauter *et al.* (2013).

[26] It can be seen at http://maps.srbc.net/wrp_fv25/.

[27] Delaware River Basin Commission, Draft Natural Gas Development regulations, http://www.nj.gov/drbc/programs/natural/draft-regulations.html.

[28] This estimate was provided to NYSDEC by the Independent Oil and Gas Association of New York (IOGA), see http://www.dec.ny.gov/docs/materials_minerals_pdf/rdsgeisch6b0911.pdf.

[29] Hazen & Sawyer (2009).

[30] See Waxman *et al.* (2011); Aminto & Olson (2012); Struchtemeyer *et al.* (2012); Hazen & Sawyer (2009).

[31] See discussion of this issue by Wilber (2012: 86 ff.) and Begos (2013).

[32] NYSDEC (2011). MSDSs are semistandard forms that contain health, safety, and chemical properties of a wide variety of substances. They were found by searching for chemicals by Chemical Abstract Service Number (CAS#) in various chemical databases and on Google®. TEDX is a not-for-profit organization that compiles and disseminates scientific information on health and environmental problems caused by low-dose exposure to chemicals that interfere with human development and growth, called endocrine disruptors; see http://www.endocrinedisruption.com/home.php.

[33] NYSDEC (2011).

[34] Bishop (2011).

[35] Eaton (2013: 161).

[36] Lutz *et al.* (2013).

[37] NYSDEC (2011); New York Water Environment Association (2011).

[38] URS Corporation (2009).

[39] NYSDEC (2011). The 3,400 gallon per day estimate represents wells still in the early phase of flowback, and the 400 gallons per day estimate represents wells that have been in production for longer.

[40] Oil and Gas Accountability Project, 2008, Shale gas: focus on the Marcellus Shale, available at http://www.earthworksaction.org/publications.cfm?pubID=334.

[41] Haluszczak *et al.* (2013), and references therein.

[42] Adams (2010).

[43] U.S. Environmental Protection Agency, Radiation Protection: Strontium, http://www.epa.gov/rpdweb00/radionuclides/strontium.html.

[44] U.S. Department of Health and Human Services, September 2005, Toxicological profile for lead, http://www.atsdr.cdc.gov/toxprofiles/tp13.pdf.

[45] Environmental Working Group, October 2009, EWG Testimony before NYC City Council on Natural Gas Drilling, http://www.ewg.org/natural_gas_drilling_new_york.

[46] U.S. Environmental Protection Agency, Radiation Protection: Strontium, http://www.epa.gov/rpdweb00/radionuclides/strontium.html.

[47] New York State Department of Health, Part 5, Subpart 5-1 Public Water Systems, http://www.health.ny.gov/environmental/water/drinking/part5/tables.htm.

[48] Iyengar (1984).

[49] U.S. Geological Survey, Toxic Substances Hydrology Program, http://toxics.usgs.gov.

[50] NYSDEC (2011); Rowan *et al.* (2011).

[51] Boyer *et al.* (2012).

[52] Schon (2011).

[53] Warner *et al.* (2012a).

[54] Warner *et al.* (2012a).

[55] Warner *et al.* (2012b).

[56] Myers (2012).

[57] NYSDEC (2011).

[58] "Tioga County cows quarantined after frack water leak," *SunGazette* (Williamsport, Pennsylvania), 2010, available at http://www.sungazette.com/page/content.detail/id/545449. html?nav=5011.

[59] U.S. Environmental Protection Agency, *Technical Overview: Volatile Organic Compounds (VOCs)*, http://www.epa.gov/iaq/voc2.html#content.

[60] Charles *et al.* (2012).

[61] NYSDEC (2011).

[62] Charles *et al.* (2012).

[63] Charles *et al.* (2012).

[64] Lutz *et al.* (2013).

[65] NYSDEC (2011).

[66] Clark & Veil (2009).

[67] Charles *et al.* (2012).

[68] Gregory *et al.* (2011); Charles *et al.* (2012).

[69] NYSDEC (2011); NYSDEC, *Wastewater Infrastructure Needs of New York State Report*, http://www.dec.ny.gov/chemical/42383.html.

[70] NYSDEC (2011: 6-62, 6-10, 6-61).

[71] NYSDEC (2011).

[72] NYSDEC (2011), Chapter 6, Potential environmental impacts, http://www.dec.ny.gov/docs/materials_minerals_pdf/rdsgeisch6a0911.pdf.

[73] *The New York Times*, 26 February 2011, Regulation lax as gas wells' tainted water hits rivers, http://www.nytimes.com/2011/02/27/us/27gas.html?_r=2&scp=2&sq=ian%20urbina&st=cse; Pennsylvania Department of Environmental Protection, 2011, DEP announces testing for radioactivity of river water downstream of marcellus water treatment plants shows water is safe, http://www.portal.state.pa.us/portal/server.pt/community/newsroom/14287?id=%20 16532%20&typeid=1.

[74] Mauter *et al.* (2013).

[75] http://www.netl.doe.gov/publications/press/2013/StudyStatement.pdf. See also media coverage of the statement in http://greenrisks.blogspot.com/2013/07/netl-fracking-research-does-not-find.html.

[76] Toxics Targeting, Inc., 2009, Hazardous Material Spills Information Requests, http://www.toxicstargeting.com/sites/default/files/pdfs/22163083-Drilling-Spills.pdf.

[77] Soeder & Kappel (2009).

[78] Moniz *et al.* (2011).

[79] Pennsylvania Land Trust Association (2008).

[80] Considine *et al.* (2012).

[81] Mosley *et al.* (2010).

[82] Anderson & Kreeger (2010).

[83] Meador (1992).

[84] Vidic *et al.* (2013).

[85] To date, migration of drilling or fracturing fluids through such fractures has not been demonstrated conclusively in Marcellus drilling. See ICF International (2009); Kargbo *et al.* (2010); EPA (2011f); Considine *et al.* (2012). At least one of these sources has been criticized as being too close to industry to be objective; see http://www.huffingtonpost.com/steve-horn/ties-that-bind-ernest_b_3045684.html and http://www.desmogblog.com/2013/08/06/fracking-ties-flawed-state-dept-keystone-xl-environmental-review.

[86] Hyne (2001); Harrison (1985).

[87] NYSDEC (2011).

[88] For discussion of potential problems or failures of standard well casing and cementing in preventing leakage of contaminants, see Harrison (1985), Ladva *et al.* (2005), and EPA (2011f).

[89] NYSDEC (2011); see discussion by Wilber (2012: 152 ff).

[90] Garfield (Colorado) Department of Oil & Gas, Phase I Hydrogeologic Characterization Mamm Creek, available at http://www.garfield-county.com/oil-gas/phase-I-hydrogeologic-characterization-mamm-creek.aspx.

[91] EPA (2010a).

[92] EPA (2010b).

[93] ProPublica, 2008, *Buried Secrets: Is Natural Gas Drilling Endangering U.S. Water Supplies?* http://www.propublica.org/article/buried-secrets-isnatural-gas-drilling-endangering-us-watersupplies-1113.

CHAPTER 5

[1] In early August 2013, the Pennsylvania Department of Environmental Protection announced that shale oil and gas wells would no longer be exempt from filing air quality plans, an exemption that they had enjoyed since 1996. See http://www.dep.state.pa.us/dep/deputate/airwaste/aq/.

[2] See, *e.g.*, Kargbo *et al.* (2010) and Petron *et al.* (2012).

[3] EPA (2012a).

[4] EPA, Ground-level Ozone (Smog) Information, http://www.epa.gov/region1/airquality/.

[5] This report was based estimates provided by the Independent Oil and Gas Association of New York (IOGA).

[6] NYSDEC (2011).

[7] NYSDEC (2011).

[8] NYSDEC (2011). Because this equipment does not run entirely continuously, these SGEIS numbers are probably overestimates.

[9] NYSDEC (2011).

[10] EPA (2011a).

[11] A recent study of waste disposal from Marcellus wells in Pennsylvania (Maloney & Yoxtheimer, 2012) found that in one year (2011), drilling fluids were mostly reused (70.7%).

[12] NYSDEC (2011).

[13] LeRoy Poff *et al.* (1997). See also Entrekin *et al.* (2011), and references therein.

[14] Bishop (2011). See also Smith *et al.* (2012), and references therein.

[15] Anderson & Kreeger (2010).

[16] Pimentel (2006).

[17] Anderson & Kreeger (2010).

[18] Anderson & Kreeger (2010).

[19] Kiviat (2013). Many species of freshwater mussels are among the most endangered invertebrate animals in the U.S. New York has at least 49 native species (Williams *et al.*, 1993; Strayer & Jirka, 1997). Four of these species are listed as threatened or endangered. Pennsylvania has 65 native species (A. Bogan, pers. comm. to WDA, 26 August 2013). Eleven of these listed as threatened or endangered. Approximately 15 species have been extirpated (become locally extinct) in Pennsylvania due to the pollution of the lower Allegheny, lower Monongahela, and upper Ohio rivers (A. Bogan, pers. comm., 26 August 2013).

[20] NYSDEC (2011).

[21] LeRoy Poff *et al.* (1997).

[22] Richter *et al.* (2003).

[23] Braun & Hanus (2005).

[24] For information on invasive species in Pennsylvania, see http://www.dcnr.state.pa.us/conservationscience/invasivespecies/; for New York, see http://www.nyis.info/.

[25] Harris (1984); Farhrig (2003); Fisher (2012); Gillen & Kiviat (2012).

[26] Farhrig (2003).

[27] Johnson (2010).

[28] Moseley *et al.* (2010); Gibbs *et al.* (2007).

[29] Braun & Hanus (2005).

[30] Braun & Hanus (2005).

[31] Smolensky & Fitzgerald (2011).

[32] Hamilton *et al.* (2011).

[33] Nasen *et al.* (2011).

[34] Smolensky & Fitzgerald (2011).

[35] NYSDEC predicts that the footprint of a multiwell pad for horizontal drilling in the Marcellus in New York would be an average size of 3.5 acres (1.4 hectares). They also predict that, with access roads included, the average multiwell pad will take up 7.4 acres (3 hectares) (NYSDEC, 2011). An aerial survey of existing Marcellus well pads in Pennsylvania shows

an average footprint of 3.1 acres (1.2 hectares) per well pad, plus 5.7 acres (2.3 hectares) cleared for access roads and other associated infrastructure for each pad. This is a total of 8.8 acres (3.5 hectares) per well. The average footprint of a vertical well pad is smaller, less than one acre (0.4 hectares) according to the aerial survey of Pennsylvania (Johnson, 2010). NYSDEC estimates that, including access roads, one vertical well covers 4.8 acres (1.9 hectares). With vertical wells spaced at 40 acres (16 hectares), there could be 400 wells in 25 square miles (65 square kilometers), with footprints covering 1,920 total acres (777 hectares). With multiwell horizontal pads, there would be 25 wells in 25 square miles, with footprints covering 185 total acres (75 hectares) using NYSDEC estimates, or 220 acres (89 hectares) using Pennsylvania data. These estimates include access roads.

[36] NYSDEC (2011).

[37] Ladlee & Jaquet (2011).

[38] From *The Marcellus Papers*, 9: table 1, source: http://www.dec.ny.gov/docs/materials_minerals_pdf/rdsgeisch6b0911.pdf.

[39] Radle (2007); Federal Highway Administration (2011).

[40] Bayne *et al.* (2008).

CHAPTER 6

[1] When methane (CH_4) is burned, it combines with oxygen, and the chemical result is carbon dioxide (CO_2) and water (the chemical equation is: $CH_4 + 2\ O_2 \rightarrow CO_2 + 2\ H_2O$). However, because natural gas contains other chemical compounds besides methane, burning it also produces various quantities of other substances, some of which can be toxic, including nitrogen oxides (NO_x), carbon monoxide (CO), sulfur dioxide (SO_2), and a variety of hydrocarbons (volatile organic compounds, VOCs), as well as uncombusted methane. The variety and volume of these combustion products depends not only on the composition of the gas but on the efficiency of the burning. In properly tuned boilers, nearly all of the fuel carbon (99.9%) in natural gas is converted to CO_2 during the combustion process (http://www.epa.gov/ttnchie1/ap42/ch01/final/c01s04.pdf). Burning coal also produces many of these same pollutants and then some (see below).

A recent study (Lu *et al.*, 2012) suggested that substitution of natural gas for coal could have contributed to a reduction in CO_2 emissions from U.S. electrical generation from 2008 to 2009 (see also Logan *et al.*, 2012). Similarly, total U.S. GHG emissions decreased by 2.6% from 2010 to 2011, and part of this could also be a result of switching from coal to gas (Derry, in Revkin, 2013a). Some portion of this decrease in emissions might also be due to decreased use of fossil fuels generally—as a result of the global recession, improved vehicle gas mileage, and unusually warm winters (R. Howarth, pers. comm. to WDA, 6 August 2013).

[2] See, *e.g.,* Pacala & Socolow (2004); Brown *et al.* (2009); Podesta & Wirth (2009); Kerr (2010); Tour *et al.* (2010); Moniz *et al.* (2011); Jenner & Lamadrid (2012).

[3] Even if all of the individual scientific issues were completely understood (which is not currently the case), making such a judgment would still be complex and difficult. This is because the decision of coal versus natural gas is not just a scientific problem. As Eaton (2013: 158) has noted: "While clarity on narrow issues is important, a sole focus on scientific and technical aspects is unlikely to have prevented [recent environmental catastrophes, which resulted] … not just from scientific uncertainty but more importantly from an avoidable reactive cascade of events driven by economic and political choices … scientifically-based decision making needs to explicitly account for non-scientific issues related to human activities … Scientists have particular responsibilities … to help develop timely, systematic approaches that consider overlapping scientific, technical, environmental, sociological, economic and political considerations, evaluate their relative importance for the issue at hand, and thereby formulate recommendations for policy decision-making… [But a broader approach is needed] to develop a proactive framework for rational, timely decision-making by weighing relative merits in the face of incomplete information, and seek a broader perspective on common ground for consensus …"

[4] Life-cycle analyses are officially standardized by the International Organization for Standardization (ISO); see ISO (2006). A useful summary of LCA for shale gas was published by Bradbury

et al. (2013: 15).

[5] The debate over the environmental impact of shale gas and hydrofracking has been aptly described as an example of "the complexity of a coupled human-nature system," characterized by "unpredictable and nonlinear dynamics in the interaction of human behaviours with natural systems" (*e.g.,* Hou *et al.,* 2012: 385).

[6] Yusuf *et al.* (2012). Major natural sources of CH_4 emissions include wetlands and peatbogs, termites, wildfires, grasslands, coalbeds, and lakes. Human sources include municipal solid waste landfills, rice paddies, coal mining, oil and gas drilling and processing, cattle ranching, manure management, agricultural products, and wastewater and sewage treatment plants.

[7] Globally, agriculture is the largest source of anthropogenic methane of these three sources (Yusuf *et al.,* 2012). In the U.S., however, "natural gas systems" (exploration, production, distribution, and use of natural gas) is currently the single largest category, followed by animal agriculture (Howarth *et al.,* 2012a).

[8] For brief general discussion of climate change science, see Allmon *et al.* (2010).

[9] As noted by Eaton (2013: 164). "...the ultimate consideration when assessing a scientific and technical issue with major public policy implications is the political and regulatory landscape. Experts tend to view the scientific and technical aspects in isolation, whereas the success of public policy decisions about these issues can depend more on politics."

[10] For example, many scientists made presentations that are very relevant to this topic at the December 2012 meeting of the American Geophysical Union (see Tollefson, 2013a, for a summary of some of these presentations), but (as of this writing, September 2013) many of these studies have not yet been published as full papers in the peer-reviewed scientific literature. This is an example of the frequent "disconnect" between the usually deliberate pace of science and the demands of the public or policy-makers for immediate answers, especially for questions of major economic or social importance. Scientific results are not generally considered valid by the general scientific community until they have been scrutinized by other scientists ("peers") with expertise in the particular field. The original researchers then respond to any criticism or questions; this can go on for months or even years before a paper is finally published. Even then, the results might not be more widely accepted, then or ever. Much of the data and arguments discussed in this and other chapters are of this type. They have been discussed by scientists informally, presented at conferences, seminars, and meetings, passed around as manuscripts, PowerPoint® presentations, or blog postings, and some have been submitted to scientific journals but have not yet been published. Individual scientists might hold strong opinions based in part on such still-unpublished work; they might eventually be shown to be correct, but it is difficult or impossible to formally evaluate the ideas until they have been subjected to this peer-review process.

[11] A lack of consensus does not mean that there is no strong evidence or opinions one way or the other; quite the contrary, and different views can be held tenaciously by equally capable scientists who cannot understand why everyone does not see things the way they do. Science ultimately works, however, by testing, reformulating, and retesting alternative ideas. This sifting process can go on for a long time, but when (or if) it eventually convinces a large majority of the scientists who are knowledgeable about the subject that one view is more likely to be correct than other competing ideas, this becomes (at least temporarily) the conclusion that is (at least provisionally) accepted, and is usually presented to the public as "what most scientists think." When there is no clear consensus among the relevant specialists, the result can look—to the public, government, media, and other scientists—like chaos or despair, but it is an unavoidable part of the scientific process. This is close to the current situation on some aspects of our understanding of the consequences of large-scale development of the Marcellus Shale. For discussion of the role of consensus in science, see *e.g.,* Ziman (2000) and Labinger & Collins (2001).

[12] Because of the controversial and rapidly changing nature of this topic, in this chapter we provide more detailed documentation of sources than in other chapters.

[13] See Montzka *et al.* (2011). The Intergovernmental Panel on Climate Change (IPCC) provides the generally accepted values for GWP, and an exact definition of how GWP is calculated is to be found in the IPCC's 2001 *Third Assessment Report* (IPCC, 2001). GWP is a convenient way of expressing the potential future climate impact of a particular greenhouse gas. It is

not, however, used in this way by climate scientists in computer models of projected future climate change (*e.g.*, Solomon *et al.*, 2010; Wigley, 2011). This in part is because it is so dependent on the time frame chosen (see endnote 14, below), and in part because the assumption of simple constant value as the basis for comparison is physically incorrect. The relative impacts of a particular emission scenario depend not only on the fuel mix used, but on how quickly the emission patterns change, on the secondary impacts on other variables, such as aerosols and ozone, and even on the feedback response of the climate system. In other words, the impact of burning more or less gas versus coal cannot be effectively boiled down to a single number. Instead, climate models run side-by-side simulations that embody different choices (*e.g.*, more gas or more coal burning) without choosing a time frame in advance. As Solomon *et al.* (2011: 424) stated: "The choice of time horizon is crudely equivalent to the imposition of a discount rate, albeit a discount rate that varies with lifetime of the gas ... and thus represents a value judgment."

[14] The GWP of a gas thus depends on the time frame (see endnote 13, above). This, therefore, in some sense might allow an analyst to pick the wanted or preferred answer; it also, however, allows an analysis to focus on effects that occur at varying time scales. If, for example, you think that processes acting over long time scales are ultimately most important, it might make sense to focus attention on GWPs at the 100-year time frame. On the other hand, if you think that processes over shorter time scales (*e.g.*, threshold effects or tipping points; see endnote 62), then you will likely focus on GWPs at shorter times frames (*e.g.*, 20 years). Understanding this difference is extremely important for understanding the controversy over the potential future climate impact of methane leakage from Marcellus and other gas production.

[15] A *joule* is a unit of energy, defined as the work required to produce one watt of power for one second, or one watt second (Ws). A watt is a measure of rate of energy conversion or transfer, defined as one joule per second. Electricity generation is commonly measured in kilowatt hours (KWh). Thus, one KWh of electricity requires the equivalent of 1,000 watts times 3,600 seconds, or 3.6 million joules (megajoules, MJ).

[16] Archer *et al.* (2009: 120).

[17] Alvarez *et al.* (2012).

[18] Alvarez *et al.* (2012).

[19] Archer *et al.* (2009); Hausfather (2010).

[20] Alvarez *et al.* (2012). Howarth *et al.* (2011: 680) noted that "The global methane budget is poorly constrained, with multiple sources and sinks all having large uncertainties." The concentration actually starts to decline the moment after the emission "spike."

[21] Shindell *et al.* (2009, 2012).

[22] See, *e.g.,* Santoro *et al.* (2011).

[23] Mostly ozone (O_3) and some aerosols.

[24] In 2012, approximately 36% of natural gas used in the U.S. was burned to produce electricity, whereas 28% was burned to heat buildings (residential and commercial) (U.S. Energy Information Agency, http://www.eia.gov/dnav/ng/ng_cons_sum_dcu_nus_a.htm). This is probably an underestimate of recent average use of natural gas for heating, because 2012 was a record warm winter in the northeast, where heating by natural gas makes up a sizeable percentage of U.S. use.

[25] See, *e.g.,* Moniz *et al.* (2011).

[26] For example, Laurenzi & Jersey (2013) expressed emissions in kg CO_2 eq/MWh. Howarth *et al.* (2011, 2012a) used g C/MJ, which Cathles *et al.* (2012a: 2) described as "less intuitive and operationally relevant but more precise."

[27] The shortage of data has been commented upon by many authors (*e.g.,* Howarth 2010a; Howarth *et al.*, 2011; Levi, 2011; Bradbury *et al.*, 2013; Levi, 2013a; Pétron *et al.*, 2013). Howarth *et al.* (2011) presented the first LCA for shale gas published in the peer-reviewed scientific literature. That study relied mainly on data from two U.S. government reports (EPA, 2010c; GAO, 2010). Howarth *et al.* (2012a) added one more (EPA, 2011a). Shortly after publication of the Howarth *et al.* (2011) study, several other LCAs of shale gas were published (Hultman *et al.*, 2011; Jiang *et al.*, 2011; Stephenson *et al.*, 2011; Burnham *et al.*, 2011). Cathles (2012) and Cathles *et al.* (2012a) summarized "five detailed analyses"

of postproduction CH_4 emissions from both conventional and shale gas wells (EPA, 1997, 2010c, 2011a; Skone *et al.*, 2011; Venkatesh *et al.*, 2011). Weber & Clavin (2012) and Bradbury *et al.* (2013) performed similar analyses of multiple previous studies. The first study to use actual air samples to address the issue was by Petron *et al.* (2012), but those results have been controversial (*e.g.*, compare the favorable treatments by Howarth *et al.*, 2012a, and Tollefson, 2013a, to the more critical treatments by Levi, 2012, 2013b, Cathles, 2012, and Cathles *et al.*, 2012a). Laurenzi & Jersey (2013: 4896, 4901), who worked for Shell at the time of publication, stated that their study made use of "the most extensive data set of any LCA of shale gas to date, encompassing data from actual gas production and power generation operations," and claimed that it was the first study to use "actual production data for the key factors that affect the life cycle GHG emissions."

EPA estimates of GHG emissions from gas wells have a somewhat tortuous history. In 1996, the EPA reported estimates of GHG emissions from gas wells, based on data voluntarily provided by industry. These estimates have been criticized as too low and out of date by Howarth *et al.* (2011, 2012a, b). In 2010, the EPA estimated that for the year 2008, production-sector leak rate was 0.16% of total production (EPA, 2010c). (This was based on data on gas captured by green completions provided to the agency by industry as part of the EPA Gas STAR program, a voluntary program to encourage the oil and natural gas industries to adopt best practices.) EPA assumed that half of these emissions were vented and half flared. Cathles *et al.* (2012a, b) criticized both Howarth *et al.* (2011) and the EPA for assuming that emissions were vented, rather than captured.

In October 2009, the EPA proposed new regulations that would require regular reporting of GHG emissions, including methane, from natural gas systems (EPA 2011c). Starting on 1 January 2010, producers were required to collect emissions data, and the first report of these data was submitted to EPA on 31 March 2011 (see http://www.gpo. gov/fdsys/pkg/FR-2009-10-30/pdf/E9-23315.pdf). In its 2011 and 2012 reports, EPA revised its estimates of emissions upward (EPA, 2011a, 2012c), and then, in 2013, back down (EPA, 2013). As discussed by Karion *et al.* (2013), the main driver for this most recent reduction in estimated emissions was a report prepared by the oil and gas industry, which contended that actual CH_4 emissions from liquid unloading were actually more than an order of magnitude lower than EPA's 2011 report estimate, and that emissions from refracturing wells in tight sands or shale formations were less than half of the EPA 2011 estimate (Shires & Lev-On, 2012). These changes in the reported emission estimates led the EPA's Office of Inspector General to release a report calling for the improvement of the agency's air emissions data for the natural gas production sector (EPA Office of Inspector General, 2013).

A very recent study (Allen *et al.*, 2013; see also http://www.nytimes.com/2013/09/17/us/gas-leaks-in-fracking-less-than-estimated.html?emc=eta1&_r=0) of leakage at 190 natural gas production sites (including 489 hydraulically fractured wells) across the U.S. concluded that methane emissions are lower than previously estimated by the EPA (2013). The study was conducted by researchers at the University of Texas, funded by the Natural Resources Defense Council, and accomplished with the cooperation of several natural gas companies. A news account of the study, including reaction from Robert Howarth, is at http://www.npr.org/2013/09/16/223122924/despite-leaks-during-production-natural-gas-still-better-than-coal.

[28] Howarth *et al.* (2011: 683).

[29] Cathles (2012: 11); see also EPA (2010c: Appendix A).

[30] Alvarez *et al.* (2012: 6467); Harrison (2012), cited by Cathles (2012).

[31] Technology evidently exists that could do so (EPA, 2010c; GAO, 2010; Alvarez *et al.*, 2012: 6438; Bradbury *et al.*, 2013), although industry has argued that there currently is not enough equipment available to service the thousands of wells that are being drilled and hydrofracked each year (http://www.schneiderdowns.com/epa-issues-new-fracking-rules).

[32] The economic incentives for capturing fugitive emissions can vary. For example, according to the EPA (2011b), the break-even price at which the cost of capturing flowback gas equals the market value of the captured gas is slightly under $4 per tcf. In other words, below this price, it might cost more to capture the gas than it is worth. (The price of natural gas has

not been at $4 per tcf since August 2011; http://www.eia.gov/dnav/ng/hist/n9190us3m.htm.) Furthermore, even if there is an incentive in price, the business structure of the gas industry can make it disappear. As described by Bradbury *et al.* (2013: 35–36), although a production company might own the gas as it leaves the wellhead, it might hire another company (a "service company") to drill and complete the well. Unless that service company is contractually obligated to reduce methane leakage, it might not be in its best interest to minimize losses. The new EPA rules (NSPS/NESHAP) are intended to address this problem (see endnotes 27, above, and 34, below). Another potential problem is that REC technology can only be used when there is a pipeline to connect a well to. Some leases with landowners, however, might require well development by a particular date, whether pipelines are there or not (Bradbury *et al.*, 2013).

[33] For example, although it is surely in the interest of companies to protect their employees and capital investment from accident, different companies have different philosophies or acceptance of risk, and smaller companies in particular can have fewer resources to devote to risk reduction (see discussions by Cathles *et al.*, 2012a, b; Howarth *et al.*, 2012a,b; Gilbert & Gold, 2013).

[34] In April 2012, the EPA released two rules which were the agency's first move to establish federal standards for emissions at natural gas production wells (EPA, 2012a). The rules took effect in October 2012, and companies must be compliant with them by 1 January 2015 (http://www.epa.gov/airquality/oilandgas/implement.html). These two rules—the New Source Performance Standards (NSPS) for volatile organic compounds (VOCs), and the National Emissions Standard for Hazardous Air Pollutants (NESHAP) for oil and natural gas production—primarily target VOC and air toxics emissions, but should have the co-benefit of reducing methane emissions. The rules require a 95% reduction in VOCs at new and restimulated natural gas wells, to be achieved through the use of technology (known as *green completion*; AKA *reduced emission completion*, REC) to capture gas that would otherwise be vented at the wellhead. A recent study concluded that the use of such technologies is likely profitable in most cases (O'Sullivan & Paltsev, 2012). A recent study from the World Resources Institute (WRI) estimated that compliance with these rules would "reduce methane emissions enough to cut all upstream GHG emissions from shale gas operations between 40 and 46 percent below their projected trajectory in the absence of the rules … For all natural gas systems (including shale gas), methane emissions reductions resulting from the NSPS/NESHAP rules are projected to lower upstream GHG emissions by 13 percent in 2015 and 25 percent by 2035 …" (Bradbury *et al.*, 2013: 5).

The WRI report further recommended implementation of three additional steps, which should be possible with existing technologies, that could reduce methane emissions by up to an additional 30%. These steps include (a) "use of plunger lift systems at new and existing wells during liquids unloading operations; (b) fugitive methane leak monitoring and repair at new and existing well sites, processing plants, and compressor stations; and (c) replacing existing high-bleed pneumatic devices with low-bleed equivalents throughout natural gas systems … [T]hese three steps would bring down the total life cycle leakage rate across all natural gas systems to just above 1 percent of total production" (Bradbury *et al.*, 2013: 6).

A number of previous studies had estimated that existing technologies could reduce methane emissions associated with natural gas development by 40–90% (EPA, 2010c; GAO, 2010; Alvarez *et al.*, 2012: 6438).

[35] EPA (2009, 2010c); Hughes (2011); Jiang *et al.* (2011); NETL (2006). This is also referred to as *liquids unloading*.

[36] See, *e.g.*, Wood *et al.* (2011: 37); Bradbury *et al.* (2013); Laurenzi & Jersey (2013).

[37] Howarth *et al.* (2011: 681).

[38] Howarth *et al.* (2012a).

[39] See detailed discussion and disagreement on this issue by Cathles *et al.* (2012b), Howarth *et al.* (2012), and Bradbury *et al.* (2013: 16). Not all studies have included liquids unloading as an explicit step in gas development, and those that have done so have used different assumptions about its frequency (Bradbury *et al.*, 2013: 17).

[40] As an example of how difficult it is to determine this one point, Howarth *et al.* (2012: 5) stated

that "While visiting Cornell [University], a Shell engineer stated [that] Shell never flares gas during well completion in its Pennsylvania Marcellus operations (Bill Langin, pers. comm.)." Cathles *et al.* (2012a), however, quoted a statement that they claimed was provided to them by Shell that indicates that Langin was misquoted. According to the statement, Langin was responding to a different question—whether Shell "routinely flares during flowback." The statement said that Langin "responded that Shell does not routinely flare flowback from its *development wells*, which are wells that are going directly into the pipeline for sale. It is important to note that flaring can occur at a Shell site during *exploration well* tests. This could happen for a number of reasons including there being no pipeline connection available for sending the product to market or the quality of the resource is not of pipeline quality and requires further processing," Accounts from several individuals who attended Langin's talk of the actual exchange between Langin and the questioner in the audience differ in exactly what was said and by whom. Based on this information, when or how often Shell flares its wells during flowback is, to say the least, unclear.

In 1996, the EPA estimated (based on industry-reported data) that 98% of flowback gas was flared (Harrison *et al.*, 1996; although it should be noted that there were no shale gas wells in production at that time, and therefore no flowback from shale gas wells in that study). Laurenzi & Jersey (2013, supplementary information: 6) stated that *all* flowback gas in Marcellus wells drilled by ExxonMobil subsidiary XTO that they considered in their study was flared.

[41] According to the U.S. Pipeline and Hazardous Materials Safety Administration (PHMSA, 2002: V-1), there are at least 17 "conditions that may contribute to unaccounted for gas." For more on UFG, see PHMSA (2002: chapter 2) and Pennsylvania Public Utilities Commission (PPUC, 2012: 1). The PPUC report concluded that gas companies "often report UFG based upon their own definition, which varies from company to company resulting in inconsistent reporting," and the "lack of a standard definition of UFG may tempt NGDCs [Natural Gas Distribution Companies] to trivialize the importance of minimizing the volume of UFG." For gas theft from pipelines, especially in eastern Europe, see Engber (2005).

[42] See Hughes (2011, 2013a, b) and Bradbury *et al.* (2013: 15) for general discussions of EUR estimates for shale gas wells. EUR is not a measurement; it is a prediction. So, it is necessarily subject to uncertainty and potential subjectivity. This uncertainty is increased because of the nature of flow out of shale gas wells, which frequently declines rapidly after an early peak initial production (Hughes, 2011, 2013a, b). According to industry geologists with whom we discussed this issue, there is usually little confidence placed on production data until there are at least two years of data from each well. This is because in the early months of production, it is difficult to know when the well has been cleared of hydrofracking fluid water and has truly begun to produce at a "normal" level. Also, in the first few months, the engineers are tinkering with the well (*e.g.*, they might turn off production for multiple days, resulting in that month's production being less, but then engineers will try to estimate what it would have been had it not been turned off). EUR estimates therefore result from a combination of actual production data and interpolation, and not all engineers will make the same interpretations.

Howarth *et al.* (2011, 2012a) argued that most EUR estimates are likely overly optimistic about total lifetime production of the average shale gas well. If this is correct, then previous estimates of methane emissions relative to production are too low. Two recent studies attempted to summarize available data, but unfortunately reached very different conclusions, illustrating the complexity of coming up with EUR values. Laurenzi & Jersey (2013) (who worked for ExxonMobil at the time of writing) reported an average EUR of a Marcellus shale gas well as 1.8 bcf. Scientists from the U.S. Geological Survey (USGS Oil and Gas Assessment Team, 2012), however, reported an average value of less than one tenth that number (0.129 bcf). The reasons for this very large difference are unclear. The USGS estimates include three values for the Marcellus Shale, from three different geographic areas (although the lack of a map in the paper makes it difficult to know exactly where they are). One of these—for the "interior Marcellus"—is not as different from the Laurenzi & Jersey value as are the other two areas, and this could be where most of the production of gas is currently focused. The difference might therefore be a result of the different purposes of the two studies; the purpose of the USGS report was to summarize the entire Marcellus rather than just the higher-producing part, whereas Laurenzi & Jersey reported on what their company had selected as the best areas for making a profit. It is also possible that if the price of natural gas rises significantly, and companies begin to produce from shale layers that have lower EUR potential, then the lower values reported by the USGS might become more relevant.

[43] Bradbury *et al.* (2013: 17).

[44] A recent convoluted estimation of leakage from transmission pipelines is another example of how difficult it can be to obtain clear information on this topic. In 1996, the EPA estimated CH_4 emissions during distribution at 0.35% of production (Harrison *et al.*, 1996). Jiang *et al.* (2011) and Burnham *et al.* (2011) reported estimates of 0.67%, based on the 2011 EPA GHG inventory (EPA 2011a), whereas NETL (2006) estimated CH_4 loss as a function of pipeline distance, yielding slightly higher estimates (0.1 GWP, g CO2e/MJ). Other recent estimates are similar (Bradbury *et al.*, 2013: 16–17). Howarth *et al.* (2011: 684; 2012a: 539) argued that most earlier estimates of pipeline emissions were too low, noting that the average long-distance gas transmission pipeline in the U.S. is more than 50 years old, and many cities have gas distribution systems 80–100 years old. They also cited a study of Russian pipelines (Lelieveld *et al.*, 2005), which reported an average overall loss rate of 1.4%, and used this number "as the likely lower limit" for such emissions. [Howarth *et al.* (2011: 684) noted that previous estimates of Russian leakage were much higher, ranging from 2.5–10%, but that the "higher value reflects poorly maintained pipelines in Russia during the Soviet collapse, and leakages in Russia are now far less."] Howarth *et al.* then stated their "conservative estimate of 1.4% to 3.6% leakage of gas during transmission," which they took as support for their argument that CH_4 emissions are much higher than previously reported. In their paper on the Russian pipelines, however, Lelieveld *et al.* (2005: 841) characterized their estimate of 1.4% as "considerably less than expected and comparable to that from systems in the United States," and took their result as support for their position that "using natural gas in preference to other fossil fuels could be useful in the short term for mitigating climate change." Cathles (2012) criticized Howarth *et al.*'s estimates of pipeline leakage, in part because, he said, they were based on "leakage in Russian pipelines that occurred during the breakup of the Soviet Union which is irrelevant to gas pipelines in the U.S.," which was not entirely an accurate characterization. Meanwhile, a recent study of gas pipelines in Boston (Phillips *et al.*, 2013) based on actual measurements reported relatively high methane emissions. Other studies, still mostly unpublished, similarly suggest that cities might be large, but previously underappreciated, sources of CH_4 (*e.g.*, the INFLUX project at Purdue University; see http://influx.psu.edu/).

[45] See, *e.g.,* Sempra Inc. (2008). Jaramillo *et al.* (2005) considered the LCA of natural gas both with and without imported LNG.

[46] See, *e.g.*, Morris & Atkinson (1986).

[47] Coal mine emissions are 11% of total U.S. emissions, compared to 37% from petroleum/gas sector (Bradbury *et al.*, 2013).

[48] Bibler *et al.* (1998).

[49] For a discussion of the climatic effects of particulates from coal burning, see Hayhoe *et al.* (2002), EPA (2012b), Wigley (2011), and Alvarez *et al.* (2012: 6437).

[50] See, *e.g.*, Levy *et al.* (2009); NRC (2010b); Epstein *et al.* (2011); Eaton (2013).

[51] NRC (2010b).

[52] For information on power plant efficiency, see, *e.g.*, http://www.naturalgas.org/overview/uses eletrical.asp, and http://www.npc.org/study_topic_papers/4-dtg-electricefficiency.pdf. It is important to note here that, because less efficient coal plants will be increasingly replaced by more efficient gas plants, this efficiency difference will increase. The efficiency of new gas plants, for example, approaches 60%. Overall effects on GHG emissions, however, could depend heavily on how many and which coal plants are retired, and when (Venkatesh *et al.*, 2012).

[53] Alvarez *et al.* (2012).

[54] This is the range reported at the 95% confidence level by the EPA (2011a); see also Jiang *et al.*

(2011) and Cathles *et al.* (2012b).

[55] Howarth *et al.* (2011).

[56] Howarth posted non-peer-reviewed information on his website in early 2010 (Howarth, 2010a, b), and a manuscript was submitted for publication to the peer-reviewed journal *Climatic Change* on 12 November 2010. Parts of that manuscript, however, were circulated prior to publication (it remains unclear exactly how or by whom), which occurred online on 12 April 2011 (Howarth *et al.*, 2011). For some of the immediate media coverage, see Zeller (2011a, b, c). Some of Howarth's critics have also communicated via non-peer-reviewed channels [*e.g.,* Cathles *et al.*, 2012a; although much of this information later appeared in a peer-reviewed paper (Cathles, 2012); see also Cathles, 2013]. The controversy between the two Cornell University groups has received its own media coverage (*e.g.,* Reilly, 2012; Revkin, 2012), and continues at the time of this writing (September 2013; *e.g.,* Ingraffea, 2013b; Revkin, 2013a).

[57] Several studies have reached conclusions similar to, or consistent with, those of Howarth and colleagues. For example, Alvarez *et al.* (2012: 6437) wrote that "… given limited current evidence, it is likely that leakage at individual natural gas well sites is high enough, when combined with leakage from downstream operations, to make the total leakage exceed the 3.2% threshold beyond which gas becomes worse for the climate than coal for at least some period of time." See also Hughes (2011, 2013b) and Hamburg (2013) for commentary and/or analysis generally supporting Howarth *et al.*'s conclusions. Recently, at least three studies based on actual air samples have reported relatively high rates of CH_4 emissions in association with natural gas production and/or transportation, lending support to Howarth *et al.*'s argument. Pétron *et al.* (2012, 2013) reported that, based on data from one county in Colorado, methane emissions from the numerous gas wells in Colorado are likely underestimated by half [but see Levi (2012, 2013b) for critiques of this work]. Karion *et al.* (2013) similarly reported an estimated CH_4 emission rate of 6.2–11.7% of the average hourly natural gas production for one county in Utah. In their study of gas pipelines in Boston, Phillips *et al.* (2013) reported CH_4 emissions up to fourteen times higher than background concentrations due to leakage in that city's aging infrastructure.

A study by Wigley (2011) agreed with Howarth *et al.* that natural gas likely does not have a lower GWP than coal. This conclusion, however, depended to a large degree on the assumption that SO_2 emissions from coal burning would not be significantly reduced in the near future. As discussed on p. 117, these emissions have a cooling effect on the Earth, thereby reducing coal's GWP.

On the other hand, several peer-reviewed studies have taken issue with Howarth *et al.*'s methods and/or conclusions. Cathles *et al.* (2012a, b; Cathles, 2012) have argued that Howarth *et al.* "significantly overestimate the fugitive emissions associated with unconventional gas extraction, undervalue the contribution of 'green technologies' to reducing those emissions … base their comparison between gas and coal on heat rather than electricity generation … and assume a time interval over which to compute the relative climate impact of gas compared to coal that does not capture the contrast between the long residence time of CO2 and the short residence time of methane in the atmosphere … Using more reasonable leakage rates and bases of comparison, shale gas has a GHG footprint that is half and perhaps a third that of coal" (Cathles *et al.*, 2012b: 525). See Howarth *et al.* (2012a) for a vigorous response to these critiques. A number of shale gas LCAs published since 2011 (*e.g.,* Fulton *et al.*, 2011; Hultman *et al.*, 2011; Stephenson *et al.*, 2011; Venkatesh *et al.*, 2011; Weber & Clavin, 2012; Jenner & Lamadrid, 2012; O'Sullivan & Paltsev, 2012) have concluded that CH_4 leakage rates are comparable in conventional and unconventional gas drilling, and not as high as suggested by Howarth *et al.* (See also Logan *et al.*, 2012, although the latter does not include emissions associated with liquids unloading.) Other scientific analyses critical of one or more of Howarth *et al.*'s methods and/or conclusions include Levi (2011); Bradbury *et al.* (2013:16); Laurenzi & Jersey (2013); Derry, in Revkin (2013a); and Pierrehumbert, in Revkin (2013b).

[58] Much has been made of the different conclusions of studies made at 20- versus 100-year time frames (*e.g.,* Howarth *et al.*, 2011, 2012; Cathles, 2012; Cathles *et al.*, 2012a, b). Yet, as very aptly noted by Bradbury *et al.* (2013: 14), the "answer" about the GWP of natural gas

is not so much a scientific question as it is "a policy question that is informed by science." The decision about whether to use the 20-, 50-, 100-, or 500-year GWP for methane "depends partly on the time scale over which you expect your policy—and affected energy infrastructure investments—to be relevant."

[59] For example, Cathles *et al.* (2012a: 9) concluded that "Scientifically the prescription for reducing green house emissions is clear: substitute gas for coal while minimizing methane emissions using proven and available technology, and then move toward low carbon energy sources as quickly as technically and economically feasible."

[60] See, *e.g.,* Hansen & Sato (2004); Hansen *et al.* (2007); Shindell *et al.* (2012).

[61] On apparently accelerating rates of some aspects and effects of climate change, see, *e.g.,* Rahmstorf *et al.* (2012). In their original paper, Howarth *et al.* (2011) did not explicitly mention tipping points as a reason to focus on the 20-year time frame, which was noted by Cathles *et al.* (2012b: 3) in their critique. [Howarth (pers. comm. to WDA, 6 August 2013) said that it was in the original manuscript but cut from the final version for reasons of length.] In their response to Cathles *et al.* (2012b), however, Howarth *et al.* (2012a) included an extended discussion of the potential consequences of tipping points. They concluded that it is important to focus on methane emissions on decadal time scales, rather than the scale of a century or more, because, as Hansen *et al.* (2007) have emphasized, methane could contribute to reaching a critical tipping point in global climate.

[62] See, *e.g.,* Whiteman *et al.* (2013); Lenton & Ciscar (2013), and references therein. Some climate scientists have suggested, however, that, although climate tipping points definitely exist, their danger has been exaggerated, specifically that those mentioned above (Greenland ice, West Antarctic ice, methane hydrates) all have time scales longer than 20–30 years (see, *e.g.,* http://www.nature.com/nature/journal/v500/n7464/full/500529a.html; http://www.nature.com/nature/journal/v500/n7464/full/500529b.html; http://www.esrl.noaa.gov/gmd/annualconference/abs.php?refnum=71-130415-A; http://www.skepticalscience.com/toward-improved-discussions-methane.html; http://dotearth.blogs.nytimes.com/2013/07/25/arctic-methane-credibility-bomb/; http://www.motherjones.com/environment/2013/08/arctic-methane-hydrate-catastrophe; http://dotearth.blogs.nytimes.com/2011/12/14/methane-time-bomb-in-arctic-seas-apocalypse-not/).

[63] See, *e.g.,* Schrag (2012); Mann (2013); Trembath & Jenkins (2013).

[64] Rogers (2011); Ryan (2013).

[65] Levi (2013a: 620). According to Levi, it does not matter very much whether methane leakage is 1–2% or 4–5% if the goal is to get to 450 ppm by a short natural gas bridge followed quickly by low- or no-carbon alternatives. If the goal is to get to 550 ppm, the bridge is longer and leakage rates might matter more. Such analyses are in contrast to most previous work (*e.g.,* Wigley, 2011), in which greatly expanded ("bridge") use of natural gas "continues indefinitely, resulting in methane emissions (and consequent radiative forcing) that also continue indefinitely."

[66] For recent assessments of the dangers of exceeding 350 ppm of CO_2 in the atmosphere, see, *e.g.,* Hansen & Sato (2004), Lovejoy & Hannah (2005); Hansen *et al.* (2007, 2008), Rockström *et al.* (2009), Lovejoy (2010), Hoegh-Guldberg & Bruno (2010); Solomon *et al.* (2010); Anderson & Bows (2011); and Steinbruner *et al.* (2012).

[67] See, e.g., Jacobson & Delucchi (2009); Jacobson *et al.* (2013).

CHAPTER 7

[1] EIA, 2012, *Annual Energy Review 2011*, DOE/EIA-0384 (2011), US EIA, Washington, DC, http://www.eia.gov/totalenergy/data/annual/pdf/aer.pdf, see tables 1.3, 2.1b–f, 10.3, and 10.4.

[2] The Energy Information Administration website (http://eia.gov) provides current statistics and a wide range of information about energy production and use.

[3] EIA, 2012, *Annual Energy Review 2011*, DOE/EIA-0384 (2011), US EIA, Washington, DC, http://www.eia.gov/totalenergy/data/annual/pdf/aer.pdf, see tables 1.3, 2.1b–f, 10.3, and 10.4.

[4] See the discussion of the difficulties of learning and teaching scale in Chapter 8.

[5] EIA, 2012, *Annual Energy Review 2011*, DOE/EIA-0384 (2011), US EIA, Washington, DC, http://www.eia.gov/totalenergy/data/annual/pecss_diagram.cfm, see tables 1.3, 2.1b–f,

10.3, and 10.4.

[6] EIA, 2013, *Annual Energy Outlook 2013 with Projections to 2040*, page 3, http://www.eia.gov/forecasts/aeo/pdf/0383(2013).pdf.

[7] EIA, 2009, *Annual Energy Review 2009*, DOE/EIA-0383 (2011), US EIA, Washington, DC, http://www.eia.gov/totalenergy/data/annual/.

[8] EIA Frequently Asked Questions: How much petroleum does the United States import and from where?, http://www.eia.gov/tools/faqs/faq.cfm?id=727&t=6.

[9] EIA Frequently Asked Questions: How much oil does the United States consume per year?, http://www.eia.gov/tools/faqs/faq.cfm?id=33&t=6.

[10] 2012 Oil Shale & Tar Sands Programmatic EIS Information Center, Argonne National Labs, http://ostseis.anl.gov/guide/tarsands/.

[11] EIA, *U.S. Natural Gas Imports & Exports 2012*, http://www.eia.gov/naturalgas/importsexports/annual/.

[12] EIA, 2011, *Annual Energy Outlook 2011 with Projections to 2035*, DOE/EIA-0383 (2011), US EIA, Washington, DC, http://www.eia.gov/forecasts/archive/aeo11/pdf/0383%282011%29.pdf.

[13] EIA, 2001, *Annual Energy Outlook 2001 with Projections to 2020*, (DOE/EIA-0383: 2001), US EIA, Washington, DC, http://www.eia.doe.gov/oiaf/archive/aeo01/pdf/0383(2001).pdf.

[14] 1 short ton = 2,000 pounds or 907 kilograms. EIA, 2013, *Quarterly Coal Report (1Q 2013)*, US EIA, Washington, DC, http://www.eia.gov/coal/data.cfm#consumption.

[15] Nuclear Energy Institute—World Statistics, http://www.nei.org/resourcesandstats/nuclearstatistics/worldstatistics/.

[16] EIA, 2009, *Annual Energy Review 2009*, DOE/EIA-0383 (2011), US EIA, Washington, DC, http://www.eia.gov/totalenergy/data/annual/, see tables 1.3, 2.1b–f, 10.3, and 10.4

[17] NRC (2010a).

[18] Manahan, M. D., & S. A. Verville, 2005 FERC and dam decommissioning, *Natural Resources & Environment*, 19(3): 45–49, doi:10.2307/40924587.

[19] Renewables 2011 Global Status Report, (REN21 Secretariat: Paris), http://www.ren21.net/REN21Activities/Publications/GlobalStatusReport/GSR2011/tabid/56142/Default.aspx.

[20] Renewables 2011 Global Status Report, (REN21 Secretariat: Paris), http://www.ren21.net/REN21Activities/Publications/GlobalStatusReport/GSR2011/tabid/56142/Default.aspx.

[21] EIA, 2011, *Renewable Energy Consumption and Electricity Preliminary Statistics 2010*, DOE/EIA 0383 (2011), US EIA, Washington, DC, http://www.eia.gov/renewable/annual/preliminary/.

[22] "Mountain top removal" is a form of surface mining commonly used in the Appalachian Mountains of the eastern U. S. It requires the removal of mountain or ridge tops to allow easy access to coal seams and has substantial environmental and human health impacts. See http://www.epa.gov/region3/mtntop/ for a more detailed description of mountain-top removal mining and about related regulations and environmental impacts.

[23] McSpirit *et al.* (2005).

[24] Manahan & Verville (2005).

[25] See Heffernan (2013).

[26] EIA, 2010, *State Energy Data System (SEDS)*, http://www.eia.gov/state/seds/seds-data-complete.cfm?sid=NY.

[27] For a range of information about production and consumption by state, see http://www.eia.gov/state/.

[28] EIA, 2010, *Electric Power Annual 2009*, DOE/EIA-0383 (2011), US EIA, Washington, DC, http://205.254.135.24/cneaf/electricity/epa/epa_sum.html.

[29] EPA, "Sources of Greenhouse Gas Emissions: Electricity Sector Emissions," 2013, http://www.epa.gov/climatechange/ghgemissions/sources/electricity.html.

[30] Lawrence Livermore National Laboratory's annual "spaghetti diagrams," produced under the auspices of the Department of Energy, show the amounts of energy rejected as waste heat and used to provide energy service for each energy source, and each demand sector. See https://flowcharts.llnl.gov/content/energy/energy_archive/energy_flow_2012/2012new2012newUSEnergy.png for the 2012 diagram. Source: Lawrence Livermore National Laboratory, 2013, with data based on DOE/EIA-0035(2013-05), May 2013, https://

flowcharts.llnl.gov/content/energy/energy_archive/energy_flow_2012/2012new2012new USEnergy.png.

[31] EIA, *Annual Electric Generator Report* (Form EIA-860), http://www.eia.gov/todayinenergy/detail.cfm?id=8250.

[32] EIA, Electricity Data Browser, http://www.eia.gov/electricity/data/browser/.

[33] EIA, 2010, *Annual Coal Report 2009*, DOE/EIA-0383 (2011), US EIA, Washington, DC, http://www.eia.gov/cneaf/coal/page/acr/acr_sum.html.

[34] EIA, 2002, *United States Energy History Annual Energy Review 2001*, DOE/EIA-0384 (2001), US EIA, Washington, DC, http://www.eia.gov/totalenergy/data/annual/archive/038401.pdf.

[35] Lawrence Livermore National Laboratory, 2013, with data based on DOE/EIA-0035(2013-05), May 2013, https://flowcharts.llnl.gov/content/energy/energy_archive/energy_flow_2012/2012new2012newUSEnergy.png.

[36] BNSF Railway, "News Release: BNSF to test liquefied natural gas in road locomotives," 6 March 2013, http://www.bnsf.com/media/news-releases/2013/march/2013-03-06a.html.

[37] Underwood, Joanna D., & Matthew P. Tomich, 2013, *Tomorrow's Trucks: Leaving the Era of Oil Behind; an Analysis of Expanded Refuse Sector Natural Gas Vehicle Use in New Jersey, New York City, and on Long Island*, Energy Vision, New York, 72 pp., available at http://energy-vision.org/wordpress/wp-content/uploads/2013/05/Tomorrows-Trucks.pdf.

[38] Lewis L. Strauss, Speech to the National Association of Science Writers, New York City, 16 September 1954 [*The New York Times*, 17 September 1954].

[39] EIA, 2001, *Annual Energy Outlook 2001: With Projections to 2020*, DOE/EIA-0383 (2001), US EIA, Washington, DC, http://www.eia.doe.gov/oiaf/archive/aeo01/pdf/0383(2001).pdf.

CHAPTER 8

[1] Aspects of what bedevils risk analysis are also importantly addressed in Chapter 9, because that chapter addresses concepts that are challenging to learn and teach, and these challenges (for example, cognitive biases) are fundamental to making sense of risk.

[2] Ropeik & Gray (2002).

[3] From Frumkin *et al.* (2008), adapted by Korfmacher *et al.* (2013).

[4] Korfmacher *et al.* (2013).

[5] CDC/ATSDR Hydraulic Fracturing Statement, 3 May 2012, http://www.cdc.gov/media/releases/2012/s0503_hydraulic_fracturing.html.

[6] Mitka (2012).

[7] Worker Exposure to Silica during Hydraulic Fracturing, 21 June 2012, https://www.osha.gov/dts/hazardalerts/hydraulic_frac_hazard_alert.html.

[8] CDC, 2013, Review of Federal Hydraulic Fracturing Research Activities, Washington DC, http://www.cdc.gov/washington/testimony/2013/t20130426.htm.

[9] EIA (2013).

[10] EPA, 2013, *Inventory of U.S. Greenhouse Gas Emissions and Sinks*, http://www.epa.gov/climatechange/Downloads/ghgemissions/US-GHG-Inventory-2013-Main-Text.pdf.

[11] See Eaton (2013) for discussion of the nature of the analogy and Dhar *et al.* (1997) for analysis of the Bangladeshi disaster.

[12] Perrow (2011: 65–66).

[13] For a discussion of Holland's rise and fall as a world power in relation to peat exploitation, see De Decker (2011).

[14] Modified from Conca (2012).

[15] Korfmacher *et al.* (2013).

[16] See http://www.culturalcognition.net/blog/2013/6/13/science-literacy-cultural-polarization-it-doesnt-happen-just.html.

[17] From U.S. Centers for Disease Control and Prevention, National Public Health Performance Standards Program (NPHPSP), *10 Essential Public Health Services*, http://www.cdc.gov/nphpsp/essentialservices.html.

[18] Fernandez, R., & D. Rodrik, 1991 (December), Resistance to reform: status quo bias in the presence of individual-specific uncertainty, *The American Economic Review*, 81: 1146–1155.

[19] See Kahan, D., 2013 (June 13), Science literacy & cultural polarization: it doesn't happen

"just"with global warming, but it also doesn't happen for *all* risks. Why?, *The Cultural Cognition Project at Yale Law School*, http://www.culturalcognition.net/blog/2013/6/13/science-literacy-cultural-polarization-it-doesnt-happen-just.html.

[20] Frumkin *et al.* (2008); Korfmacher *et al.* (2013).

CHAPTER 9

[1] Shulman, L. S., 1987, Knowledge and teaching: foundations of the new reform, *Harvard Educational Review*, 57(1): 1–22; Shulman, L. S., 1986, Paradigms and research programs in the study of teaching: a contemporary perspective, Pages 3–36, in: *Handbook of Research on Teaching*, M. C Wittrock (ed.), Macmillan, New York.

[2] See more about Technological and Pedagogical Content Knowledge on Punya Mishra's website: http://punya.educ.msu.edu/research/tpck/.

[3] See the entire essay at http://www.museumoftheearth.org/outreach.php?page=Edu_Prog/92387/430947.

[4] Sturgis, P., & N. Allum, 2004, Science in society: re-evaluating the deficit model of public attitudes, *Public Understanding of Science*, 13(1): 55–74. This work explores the deficit model, a way of describing the currently dominant educational practice in which students are seen as having a deficit of information to be filled by the instructor providing the missing information. This too is a controversial issue and Sturgis & Allum saw both utility and problems with the approach, arguing in part that a deficit that can be filled is related to the understanding of context.

[5] Posner, G. J., K. A. Strike, P. W. Hewson, & W. A. Gertzog, 1982, Accommodation of a scientific conception: toward a theory of conceptual change, *Science Education*, 66(2): 211–227. Available at http://www.fisica.uniud.it/URDF/laurea/idifo1/materiali/g5/Posner%20et%20al.pdf.

[6] The presentation that begins with this question is, "There's No Such Thing as a Free Megawatt: Hydrofracking as a Gateway Drug to Energy Literacy"; it is regularly updated and available online at http://bit.ly/MarcellusGateway.

[7] Paulos, J. A., 2001, *Innumeracy: Mathematical Illiteracy and its Consequences*, Hill and Wang, New York, 180 pp.

[8] Gaylord Nelson (1916–2005) was a U.S. Senator from Wisconsin, environmental advocate, and principal founder of Earth Day; see Nelson (2002).

[9] McGraw (2012).

[10] Wilber (2012).

[11] Shale Gas Review, http://tomwilber.blogspot.com

[12] PRI's Marcellus Shale website, http://www.museumoftheearth.org/marcellusshale.

[13] Cornell Cooperative Extension Natural Gas Resource Center, http://cce.cornell.edu/EnergyClimateChange/NaturalGasDev/Pages/default.aspx.

[14] New York State Water Resources Institute, http://wri.eas.cornell.edu/.

[15] Penn State Extension Natural Gas website, http://extension.psu.edu/natural-resources/natural-gas.

[16] "There's no such thing as a free megawatt: The Marcellus Shale as a Gateway Drug to Energy Literacy," http://bit.ly/MarcellusGateway.

[17] *A Research Guide to the Marcellus and Utica Shales*, http://www.andrew.cmu.edu/org/marcellus-biblio.

[18] WSKG Marcellus Resource Page, http://wskgmarcellus.tumblr.com/.

[19] Institute for Energy and Environmental Research for Northeastern Pennsylvania at Wilkes University, http://energy.wilkes.edu.

[20] PRI's Marcellus Shale website, http://www.museumoftheearth.org/marcellusshale.

[21] Donovan, M. S., J. D. Bransford, & J. W. Pellegrino (eds), 1999, *How People Learn: Bridging Research and Practice*, National Academy Press, Washington DC, 10 + 78 pp. Available at http://www.nap.edu/openbook.php?record_id=9457&page=R1.

[22] Donovan, M. S., & J. D. Bransford (eds), 2005, *How Students Learn: History in the Classroom*, National Academy Press, Washington, DC, 16 + 264 pp., available at http://www.nap.edu/openbook.php?record_id=11100; Donovan, M. S., & J. D. Bransford (eds), 2005, *How Students Learn: Science in the Classroom*, National Academy Press, Washington, DC, 16

+ 248 pp., available at http://www.nap.edu/openbook.php?isbn=0309089506; Donovan, M. S., & J. D. Bransford (eds), 2005, *How Students Learn: Mathematics in the Classroom*, National Academy Press, Washington, DC, 16 + 256 pp., available at http://www.nap.edu/openbook.php?record_id=11101.

[23] Fenichel, M., & H. A. Schweingruber, 2010, *Surrounded by Science: Learning Science in Informal Environments*, National Academies Press, Washington, DC, 18 + 222 pp. Available at http://www.nap.edu/openbook.php?record_id=12614.

[24] Wiggins & McTighe (2005); supporting resources, http://www.ascd.org/research-a-topic/understanding-by-design-resources.aspx.

[25] Bateson, G., 2000, *Steps to an Ecology of Mind: Collected Essays in Anthropology, Psychiatry, Evolution, and Epistemology*, University of Chicago Press, Chicago, 565 pp.

[26] Meadows, D. H., 2008, *Thinking in Systems: a Primer*. Chelsea Green Publishing, White River Junction, Vermont, 240 pp.

[27] *The Next Generation Science Standards* (NGSS), http://nextgenscience.org.

[28] *A Framework for K-12 Science Education*, http://www.nap.edu/catalog.php?record_id=13165.

[29] *National Science Education Standards*, http://www.nap.edu/catalog.php?record_id=4962#.

[30] Centers for Ocean Science Education Excellence (2005).

[31] The *Overarching Questions* and *Bigger Ideas* are mapped onto the different essential principles at http://virtualfieldwork.org/Big_Ideas.html.

[32] Energy Information Administration, http://www.eia.gov/.

[33] A brief overview of relevant strategies for teaching and talking about climate change can be found at http://growwny.org/whats-new/1294-resolve-to-be-an-effective-climate-communicator-some-tips; a large collection of reviewed resources can be found through the Climate Literacy and Energy Awareness Network at http://cleanet.org/. See also Allmon *et al.* (2010). Of course, this is a huge issue, so these are just the barest of introductions.

[34] NOAA, http://www.education.noaa.gov/climate.

[35] NCDC, http://www.ncdc.noaa.gov.

[36] IPCC, http://ipcc.ch.

[37] Climate Literacy and Energy Awareness Network, http://cleanet.org/index.html.

[38] Ropeik & Grey (2002).

[39] Bond (2009).

[40] Cook, J., & S. Lewandowsky, 2011, *The Debunking Handbook*, University of Queensland, St. Lucia, Australia, available at http://sks.to/debunk.

[41] Irfan, U., 2011 (December 19), *Report Finds 'Motivated Avoidance' Plays a Role in Climate Change Politics*, E & E Publishing, http://www.eenews.net/stories/1059957806; Shepherd, S., & A. C. Kay, 2012, On the perpetuation of ignorance, *Journal of Personality and Social Psychology*, 102(2): 264–280.

[42] Kahneman, D., 2011, *Thinking, Fast and Slow*, Farrar, Straus and Giroux, New York, 499 pp.

[43] McGraw (2012).

[44] Navarro, M., 2011 (December 27), With gas drilling next door, county in New York gets an economic lift, *The New York Times*, http://www.nytimes.com/2011/12/28/nyregion/hydrofracking-gives-chemung-county-ny-economic-boost.html.

FIGURE CREDITS

Introduction leading image. The Earth from space, with Hurricane Linda west of Mexico, 9 September 1997. Image by Nelson Stöckli, Haller Laboratory for Atmospheres, Goddard Space Flight Center, National Aeronautics and Space Administration.

Figure 1.1. Marcellus Shale at a quarry in Seneca County, New York. Photograph by Robert Ross.

Figure 1.2. Artist's reconstruction of a typical Middle Devonian shallow sea environment. Original painting (on wood) by Gloria Royer, PRI Art Collection.

Figure 1.3. The Appalachian Basin and the distribution of the Marcellus Shale in the subsurface. Graphic by Alex Wall.

Figure 1.4. (A) Geological time scale, with Devonian Period shaded. (B) Block diagram showing the major units of sedimentary rock that accumulated in central New York State between approximately 500 million and 360 million years ago. Shales that contain significant amounts of natural gas are marked in black. (C) Detailed stratigraphy of the Hamilton Group, including the Marcellus Shale. Modified from *The Marcellus Papers*, 2: fig. 4; graphic by J. Houghton. Graphic by Sally Vann.

Figure 1.5. A paleogeographic map, showing what North America might have looked like during the middle part of the Devonian Period, approximately 390 million years ago. Modified from http://www2.nau.edu/rcb7/namD385.jpg; map by Ron Blakey. Graphic by Yuka Sagar.

Figure 1.6. Fossils brachiopods. (Left, top and bottom) from Pecksport Member of the Oatka Creek Formation, 3 miles north of Morrisville, New York, PRI collections acc. 1635. (Right) from Union Springs Member, Seneca County, New York, PRI collection acc. 1657.

Figure 1.7. Diagram showing how the formation of oil and gas depend on temperature and pressure. Modified from http://www.oilandgasgeology.com/oil_gas_window.jpg.

Figure 1.8. Flaming gas seep. Photograph by Don Duggan-Haas.

Figure 1.9. Aerial view of the creek near Taughannock Falls near Ithaca, NY. From *The Marcellus Papers*, 5: fig. 1. Photograph by the PRI Marcellus Shale Team.

Figure 1.10. (A) Surface of central New York State. Image from Richard W. Allmendinger, Cornell University, modified slightly to show dipping layers. (B) The Marcellus Shale in New York is beneath the surface in most of the southern tier and is exposed near Buffalo, Rochester, and Syracuse. From *The Marcellus Papers*, 2: fig. 1; Source: http://www.shalenetwork.org/image/view/9/_original (modified from USGS).

Figure 1.11. Growth of shale gas production. Data from http://www.eia.gov/naturalgas/weekly/#tabs-rigs-2. Graphic by Don Duggan-Haas.

Figure 2.1. Drill cuttings added to waste container. Photograph by Don Duggan-Haas.

Figure 2.2. (A) Gamma-ray log. Modified after Wang & Carr, 2012: fig. 10. (B) Geiger counter and Union Springs shale. Photograph by Warren Allmon.

Figure 2.3. Scale build-up in a drilling pipe. Reproduced with permission, N.E.T. Waterjet Ltd., http://www.nctwaterjet.co.uk/.

Figure 2.4. The location of active and inactive faults within New York State. From The Marcellus Papers 3: fig. 2. Modified from Isachsen & McKendree (1977); digitized for GIS http://www.nysm.nysed.gov/gis; image courtesy of M. Weltman-Fahs.

Figure 2.5. Injection-induced seismicity. Modified after fig. 2 at http://esd.lbl.gov/research/projects/

induced_seismicity/primer.html. Graphic by Sally Vann.

Figure 2.6. Injection well. Modified after *Injection Wells and Induced Seismicity*, American Petroleum Institute, fig. 2, http://www.api.org/~/media/Files/Policy/Hydraulic_Fracturing/UIC-amd-Seismicity.ashx. Graphic by Alex Wall.

Figure 3.1. A Marcellus Shale drilling rig outside Towanda, Pennsylvania. Photograph by Don Duggan-Haas.

Figure 3.2. Gas production in New York State. Modified from maps 2 and 4 in NYSDEC (New York State Department of Environmental Conservation), 2010, *New York State Oil, Gas and Mineral Resources 2010.* Available at http://www.dec.ny.gov/docs/materials_minerals_pdf/10anrpt1.pdf. Graphic by Sally Vann.

Figure 3.3. A conventional vertical well, and an unconventional horizontal well. From *The Marcellus Papers*, 7: fig. 1; graphic by J. Houghton.

Figure 3.4. Natural gas prices through time. Modified after a figure at http://www.eia.gov/dnav/ng/hist/n9190us3a.htm. Graphic by Sally Vann.

Figure 3.5. Simplified, generalized summary of the stages by which hydrofracked wells are developed. Graphic by Warren Allmon.

Figure 3.6. A Marcellus Shale well pad during drilling operations. Photograph by Don Duggan-Haas.

Figure 3.7. Components of a typical drilling rig. Modified from a diagram by "Mudgineer" via Wikimedia Commons, http://commons.wikimedia.org/wiki/File:Oil_Rig_NT8.jpg. Graphic by Sally Vann.

Figure 3.8. Fixed cutter drill bit. Photograph by Don Duggan-Haas.

Figure 3.9. Drill pipe stacked below a rig near Sayre, Pennsylvania. Photograph by Don Duggan-Haas.

Figure 3.10. Drilling and casing a well. From *The Marcellus Papers*, 6: fig. 1; graphic by J. Houghton.

Figure 3.11. Schematic summary of the fluids added to a typical hydrofracked well, and the fluids that come back out. Graphic by Warren Allmon.

Figure 3.12. Fracture propagation. From *The Marcellus Papers*, 5: fig. 6; graphic by J. Houghton.

Figure 4.1. Reflecting Pool on the National Mall. Photograph by Hu Totya, 2006, via Wikimedia Commons.

Figure 4.2. The Marcellus Shale and major river basins in New York. From *The Marcellus Papers*, 7: fig. 2; graphic by J. Houghton.

Figure 4.3. The proportion of flowback fluid to produced water over the life of a well. From *The Marcellus Papers*, 8: fig. 1; graphic by J. Houghton.

Figure 4.4. Abington Regional Waste Water Treatment Plant, Chinchilla, Pennsylvania. Image © 2013 Google, via Google Earth.

Figure 4.5. Drilling explosion/blowout near Moundsville, West Virginia, June 2010. Photograph by AP Images, used by permission.

Figure 5.1. Service trucks on a Marcellus Shale well pad. Photograph by Doug Duncan, U.S. Geological Survey, http://energy.usgs.gov/GeneralInfo/HelpfulResources/MultimediaGallery/HydraulicFracturingGallery.aspx.

Figure 5.2. Summary of the major environmental impacts resulting from well pad (and other) construction. Graphic by Warren Allmon.

Figure 5.3. Freshwater mussel. *Lampsilis radiata* from Plum Point, western shore of Seneca Lake, Yates County, New York, Mary Wheeler collection, 1960, PRI collections 1492.

Figure 5.4. Habitat fragmentation, Chartiers Township, Washington County, Pennsylvania. Photograph from PA Shale Viewer (11 September 2013). Data mapped by The FracTracker Alliance on http://www.fractracker.org. Original data source (drilled wells and compressor stations): Pennsylvania Department of Environmental Protection and GASP (Group Against Smog and Pollution, http://gasp-pgh.org/). Accessed on 14 September 2013: http://maps.fractracker.org/latest/?appid=28041aae3e674e04b0f987f047f3fe59.

Figure 5.5. American Toad (*Bufo americanus*), Fairfax, Virginia, 2009, photographer Jarek Tuszynski, via Wikimedia Commons; Northern Dusky Salamander (*Desmognathus fuscus*), reproduced with permission from *Field Guide to the Cayuga Lake Region*, by James Dake, 2009, Paleontological Research Institution, Ithaca, New York; photograph by James Dake.

Figure 6.1. Methane cloud. From Howarth *et al.* (2012a), by permission of the senior author.

Figure 6.2. Human-caused sources of atmospheric methane emissions. Modified from Yusuf *et al.* (2012). Graphic by Sally Vann.

Figure 6.3. Schematic diagram representing the major variables in a life-cycle analysis (LCA) of greenhouse gas emissions during natural gas development. Graphic by Yutka Sagar.

Figure 6.4. Simplified schematic diagram of the major phases of natural gas development in which methane emissions can occur. Graphic by Sally Vann.

Figure 7.1. Hydropower on the Niagara River. Photograph by Don Duggan-Haas.

Figure 7.2. Primary energy flow by source and sector 2009. From *The Marcellus Papers*, 11: fig. 1. EIA, 2009, *Annual Energy Review 2009*, DOE/EIA-0383 (2011), US EIA, Washington, DC, http://www.eia.gov/totalenergy/data/annual/, tables 1.3, 2.1b–f, 10.3, and 10.4.

Figure 7.3. Comparing the energy demand for different light bulb types and fuel sources. From *The Marcellus Papers*, 11: fig. 2; graphic by J. Houghton.

Figure 7.4. U.S. net electric generation by source, 2001–2012. Data from EIA, Electricity Data Browser, http://www.eia.gov/electricity/data/browser/.

Figure 7.5. U.S. renewable energy consumption by energy source, 2010. From *The Marcellus Papers*, 11: fig. 3. Source: EIA, 2011, *Renewable Energy Consumption and Electricity Preliminary Statistics 2010*, http://www.eia.gov/renewable/annual/preliminary/.

Figure 7.6. Electric power industry net generation by state within the Marcellus region. Modified from *The Marcellus Papers*, 11: fig. 4; source: EIA, 2011, U.S. Energy Information Administration (EIA), Energy Information Administration, http://www.eia.gov/state/. Graphic by Sally Vann.

Figure 7.7. U.S. Energy capacity by energy type, 2010. Source: EIA, 2011, *Today in Energy: Age of Electric Power Generators Varies Widely*, June 6, http://www.eia.gov/todayinenergy/detail.cfm?id=1830#.

Figure 8.1. "Grand ball given by the whales in honor of the discovery of oil wells in Pennsylvania," *Vanity Fair*, 1861

Figure 8.2. (A) New York State energy consumption estimates. (B) New York State energy production estimates. Data from EIA, State Energy Data System. Comparable data are available for all 50 states at http://www.eia.gov/state/.

Figure 8.3. The relationship between science literacy and cultural polarization. See http://www.culturalcognition.net/blog/2013/6/13/science-literacy-cultural-polarization-it-doesnt-happen-just.html, 2002.

Figure 9.1. A piece of the Marcellus Shale from Seneca County, New York. Photograph by Don Duggan-Haas.

Figure 10.1. Hydrofracking signs, pro and con: clockwise from upper left, graffiti on a condemned building in Ithaca, New York (photograph by Warren Allmon); advertisement on a message board in a Philadelphia coffee shop for a 2012 rally against hydraulic fracturing in Washington, DC (photograph by "Little Gun" via Wikimedia Commons); bumper sticker in Ithaca, New York (photograph by Alex Wall); a young man in Washington, DC, participates in the largest rally on global warming in U.S. history on 17 February 2013 (photograph by Michael G McKinne / Shutterstock.com); bumper sticker in Ithaca, New York (photograph by Alex Wall); roadside "no fracking" sign (photograph by Alex Wall); pro-drilling road signs in upstate New York (top and bottom three photographs by Sally Vann, second from top by Joe Henderson).

REFERENCES

Adams, J. A. S., & C. E. Weaver. 1958. Thorium-to uranium ratios as indicators of sedimentary processes: example of concept of geochemical facies. *American Association of Petroleum Geologists Bulletin*, 42(2): 387–430.

Adams, M. 2010. *Evaluation of Erosion and Sediment Control and Stormwater Management for Gas Exploration and Extraction Facilities in Pennsylvania Under Existing Regulations and Policies to Determine if Existing Safeguards Protect Water Quality in Special Protection Waters of the Delaware Basin.* Delaware Riverkeeper Network, Bristol, Pennsylvania, 151 pp. Available at http://www.delawareriverkeeper.org/resources/Reports/DRN_DCS_Expert_Reports.pdf.

Advanced Resources International, Inc. 2012. Estimate of impacts of EPA proposals to reduce air emissions from hydraulic fracturing operations. Final report for American Petroleum Institute, Washington, DC, 23 pp. Available at: http://www.api.org/~/media/Files/Policy/Hydraulic_Fracturing/NSPS-OG-ARI-Impacts-of-EPA-Air-Rules-Final-Report.ashx.

Allen, D. T., V. M. Torres, J. Thomas, D. W. Sullivan, M. Harrison, A. Hendler, S. C. Herndon, C. E. Kolb, M. P. Fraser, A. D. Hill, B. K. Lamb, J. Miskimins, R. F. Sawyer, & J. H. Seinfeld. 2013. Measurements of methane emissions at natural gas production sites in the United States. *Proceedings of the National Academy of Sciences of the USA*, published online ahead of print, September 16, doi:10.1073/pnas.1304880110.

Allmon, W. D. 2007. *The First 75 Years: a History of the Paleontological Research Institution.* Paleontological Research Institution, Ithaca, New York, Special Publication No. 29, 135 pp.

Allmon, W. D. 2009. *Evolution and Creationism: a Very Short Guide, 2nd ed.* Paleontological Research Institution, Ithaca, New York, Special Publication No. 35, 128 pp.

Allmon, W. D., & R. M. Ross. 2011. Paleontology, nature, and natural history: an old approach to "environmental education." *American Paleontologist*, 19(2): 22–25.

Allmon, W. D., T. Smrecak, & R.M. Ross. 2010. *Climate Change—Past, Present, and Future: a Very Short Guide.* Paleontological Research Institution, Ithaca, New York Special Publication No. 38, 200 pp.

Alvarez, R. A., S. W. Pacala, J. J. Winebrake, W. L. Chameides, & S. P. Hamburg. 2012. Greater focus needed on methane leakage from natural gas infrastructure. *Proceedings of the National Academy of Sciences*, 109(17): 6435–6440.

Aminto, A., & M.S. Olson. 2012. Four-compartment partition model of hazardous components in hydraulic fracturing fluid additives. *Journal of Natural Gas Science and Engineering*, 7: 16–21. Available at http://dx.doi.org/10.1016/j.jngse.2012.03.0006.

Anderson, E. 2011. Democracy, public policy, and lay assessments of scientific testimony. *Episteme*, 8(02): 144–164.

Anderson, K., & A. Bows. 2011. Beyond 'dangerous' climate change: emission scenarios in a new world. *Philosophical Transactions of the Royal Society*, 369A: 20–44.

Anderson, R. M., & D. A. Kreeger. 2010. *Potential for Impairment of Freshwater Mussel Populations in DRBC Special Protection Waters as a Consequence of Natural Gas Exploratory Well Development.* Delaware Riverkeeper Network, Bristol, Pennsylvania, 82 pp.

Andren, H. 1994. Effects of habitat fragmentation on birds and mammals in landscapes with different proportions of suitable habitat: a review. *Oikos*, 71(3): 355–366.

Andrews, A., P. Folger, M. Humphries, C. Copeland, M. Tiemann, R. Melt, & C. Brougher. 2009. *Unconventional Gas Shales: Development, Technology and Policy Issues*. Congressional Research Service Report for U.S. Congress, 30 October 2009, R40894, 49 pp. Available at http://www.fas.org/sgp/crs/misc/R40894.pdf.

Archer, D., M. Eby, V. Brovkin, A. Ridgwell, L. Cao, U. Mikolajewicz, K. Caldeira, K. Matsumoto, G. Munhoven, A. Montenegro, & K. Tokos. 2009. Atmospheric lifetime of fossil fuel carbon dioxide. *Annual Reviews of Earth and Planetary Sciences*, 37: 117–134.

Arthur, J. D., B. Bohm, B. J. Coughlin, & M. Layne. 2008a. *Evaluating the Environmental Implications of Hydraulic Fracturing in Shale Gas Reservoirs*. ALL Consulting, ALL Consulting, Tulsa, Oklahoma, 21 pp. Available at http://www.all-llc.com/publicdownloads/ArthurHydrFracPaperFINAL.pdf.

Arthur, J. D., B. Bohm, & M. Layne. 2008b. *Hydraulic Fracturing Considerations for Natural Gas Wells of the Marcellus Shale*. ALL Consulting, Tulsa, Oklahoma, 16 pp. Available at http://www.dec.ny.gov/docs/materials_minerals_pdf/GWPCMarcellus.pdf.

Arthur, J. D., B. Langus, & D. Aleman. 2008c. *An Overview of Modern Shale Gas Development in the United States*. ALL Consulting, Tulsa, Oklahoma, 21 pp. Available at http://www.all-llc.com/publicdownloads/ALLShaleOverviewFINAL.pdf.

Bayne, E., M. L. Habib, & S. Boutin. 2008. Impacts of chronic anthropogenic noise from energy-sector activity on abundance of songbirds in the boreal forest. *Conservation Biology*, 22: 1186–1193.

BC Oil and Gas Commission. 2012. Investigation of observed seismicity in the Horn River Basin. British Columbia Oil and Gas Commission, Fort St John, British Columbia, Canada, 29 pp. Available at http://www.bcogc.ca/investigation observed-seismicity-horn-river-basin.

Begos, K. 2013. Some say industry arrogance fueled anger toward fracking. *The Ithaca Journal*, 13 August.

Biblei, C. J., J. S. Marshall, & R. C. Pilcher. 1998. Status of worldwide coal mine methane emissions and use. *International Journal of Coal Geology*, 35(1–4): 283–310.

Bishop, R. E. 2011 *Chemical and Biological Risk Assessment for Natural Gas Extraction in New York*. Sustainable Otsego, Otsego, New York, 28 pp. Available at http://www.sustainableotsego.org/Risk%20Assessment%20Natural%20Gas%20Extraction-1.htm.

Bistline, J. E. 2012. *Electric Sector Capacity Planning Under Uncertainty: Shale Gas and Climate Policy in the U.S.* 31st USAEE/IAEE North American Conference, Austin, Texas, 26 pp.

Bond, M. 2009. Risk school. *Nature*, 461(29): 1189–1192. Available at http://www.nature.com/news/2009/091028/pdf/4611189a.pdf.

Boyer, C., J. Kieschnick, R. Suarez-Rivera, R. E. Lewis, & G. Walters. 2006. Producing gas from its source. *Oilfield Review*, 18(3): 36 49.

Boyer, E. W., B. R. Swistock, J. Clark, M. Madden, & D. E. Rizzo. 2012. *The Impact of Marcellus Gas Drilling on Rural Drinking Water Supplies*. The Center for Rural Pennsylvania, Harrisburg, Pennsylvania, 26 pp. Available at http://www.rural.palegislature.us/documents/reports/Marcellus_and_drinking_water_2012.pdf.

Bradbury, J., M. Obeiter, L. Draucker, W. Wang, & A. Stevens. 2013 (April). *Clearing the Air: Reducing Upstream Greenhouse Gas Emissions from U.S. Natural Gas Systems*. Working Paper, World Resources Institute, Washington, DC, 61 pp. Available at http://www.wri.org/publication/clearing-the-air.

Brasier, K., M. Filteau, J. Jacquet, S. Goetz, T. Kelsey, D. McLaughlin, & R. Stedman. 2011. Residents' perceptions of community and environmental impacts from development of natural gas in the Marcellus Shale: a comparison of Pennsylvania and New York case studies. *Journal of Rural Social Sciences*, 26(1): 32–61.

Braun, T., & S. Hanus. 2005. *Forest Fragmentation—Effects of Oil and Gas activities on Alberta Forests*. University of Alberta, Calgary, 16 pp. Available at http://129.116.232.161/energyecon/thinkcorner/Forest_Fragmentation_Alberta.pdf.

Brett, C. E., G. C. Baird, A. J. Bartholomew, M. K. DeSantis, & C. A. Ver Straeten. 2011. Sequence stratigraphy and a revised sea-level curve for the Middle Devonian of eastern North America. *Palaeogeography, Palaeoclimatology, Palaeoecology*, 304: 21–53.

Brice, W. R. 2009. *Myth, Legend, Reality. Edwin Laurentine Drake and the Early Oil Industry*. Oil Region Alliance, Oil City, Pennsylvania, 661 pp.

Brown, S. P. A., A. Krupnick, & M. A. Walls. 2009. *Natural Gas: A Bridge to a Low-Carbon Future?* RFF Issue Brief 09-11, Resources for the Future, Washington, DC, 14 pp.

Burkhardt, J., G. Heath, & E. Cohen. 2012. Life cycle greenhouse gas emissions from trough and tower concentrating solar power electricity generation: systematic review and harmonization. *Journal of Industrial Ecology*, 16(S1): S93–S109.

Burnham, A., & C. Clark. 2012. Examining the impacts of methane leakage. *EM (Air and Waste Management Association)*, June: 8–13.

Burnham, A., J. Han, C. E. Clark, M. Wang, J. B. Dunn, & I. P. Rivera. 2011. Life-cycle greenhouse gas emissions of shale gas, natural gas, coal, and petroleum. *Environmental Science and Technology*, 46(2): 619–627, doi: 10.1021/es201942m.

Caenn, R., H. C. H. Darley, & G. R. Gray. 2011. *Composition and Properties of Drilling and Completion Fluids*. Gulf Professional Publishing, Waltham, Massachusetts, 720 pp.

Carter, B. J., J. Desroches, A. R. Ingraffea, & P.A. Wawrzynek. 2000. Simulating fully 3D hydraulic fracturing. Pp 525–557, in: *Modeling in Geomechanics*, M. Zaman, G. Gioda, & J. Booker (eds), John Wiley & Sons, New York.

Cathles, L. M. 2012 (19 June). Assessing the greenhouse impact of natural gas. *Geochemistry, Geophysics, Geosystems*, 13(6): Q06013, doi:10.1029/2012GC004032.

Cathles, L. 2013. Posting to *The New York Times* Dot Earth blog, temporarily posted at http://www.slideshare.net/Revkin/cathles-submission-to-revkin-dotearth.

Cathles, L. M., L. Brown, A. Hunter, & M. Taam. 2012a. Press release: Response to Howarth *et al.*'s reply. 29 February 2012. Available at http://www.geo.cornell.edu/eas/PeoplePlaces/Faculty/cathles/Natural%20Gas/Response%20to%20Howarth's%20Reply%20Distributed%20Feb%2030,%202012.

Cathles, L. M., L. Brown, M. Taam, & A. Hunter. 2012b. A commentary on "The greenhouse-gas footprint of natural gas in shale formations" by R. W. Howarth, R. Santoro, and Anthony Ingraffea. *Climatic Change*, 113(2): 525–535, doi: 10.1007/s10584-011-0333-0.

Centers for Ocean Science Education Excellence (National Geographic Society, National Oceanic and Atmospheric Administration, and College of Exploration). 2005. Ocean Literacy: The Essential Principles of Ocean Sciences K-12. Ver. 2 (2013) available at http://www.coexploration.org/oceanliteracy/documents/OceanLitChart.pdf.

Charles A., J. Drohan, B. Rahm, J. Jacquet, J. Becker, A. Collins, A. Klaiber, G. Poe, & D. Grantham. 2012. *Water's Journey Through the Shale Gas Drilling and Production Processes in the Mid-Atlantic Region*. Mid-Atlantic Water Program, Penn State Extension, State College, Pennsylvania, 12 p.

Clark, C. E., A. J. Burnham, C. B. Haro, & R. M. Horner. 2012. The technology and policy of hydraulic fracturing and potential environmental impacts of shale gas development. *Environmental Practice*, 14: 249–261.

Clark, C. E., J. Han, A. Burnham, J. B. Dunn, & M. Wang. 2011. *Life-Cycle Analysis of Shale Gas and Natural Gas*. Argonne National Laboratory report ANL/ESD/11-11, 38 Pp. Available at http://www.osti.gov/bridge.

Clark, C. E., & J. A. Veil. 2009. Produced water volumes and management practices in the United States. United States Department of Energy, Argonne National Laboratory ANL/EVS/R-09/1, 57 p. Available at http://www.ipd.anl.gov/anlpubs/2009/07/64622.pdf.

Coburn, T., C. Kwiatkowski, K. Schultz, & M. Bachran. 2011. Natural gas operations from a public health perspective. *Human and Ecological Risk Assessment*, 17(5): 1039–1056, doi:10.1080/108 07039.2011.605662.

Colburn, T. K. Schultz, L. Herrick, & C. Kwiatkowski. 2012. An exploratory study of air quality near natural gas operations. *Human and Ecological Risk Assessment*, doi: 10.1080/10807039.2012.749447.

Conca, J. 2012. How deadly is your kilowatt? We rank the killer energy sources. *Forbes*, June 10, available at http://www.forbes.com/sites/jamesconca/2012/06/10/energys-deathprint-a-price-always-paid/.

Considine, T., R. Watson, N. Considine, & J. Martin. 2012. *Environmental Impacts During Marcellus Shale Gas Drilling: Causes, Impacts, and Remedies*. Shale Resources and Society Institute, University at Buffalo, Buffalo, New York, 52 pp. Available at http://cewc.colostate.edu/2012/05/environmental-impacts-during-marcellus-shale-gas-drilling-causes-impacts-and-remedies/.

De Decker, K. 2011. Medieval smokestacks: fossil fuels in pre-industrial times. *Low-tech Magazine*, September 29. Available at http://www.lowtechmagazine.com/2011/09/peat-and-coal-fossil-fuels-in-pre-industrial-times.html.

216

Dietl, G. P., & K. W. Flessa (eds). 2009. *Conservation Paleobiology: Using the Past to Manage for the Future*. Paleontological Society Papers no. 15, 285 pp.

Dietl, G. P., S. Kidwell, M. Brenner, D. Burney, K. Flessa, S. Jackson, & P. Koch. 2012, *Conservation Paleobiology: Opportunities for the Earth Sciences*. Report to the Division of Earth Sciences, National Science Foundation. Paleontological Research Institution, Ithaca, New York, 32 pp.

Eaton, T. T. 2013. Science-based decision-making on complex issues: Marcellus Shale gas hydrofracking and New York City water supply. *The Science of the Total Environment*, 461–462: 158–169.

EIA (U. S. Department of Energy, Energy Information Agency). 2011a. *U. S. Natural Gas Wellhead Price (Dollars per Thousand Cubic Feet)*. Available at http://www.eia.gov/dnav/ng/hist/n9190us3m.htm.

EIA (U. S. Department of Energy, Energy Information Agency). 2011b (April). *Annual Energy Outlook 2011*. Available at ftp://ftp.eia.doe.gov/forecasting/0554(2011).pdf.

EIA (U. S. Department of Energy, Energy Information Agency). 2012 (20 July). *Geology and Technology Drive Estimates of Technically Recoverable Resources*. Available at http://www.eia.gov/todayinenergy/detail.cfm?id-7190.

EIA (U. S. Department of Energy, Energy Information Agency). 2013. *Quarterly Coal Report*. Available at http://www.eia.gov/coal/production/quarterly/index.cfm.

Ellsworth, W. L. 2013. Injection-induced earthquakes. *Science*, 341: 142, doi: 10.1126/science.1225942.

Engber, D. 2005. How do you steal gas from a pipeline? *Slate Magazine*, December 30. Available at http://www.slate.com/articles/news_and_politics/explainer/2005/12/how_do_you_steal_gas_from_a_pipeline.html.

Engelder, T. 1985. Loading paths to joint propagation during a tectonic cycle: an example from the Appalachian Plateau, U.S.A. *Journal of Structural Geology*, 7: 459–476.

Engelder, T. 2011. Should fracking stop? No, it's too valuable. *Nature*, 477: 271, 274–275.

Engelder, T. 2012. Capillary tension and imbibition sequester frack fluid in Marcellus gas shale. *Proceedings of the National Academy of Sciences*, 109(52): F3625

Engelder, T., & G. G. Lash. 2008. Unconventional natural gas reservoir could boost U. S. supply. *Penn State Live*, available at http://live.psu.edu.

Engelder, T., G. G. Lash, & S. Uzcategui. 2009. Joint sets that enhance production from Middle and Upper Devonian gas shales of the Appalachian Basin. *American Association of Petroleum Geologists Bulletin*, 93(7): 857–889.

Entrekin, S., M. Evans-White, B. Johnson, & E. Hagenbuch. 2011. Rapid expansion of natural gas development poses a threat to surface waters. *Frontiers in Ecology and the Environment*, 9(9): 503–511.

EPA (U. S. Environmental Protection Agency). 2009. *Inventory of U. S. Greenhouse Gas Emissions and Sinks: 1990–2007*. Available at http://www.epa.gov/climatechange/ghgemissions/usinventoryreport/archive.html.

EPA (U. S. Environmental Protection Agency). 2010a. *Pavilion, Wyoming Groundwater Investigation, January 2010 Sampling Results and Site Update*. Available at http://www.epa.gov/region8/superfund/wy/pavillion/PavillionWyomingFactSheet.pdf.

EPA (U. S. Environmental Protection Agency). 2010b. *Pavilion, Wyoming EPA Sampling Results*. Available at http://www.epa.gov/region8/superfund/wy/pavillion/Pavillion_Ph2PublicPresentation083110.pdf.

EPA (U. S. Environmental Protection Agency). 2010c. *Greenhouse Gas Emissions Reporting from the Petroleum and Natural Gas Industry. Background Technical Support Document*. Available at http://www.epa.gov/climatechange/emissions/downloads10/Subpart-W_TSD.pdf.

EPA (U. S. Environmental Protection Agency). 2011a (14 April). *Inventory of U. S. Greenhouse Gas Emissions and Sinks: 1990–2009*. Available at http://epa.gov/climatechange/emissions/usinventoryreport.html.

EPA (U. S. Environmental Protection Agency). 2011b (July). *Regulatory Impact Analysis: Proposed New Source Performance Standards and Amendments to the National Emissions Standards for Hazardous Air Pollutants for the Oil and Gas Industry*. Office of Air and Radiation, available at http://www.epa.gov/ttnecas1/regdata/RIAs/oil_natural_gas_final_neshap_nsps_ria.pdf.

EPA (U. S. Environmental Protection Agency). 2011c. *Climate Change—Regulatory Initiatives*. Available at http://www.epa.gov/climatechange/emissions/ghgrulemaking.html.

EPA (U. S. Environmental Protection Agency). 2011d. *Oil and Natural Gas Sector: Standards of Performance for Crude Oil and Natural Gas Production, Transmission, and Distribution.* EPA-453/R-11-002. Available at http://www.epa.gov/airquality/oilandgas/pdfs/20120418tsd.pdf.

EPA (U. S. Environmental Protection Agency). 2011e. *Proposed Amendments to Air Regulations for the Oil and Gas Industry Fact Sheet.* Available at http://www.epa.gov/airquality/oilandgas/pdfs/20110728factsheet.pdf.

EPA (U. S. Environmental Protection Agency). 2011f. *Investigation of Ground Water Contamination Near Pavillion, Wyoming.* U.S. Environmental Protection Agency draft report EPA 600/R-00/000. Available at http://www.epa.gov/region8/superfund/wy/pavillion/index.html.

EPA (U. S. Environmental Protection Agency). 2012a. *Overview of Final Amendments to Air Regulations for the Oil and Natural Gas Industry Fact Sheet.* Available at http://www.epa.gov/airquality/oilandgas/pdfs/20120417fs.pdf.

EPA (U. S. Environmental Protection Agency). 2012b. *Report to Congress on Black Carbon.* EPA-450/R-12-001, 388 pp. Available at http://www.epa.gov/blackcarbon/2012report/fullreport.pdf.

EPA (U. S. Environmental Protection Agency). 2012c (15 April). *Inventory of U.S. Greenhouse Gas Emissions and Sinks: 1990-2010.* EPA 430-12-R-001, 481 pp. Available at http://www.epa.gov/climatechange/Downloads/ghgemissions/US-GHG-Inventory-2012-Main-Text.pdf.

EPA (U. S. Environmental Protection Agency). 2013. *Inventory of U. S. Greenhouse Gas Emissions and Sinks: 1990–2011.* EPA 430-R-13-001, 61 pp. Available at http://www.epa.gov/climatechange/emissions/usinventoryreport.html.

EPA (U. S. Environmental Protection Ageny) Gas Research Institute. 1997. *Methane Emissions from the Natural Gas Industry, Project Summary,* by N. R. Harrison, T. M. Shires, J. K. Wessels, & R. M. Cowgill. EPA/600/SR-96/080, http://www.docstoc.com/docs/19963708/Methane-Emissions-from-the-Natural-Gas-Industry.

EPA (U. S. Environmental Protection Agency) Office of Inspector General. 2013. *EPA Needs to Improve Air Emissions Data for the Oil and Natural Gas Production Sector.* U.S. Environmental Protection Agency Office of the Inspector General, Washington, DC, 36 pp. Available at http://www.epa.gov/oig/reports/2013/20130220-13-P-0161.pdf.

Epstein, P. R., J. J. Buonocore, K. Eckerle, M. Hendryx, B. M. Stout, III, R. Heinberg, R. W. Clapp, B. May, N. L. Reinhart, M. M. Ahern, S. K. Doshi, & L. Glustrom. 2011. Full cost accounting for the life cycle of coal. In *Ecological Economics Reviews*, R. Costanza, K. Limburg, & I. Kubiszewski (eds). *Annals of the New York Academy of Sciences*, 1219: 73–98.

Fakhru'l-Razi, A., A. Pendashteh, L.,C. Abdullah, D.,R.,A. Biak, S.,S. Madaeni, & Z. Z. Abidin. 2009. Review of technologies for oil and gas produced water treatment. *Journal of Hazardous Materials*, 170: 530–551.

Farhrig, L. 2003. Effects of habitat fragmentation on biodiversity. *Annual Review of Ecology, Evolution, and Systematics*, 34: 487–515.

Federal Highway Administration. 2011. *Noise Effect on Wildlife.* Available at http://www.fhwa.dot.gov/environment/noise/noise_effect_on_wildlife/effects/index.cfm.

Fisher, K. 2010. Data confirm safety of well fracturing. *The American Oil and Gas Reporter*, July, 4 pp.

Fisher, M. 2012. Fracking's footprint. *CSA [Crop Society of America] News*, July: 4–11.

Flessa, K. W. 2002. Conservation paleobiology. *American Paleontologist*, 10(1): 2–5.

Fletcher, J. B., & L. R. Sykes. 1977. Earthquakes related to hydraulic mining and natural seismic activity in western New York State. *Journal of Geophysical Research*, 82(26): 3767–3780.

Freyman, M., & R. Salmon. 2013. *Hydraulic Fracturing and Water Stress: Growing Competitive Pressures for Water.* Ceres, Boston, Massachusetts, 13 pp. Available at http://www.ceres.org/resources/reports/hydraulic-fracturing-water-stress-growing-competitive-pressures-for-water.

Frohlich, C. 2012. Two-year survey comparing earthquake activity and injection-well locations in the Barnett Shale, Texas. *Proceedings of the National Academy of Sciences*, 109(35): 13934–13938.

Frumkin, H., J. Hess, G. Luber, J. Malilay, & M. McGeehin. 2008. Climate change: the public health response. *American Journal of Public Health*, 98(3): 435–445.

Fulton, M., N. Mellquist, S. Kitasei, & J. Bluestein. 2011. *Comparing Life-Cycle Greenhouse Gas Emissions from Natural Gas and Coal.* Report by the Worldwatch Institute for Deutsche Bank Group/DB Climate Change Advisors, Frankfurt am Main, Germany, 29 pp. Available at http://www.worldwatch.org/system/files/pdf/Natural_Gas_LCA_Update_082511.pdf.

Galbraith, K. 2013. Ready (or not?) for a great coming shale boom. *The New York Times*, 28 April 2013, p. A27A. Available at http://www.nytimes.com/2013/04/28/us/time-for-texas-to-get-ready-for-the-shale-boom.html?pagewanted=all&_r=0.

GAO (U. S. Government Accountability Office). 2010. Federal oil and gas leases: opportunities exist to capture vented and flared natural gas, which would increase royalty payments and reduce greenhouse gases. GAO-11-34, 36 pp. + appendices. Available at http://www.gao.gov/new.items/d1134.pdf.

Gibbs, J. P., A. R. Breisch, P. K. Ducey, G.Johnson, J. Behler, & R. Bothner. 2007. *The Amphibians and Reptiles of New York State: Identification, Natural History, and Conservation*. Oxford University Press, New York, 504 pp.

Gies, E. 2012. Race is on to clean up hydraulic fracturing. *The New York Times*, December 4. Available at http://www.nytimes.com/2012/12/05/business/energy-environment/race-is-on-to-clean-up-hydraulic-fracturing.html?smid=fb-share&_r=4&.

Gilbert, D., & R. Gold. 2013. As big drillers move in, safety goes up. *The Wall Street Journal*, April 2.

Gillen, J. L., & E. Kiviat. 2012. Hydraulic fracturing threats to species with restricted ranges in the eastern United States. *Environmental Practice*, 14: 320–331.

Goodstein, E. 2011. Reconciling the science and economics of climate change. *Climatic Change*, 106: 661–665. Available at http://dx.doi.org/10.1007/s10584-011-0039-3.

Gowan, S. W., & S. M. Trader. 2000. Mine failure associated with a pressurized brine horizon Retsof Salt Mine, western New York. *Environmental & Engineering Geoscience*, 6(1): 57–70.

Gregory, K. B., R. D. Vidic, & D. A. Dzombak. 2011. Water management challenges associated with the production of shale gas by hydraulic fracturing. *Elements*, 7: 181–186.

Ground Water Protection Council and ALL Consulting. 2009. *Modern Shale Gas Development in the United States: A Primer*. Report prepared for the U.S. Department of Energy, Office of Fossil Energy, National Energy Technology Laboratory (NETL) under Award Number DE-FG26-04NT15455. 96 p. Available at http://www.netl.doe.gov/technologies/oil-gas/publications/epreports/shale_gas_primer_2009.pdf.

Groat, C. G., & T. W. Grimshaw. 2012. *Fact-Based Regulation for Environmental Protection in Shale Gas Development*. The Energy Institute, The University of Texas at Austin, 51 pp. + supplemental information and appendices. Available at http://heartland.org/sites/default/files/texas_fracking_study_feb_2012.pdf.

Haluszczak, L. O., A. W. Rose, & L. R. Kump. 2013. Geochemical evaluation of flowback brine from Marcellus gas wells in Pennsylvania, USA. *Applied Geochemistry*, 28: 5561. Available at http://dx.doi.org/10.1016/j.apgeochem.2012.10.002.

Hamburg, S. 2013. *Measuring Fugitive Methane Emissions*. Energy Exchange blog, Environmental Defense Fund, Washington, DC, available at http://blogs.edf.org/energyexchange/2013/01/04/measuring-fugitive-methane-emissions/.

Hamilton, L. E., B. C. Dale, & C. A. Paszkowski. 2011. Effects of disturbance associated with natural gas extraction on the occurrence of three grassland songbirds. *Avian Conservation and Ecology*, 6(1): 7.

Hansen, J., & M. Sato. 2004. Greenhouse gas growth rates. *Proceedings of the National Academy of Sciences*, 101: 16109–16114, doi:10.1073/pnas.0406982101.

Hansen, J., M. Sato, P. Kharecha, G. Russell, D. W. Lea, & M. Siddall. 2007. Climate change and trace gasses. *Philosophical Transactions of the Royal Society A*, 365: 1925–1954.

Hansen, J., M. Sato, P. Kharecha, D. Beerling, R. Berner, V. Masson-Delmotte, M. Pagani, M. Raymo, D. L. Royer, & J. C. Zachos. 2008. Target atmospheric CO_2: where should humanity aim? *Open Atmospheric Science Journal*, 2: 217–231.

Harris, L. 1984. *The Fragmented Forest. Island Biogeography Theory and the Preservation of Biotic Diversity*. University of Chicago Press, Chicago, 230 pp.

Harrison, M. 2012. *Revised Attachment 3: Gas Well Completion Emissions Data*. URS Corporation report (aka the URS Devon Study), Devon Energy Corporation, Oklahoma City, Oklahoma. Available at http://anga.us/media/241555/anga-axpc%20nsps%20memo%20revised.pdf.

Harrison, M. R., L. M. Campbell, T. M. Shires, & R. M. Cowgill. 1996. *Methane Emissions from the Natural Gas Industry. Vol. 3*. EPA/600/R-96/080C, U.S. Environmental Protection Agency, Washington, DC. Available at http://www.epa.gov/gasstar/documents/emissions_report/3_generalmeth.pdf.

Harrison, S. S. 1985. Contamination of aquifers by overpressuring the annulus of oil and gas wells. *Groundwater*, 23(3): 317–324 [referenced by Cathles, 2012].

Hausfather, Z. 2010. *Common Climate Misconceptions: Atmospheric Carbon Dioxide*. Yale Forum on Climate Change and the Media, Yale University, New Haven, Connecticut. Available at: http://www.yaleclimatemediaforum.org/2010/12/common-climate-misconceptions-atmospheric-carbon-dioxide/.

Hayhoe, K., H. S. Kheshgi, A. K. Jain, & D. J. Wuebbles. 2002. Substitution of natural gas for coal: climatic effects of utility sector emissions. *Climatic Change*, 54: 107–139.

Hazen, X., & X. Sawyer. 2009. Final impact assessment report: impact assessment of natural gas production in the New York City water supply watershed. Report commissioned by the New York City Department of Environmental Protection, New York. Available at http://www.nyc.gov/html/dep/html/press_releases/09-15pr.shtml.

Heffernan, T. 2013. The new Bronze Age: we're entering the era of tough ore. *Pacific Standard*, 8 July. Available at http://www.psmag.com/environment/the-new-bronze-age-entering-the-era-of-tough-ore-60868/.

Hill, D., T. E. Lombardi, & J. P. Martin. 2002. *Fractured Shale Gas Potential in New York*. Ticora Geosciences, Inc., Arvarda, Colorado, 114 pp.

Hoegh-Guldberg, O., & J. F. Bruno. 2010. The impact of climate change on the world's marine ecosystems. *Science*, 328: 1523–1528.

Hou, D., J. Luo, & A. Al-Tabbaa. 2012. Shale gas can be a double-edged sword for climate change. *Nature Climate Change*, 2: 385–387.

Howarth, R.W. 2010a (1 April). *Preliminary Assessment of the Greenhouse Gas Emissions from Natural Gas Obtained by Hydraulic Fracturing (Draft)*. Available at http://www.technologyreview.com/sites/default/files/legacy/ghg.emissions.from.marcellus.shale.april12010_draft.pdf.

Howarth, R.W. 2010b. Gas and drilling not clean choices. Environmental risks too great; alternative fuels a better option. *The Ithaca Journal*, March 28.

Howarth, R., & A. Ingraffea. 2011. Should fracking stop? Yes, it is too high risk. *Nature*, 477: 271–275.

Howarth, R., R. Santoro, & A. Ingraffea. 2011. Methane and the greenhouse-gas footprint of natural gas from shale formations. *Climatic Change*, 106: 679–690.

Howarth, R. W., R. Santoro, & A. Ingraffea. 2012a. Venting and leaking of methane from shale gas development: response to Cathles *et al*. *Climatic Change*, 106(4): 679–690, doi: 10.1007/s10584-012-0401-0.

Howarth, R., D. Shindell, R. Santoro, A. Ingraffea, N. Phillips, and A. Townsend-Small. 2012b. *Methane Emissions from Natural Gas Systems. Background Paper Prepared for the National Climate Assessment*. Available at http://www.eeb.cornell.edu/howarth/publications/Howarth_et_al_2012_National_Climate_Assessment.pdf.

Hughes, J. D. 2011. *Lifecycle Greenhouse Gas Emissions from Shale Gas Compared to Coal: an Analysis of Two Conflicting Studies*. Post Carbon Institute, Santa Rosa, California. Available at: http://www.postcarbon.org/report/390308-life-cycle-greenhouse-gas-emissions-from.

Hughes, J. D. 2013a. A reality check on the shale revolution. *Nature*, 494: 307–308.

Hughes, J. D. 2013b. *Drill, Baby, Drill: Can Unconventional Fuels Usher in a New Era of Energy Abundance?* Post Carbon Institute, Santa Rosa, California, 178 pp.

Hultman, N., D. Rebois, M. Scholten, & C. Ramig. 2011. The greenhouse impact of unconventional gas for electricity generation. *Environmental Research Letters*, 6: 044008, doi: 10.1088/1748-9326/6/4/044008.

Hyne, N. J. 2001. *Nontechnical Guide to Petroleum Geology, Exploration, Drilling, and Production, 2nd ed.* PennWell Corporation, Tulsa, Oklanoma, 598 pp.

ICF International. 2009. *Technical Assistance for the Draft Supplemental Generic EIS: Oil, Gas and Solution Mining Regulatory Program* (well permit issuance for horizontal drilling and high-volume hydraulic fracturing to develop the Marcellus Shale and other low permeability gas reservoirs—task 2). New York State Energy Research and Development Authority (NYSERDA), Albany, New York, http://www.nyserda.org/publications/ICF%20task%202%20Report_Final.pdf.

Ingraffea, A. R. 2013a. *The Carbon Footprint of Shale Gas Development and the Remedial Measures Necessary to Address It*. Comments prepared for Ontario Energy Board Proceedings, June 26. Available at http://www.cleanairalliance.org/files/Ingraffea%20Evidence%20L%20EGD%20COC%201.pdf.

Ingraffea, A. R. 2013b. Gangplank to a warm future. *The New York Times*, 28 July. Available at http://www.nytimes.com/2013/07/29/opinion/gangplank-to-a-warm-future.html?_r=0.

International Organization for Standardization (ISO). 2006. *ISO 14044—Environmental Management—Life Cycle Assessment—Principles and Framework*. ISO, Geneva, Switzerland, 20 pp.

IPCC (Intergovernmental Panel on Climate Change). 2001. *Climate Change 2001: The Scientific Basis. Contribution of Working Group I to the Third Assessment Report of the Intergovernmental Panel on Climate Change*, J. T. Houghton, Y. Ding, D. J. Griggs, M. Noguer, P. J. van der Linden, X. Dai, K. Maskell, & C.A. Johnson (eds). Cambridge University Press, Cambridge, United Kingdom and New York, 881 pp.

Isachsen, Y. W., & W. G. McKendree. 1977. Preliminary brittle structures map of New York, and generalized map of recorded joint systems in New York. *New York State Museum, Map and Chart Series* no. 31G.

Iyengar, M. A. R. 1984. *Distribution in Nature—The Behavior of Radium in Waterways and Aquifers*. TEC DOC 301, International Atomic Energy Agency, Vienna, Austria, 262 pp.

Jacobson, M. Z., & M. A. Delucchi. 2009. A path to sustainable energy by 2030. *Scientific American*, 301: 58–65.

Jacobson, M. Z., R. W. Howarth, M. A. Delucchi, S. R. Scobie, J. M. Barth, M. J. Dvorak, M. Klevze, H. Katkhuda, B. Miranda, N. A. Chowdhury, R. Jones, L. Plano, & A. R. Ingraffea. 2013. Examining the feasibility of converting New York State's all-purpose energy infrastructure to one using wind, water, and sunlight. *Energy Policy*, 57: 585–601.

Jaramillo, P., & H. S. Matthews. 2005. Landfill-gas-to-energy projects: Analysis of net private and social benefits. *Environmental Science & Technology*, 39(19): 7365–7373.

Jenkins, C., A. Ouenes, A. Zellou, & J. Wingard. 2009. Quantifying and predicting naturally fractured reservoir behavior with continuous fracture models. *American Association of Petroleum Geologists Bulletin*, 93(11): 1597–1608.

Jenkins, C. D., & C. M. Boyer. 2008. Coal bed and shale-gas reservoirs. *Journal of Petroleum Technology*, 60: 92–99.

Jenner, S., & A. J. Lamadrid. 2012. Shale gas vs. coal: policy implications from environmental impact comparisons of shale gas, conventional gas, and coal on air, water and land in the United States. *Energy Policy*, 53; 442–453. Available at http://dx.doi.org/10.1016/j.enpol.2012.11.010.

Jiang, M., W. M. Griffin, C. Hendrickson, P. Jaramillo, J. VanBriesen, & A. Venkatesh. 2011. Life cycle greenhouse gas emissions of Marcellus shale gas. *Environmental Research Letters*, 6(3): 034014, doi: 10.1088/1748-9326/6/3/034014.

Johnson, N. 2010. *Pennsylvania Energy Impacts Assessment – Report 1. Marcellus Shale Natural Gas and Wind*. The Nature Conservancy and Audubon Pennsylvania, Audubon, Pennsylvania, 47 pp.

Kahneman, D. 2011. *Thinking, Fast and Slow*. Farrar, Straus and Giroux, New York, 512 pp.

Kappel, W. M., & E. A. Nystrom. 2012. Dissolved methane in New York groundwater, 1999–2011. *U.S. Geological Survey Open File Report* 2012-1162. Available at http://pubs.usgs.gov/of/2012/1162.

Kargbo, D. M., R. G. Wilhelm, & D. J. Campbell. 2010. Natural gas plays in the Marcellus Shale: challenges and potential opportunities. *Environmental Science & Technology*, 44(15). 5679–5684.

Karion, A., C. Sweeney, G. Pétron, G. Frost, R. M. Hardesty, J. Kofler, B. R. Miller, T. Newberger, S. Wolter, R. Banta, A. Brewer, E. Dlugokencky, P. Lang, S. A. Montzka, R. Schnell, P. Tans, M. Trainer, R. Zamora, & S. Conley. 2013. Methane emissions estimate from airborne measurements over a western United States natural gas field. *Geophysical Research Letters*. Accepted manuscript online, 3 August 2013, doi: 10.1002/grl.50811.

Kasey, P. 2012. Which county leads WV's Marcellus production? *The State Journal*, November 17. Available at http://www.statejournal.com/story/19853093/which-county-leads-wvs-marcellus-production.

Kelso, M. 2012. Drilling wells by operator over time in PA's Marcellus. Available at http://www.fractracker.org/2012/05/drilled-wells-by-operator-over-time-in-pas-marcellus.

Keranen, K. M., H. M. Savage, G. A. Abers, & E. S. Cochran. 2013. Potentially induced earthquakes in Oklahoma, USA: links between wastewater injection and the 2011 Mw 5.7 earthquake sequence. *Geology*, 41(6): 699–702.

Kerr, R. A. 2010. Natural gas from shale bursts onto the scene. *Science*, 328: 1624–1626.

Khodja, M., M. Khodja-Saber, J. P. Canselier, N. Cohaut, & E. Bergaya. 2010. *Drilling fluid technology: performances and environmental considerations, Product and Services, From R&D to Final Solutions,* http://cdn.intechopen.com/pdfs/12330/InTech-Drilling_fluid_technology_performances_and_environmental_considerations.pdf.

Kim, Won-Young. 2001. *The Lamont Cooperative Seismic Network and the National Seismic System: Earthquake Hazard Studies in the Northeastern United States.* Available at http://www.ldeo.columbia.edu/LCSN/Report/LCSN Tech Report-98-01.pdf.

King, R. F., & D. F. Morehouse. 1993. *Drilling Sideways—A Review of Horizontal Well Technology and its Domestic Application.* U. S. Department of Energy, Energy Information Administration, Washington, DC, 30 pp. Available at http://www.eia.doe.gov/pub/oil_gas/natural_gas/analysis_publications/drilling_sideways_well_technology/pdf/tr0565.pdf.

Kinnaman, T. C. 2011. The economic impact of shale gas extraction: a review of existing studies. *Ecological Econonmics,* 70: 1243–1249. Available at http://dx.doi.org/10.1016/j.ecolecon.2011.02.005.

Kiviat, E. 2013. Risks to biodiversity from hydraulic fracturing for natural gas in the Marcellus and Utica shales. *Annals of the New York Academy of Sciences,* 1286: 1–14.

Korfmacher, K. S., W. A. Jones, S. L. Malone, & L. F. Vinci. 2013. Public health and high volume hydraulic fracturing. *New Solutions: A Journal of Environmental and Occupational Health Policy,* 23(1): 13–31.

Labinger, J. A., & H. Collins (eds). 2001. *The One Culture? A Conversation About Science.* University of Chicago Press, Chicago, 296 pp.

Ladlee, J., & J. Jaquet. 2011. The implications of multi-well pads in the Marcellus Shale. *Research and Policy Brief Series, Penn State College of Agricultural Sciences Cooperative Extension,* Issue 43. Available at http://devsoc.cals.cornell.edu/cals/devsoc/outreach/cardi/publications/loader.cfm?csModule=security/getfile&PageID=1016988.

Ladva, H. K. J., B. Craster, T. G. J. Jones, G. Goldsmith, & D. Scott. 2005. The cement-to-formation interface in zonal isolation. *SPE (Society of Petroleum Engineers) Drilling and Completion,* 20(3): 186–197.

Lash, G. G. 2008. Pyrite laminae in black shale—an additional source of permeability in unconventional reservoirs, *Geological Society of America Annual Meeting, Abstracts with Program,* 40(6): 233.

Lash, E., & G. Lash. 2011. Early history of the gas industry: "kicking down the well." *AAPG Explorer,* News & Features, September, http://www.aapg.org/explorer/2011/09sep/natgashist0911.cfm.

Laurenzi, I. J., & G. R. Jersey. 2013. Life cycle greenhouse gas emissions and freshwater consumption of Marcellus Shale gas. *Environmental Science and Technology,* 47(9): 4896–4903, doi: 10.1021/es305162w.

Lavelle, M. 2010. Forcing gas out of the rock with water. *National Geographic News,* 17 Octoberr, available at http://news.nationalgeographic.com/news/2010/10/101022-energy-marcellus-shale-gas-science-technology-water/.

Lee, D. S., J. D. Herman, D. Elsworth, H. T. Kim, & H. S. Lee. 2011. A critical evaluation of unconventional shale gas recovery from the Marcellus Shale, Nnrtheastern United States. *KSCE Journal of Civil Engineering,* 15(4): 679–687.

Lelieveld, J., S. Lechtenböhmer, S. S. Assonov, C. A. M. Brenninkmeijer, C. Dienst, M. Fischedick, & T. Hanke. 2005. Greenhouse gases: low methane leakage from gas pipeline. *Nature,* 434: 841–842, doi:10.1038/434841a.

Lenton, T. M., & J.-C. Ciscar. 2013. Integrating tipping points into climate impact assessments. *Climatic Change,* 117: 585–597.

LeRoy Poff, N., J. D. Allan, M. B. Bain, J. R. Karr, K. L. Prestegaard, B. D. Richter, R. E. Sparks, & J. C. Stromberg. 1997. The natural flow regime. *BioScience,* 47(11): 769–784.

Levi, M. 2011. *Some Thoughts on the Howarth Shale Gas Paper.* Council on Foreign Relations, available at blogs.cfr.org/levi/2011/04/15/some-thoughts-on-the-howarth-shale-gas-paper/.

Levi, M. 2012. Comment on "Hydrocarbon emissions characterization in the Colorado Front Range – a pilot study." *Journal of Geophysical Research: Atmospheres,* 117: D21203, doi: 10.1029/2012JD017686.

Levi, M. 2013a. Climate consequences of natural gas as a bridge fuel. *Climatic Change,* 118(3-4): 609–623, doi: 10.1007/s10584-012-0658-3.

Levi, M. 2013b. Reply to "Reply to 'Comment on "Hydrocarbon emissions characterization in the Colorado Front Range – a pilot study"' by Michael A. Levi' by Gabirelle Pétron *et al. Journal of*

Geophysical Research: Atmospheres, 118: 3044–3046.

Levy, J. I., L. K. Baxter, & J. Schwartz. 2009. Uncertainty and variability in health-related damages from coal-fired power plants in the United States. *Risk Analysis*, 29(7): 1000–1014, doi: 10.1111/j.1539-6924.2009.01227.x.

Lichtner, P. C., C. I. Steefel, & E. H. Oelkers (eds). 1996. *Reactive Transport in Porous Media. Reviews in Mineralogy*, 34: 438 pp.

Logan, J., G. Heath, E. Paranhos, W. Boyd, K. Carlson, & J. Macknick. 2012. *Natural Gas and the Transformation of the U.S. Energy Sector: Electricity.* Technical Report NREL/TP-6A50-55538. Joint Institute for Strategic Energy Analysis (JISEA), Golden, Colorado, 240 pp.

Lovejoy, T. E. 2010. Climate change. Pp 153–162, in: *Conservation Biology for All*, N. S. Sodhi & P. R. Ehrlich (eds), Oxford University Press, Oxford, UK.

Lovejoy, T. E., & L. Hanna. 2005. Global greenhouse gas levels and the future of biodiversity. Pp 387–396, in: *Climate Change and Biodiversity*, T. E. Lovejoy & L. Hannah (eds), Yale University Press, New Haven, Connecticut.

Lu, X., J. Salovaara, & M. B. McElroy. 2012. Implications of the recent reductions in natural gas prices for emissions of CO_2 from the US power sector. *Environmental Science and Technology*, 46(5): 3014–3021. Available at http://dx.doi.org/10.1021/es203750k.

Lustgarten, A. 2011. Climate benefits of natural gas may be overstated. *ProPublica*, January 25, http://www.propublica.org/article/natural-gas-and-coal-pollution-gap-in-doubt.

Lutz, B. H., A. N. Lewis, & M. W. Doyle. 2013. Generation, transport, and disposal of wastewater associated with Marcellus Shale gas development. *Water Resources Research*, 49(2): 647–656, doi: 10.1002/wrcr.20096.

Maloney, K. O., & D. A. Yoxtheimer. 2012. Production and disposal of waste materials from gas and oil extraction from the Marcellus Shale play in Pennsylvania. *Environmental Practice*, 14(4): 270–287.

Manahan, M. D., & S. A. Verville. 2005. FERG and dam decommissioning. *Natural Resources & Environment*, 19(3): 45–49, doi:10.2307/40924587.

Mann, C. C. 2013. What if we never run out of oil? *The Atlantic Monthly*, May, pp. 48–63.

Marriott, J. 2007. *An Electricity-Focused Economic Input-Output Model: Life Cycle Assessment and Policy Implications of Future Electricity Generation Scenarios.* Unpublished Ph.D. Dissertation, Carnegie Mellon University, Pittsburgh, Pennsylvania, 116 pp.

Mauter, M. S., V. R. Palmer, Y. Tang, & A. P. Behrer. 2013. *The Next Frontier in United States Shale Gas and Tight Oil Extraction: Strategic Reduction of Environmental Impacts.* Belfer Center for Science and International Affairs, Kennedy School of Government, Harvard University, Cambridge, Massachusetts, 81 pp. Available at http://belfercenter.ksg.harvard.edu/files/mauter-dp-2013-04-final.pdf.

McGraw, S. 2012. *The End of Country: Dispatches from the Frack Zone.* Random House, New York, 256 pp.

McSpirit, S., S. L. Scott, S. Hardesty, & R. Welch. 2005. EPA actions in post disaster Martin County, Kentucky: an analysis of bureaucratic slippage and agency recreancy. *Journal of Appalachian Studies*, 11(1/2): 30–59, doi:10.2307/41446653.

Meador, M. R. 1992. Inter-basin water transfer: ecological concerns. *Fisheries*, 17(2): 17–22.

Meadows, D. 2008. *Thinking in Systems: A Primer.* Chelsea Green Publishing, White River Junction, Vermont, 240 pp.

Mielke, E., L. D. Anadon, & V. Narayanamurti. 2010. *Water Consumption of Energy Resource Extraction, Processing, and Conversion.* Belfer Center for Science and International Affairs, Kennedy School of Government, Harvard University, Cambridge, Massachusetts, 52 pp. Available at http://belfercenter.ksg.harvard.edu/files/ETIP-DP-2010-15-final-4.pdf.

Mitchell, A. L., & E. A. Casman. 2011. Economic incentives and regulatory framework for shale gas well site reclamation in Pennsylvania. *Environmental Science and Technology*, 45: 9506–9514. Available at http://dx.doi.org/10.1021/es2021796.

Mitka, M. 2012 (23 May). Rigorous evidence slim for determining health risks from natural gas fracking. *Journal of the American Medical Association*, 307(20): 2135–2136.

Moniz, E. J., H. D. Jacoby, & A. J. M. Meggs. 2011. *The Future of Natural Gas—An Interdisciplinary Study.* Massachusetts Institute of Technology, Cambridge, Massachusetts, available at http://mitei.mit.edu/publications/reports-studies.

Montgomery, C. T., & M. B. Smith. 2010. Hydraulic fracturing. History of an enduring technology. *Journal of Petroleum Technology Online*, 105: 26–41. Available at http://www.spe.org/jpt/print/archives/2010/12/10Hydraulic.pdf.

Montzka, S. A., E. J. Dlugokencky, & J. H. Butler. 2011. Non-CO_2 greenhouse gases and climate change. *Nature*, 476: 43–50.

Morris, R., & T. Atkinson. 1986. Geological and mining factors affecting spontaneous heating of coal. *Mining Science and Technology*, 3: 217–231.

Mosley, K., W. M. Ford, J. W. Edwards, & M. B. Adams. 2010. *Reptile, Amphibian and Small Mammal Species Associated with Natural Gas Development in the Monongahela National Forest, West Virginia*. U.S. Forest Service, Washington, DC, Research Paper NRS-10, 18 pp.

Myers, T. 2012. Potential contaminant pathways from hydraulically fractured shale to aquifers. *Ground Water*, 50: 872–882.

Myhrvold, N. P., & K. Caldeira. 2012. Greenhouse gases, climate change and the transition from coal to low-carbon electricity. *Environmental Research Letters*, 7: 014019.

Nasen, L. C., B. F. Noble, & J. F. Johnstone. 2011. Environmental effects of oil and gas lease sites in a grassland ecosystem. *Journal of Environmental Management*, 92(1): 195–204.

Nelson, G. 2002. *Beyond Earth Day: Fulfilling the Promise*. University of Wisconsin Press, Madison, 222 pp.

NETL (National Energy Technology Laboratory, U.S. Department of Energy). 2006. *Life-cycle Analysis of Greenhouse Emissions for Hydrogen Fuel Production in the United States from LGN and Coal*. 18 pp. Available at http://www.netl.doe.gov/energy-analyses/pubs/H2_from_Coal_LNG_Final.pdf.

NETL (National Energy Technology Laboratory, U.S. Department of Energy). 2012. *Role of Alternative Energy Sources: Natural Gas Technology Assessment*. 72 pp. Available at http://www.netl.doe.gov/energy-analyses/pubs/NGTechAssess.pdf.

New York Water Environment Association. 2011. *Evaluating the Acceptability of Gas Well Development and Production-Related Wastewater at New York Wastewater Treatment Plants*. http://nywea.org/gac/HFSCEvaluatingAcceptability.pdf.

NRC (National Research Council). 2010a. *Hidden Costs of Energy: Unpriced Consequences of Energy Production and Use*. The National Academies Press, Washington, DC, 399 pp. + supplemental information and appendices. Available at http://www.nap.edu/catalog.php?record_id=12794.

NRC (National Research Council). 2010b. *Management and Effects of Coalbed Methane Development and Produced Water in the Western United States*. National Academies Academic Press, Washington, DC, 217 pp.

NRC (National Research Council). 2012. *Induced Seismicity Potential in Energy Technologies*. The National Academies Press, Washington, DC, 300 pp.

NYSDEC (New York State Department of Environmental Conservation). 2011. *Revised Draft Supplemental Generic Environmental Impact Statement on the Oil, Gas and Solution Mining Regulatory Program*. Available at http://www.dec.ny.gov/energy/58440.html.

NYSERDA (New York State Energy Research and Development Authority). 2007. *New York's Natural Gas and Oil Resource Endowment: Past, Present and Potential*. New York State Energy Research and Development Authority, Albany, New York, 41 pp. Available at http://www.dec.ny.gov/about/37805.html.

Ohio Department of Natural Resources. 2012a. *Horizontal Marcellus Shale well activity of Ohio*. 1 p. Available at http://www.dnr.state.oh.us/Portals/10/Energy/Marcellus/MarcellusWells Activity_02142012.pdf.

Ohio Department of Natural Resources. 2012b. *Preliminary Report on the Northstar 1 Class II Injection Well and the Seismic Events in the Youngstown, Ohio, Area 13*. 24 pp. Available at http://ohiodnr.com/downloads/northstar/UICreport.pdf.

Oil and Gas Accountability Project. 2008. *Shale Gas: Focus on the Marcellus Shale*. Available at http://www.earthworksaction.org/publications.cfm?pubID=354.

Osborn, S. G., A. Vengosh, N. R. Warner, & R. B. Jackson. 2011. Methane contamination of drinking water accompanying gas-well drilling and hydraulic fracturing. *Proceedings of the National Academy of Sciences*, 108: 8172–8176.

O'Sullivan, F., & S. Paltsev. 2012. *Shale Gas Production: Potential Versus Actual GHG Emissions*. MIT Joint Program on the Science and Policy of Global Change, Report No. 234, 14 p.

224

Pacala, S., & R. Sokolow. 2004. Stabilization wedges: solving the climate problem for the next 50 years with current technologies. *Science*, 305: 968–972.

Penningroth, S. M., M. M. Yarrow, A. X. Figueroa, R. J. Bowen, & S. Delgado. 2013. Community-based risk assessment of water contamination of high-volume horizontal hydraulic fracturing. *New Solutions: a Journal of Environmental and Occupational Health Policy*, 23(1): 137–166.

Pennsylvania Land Trust Association. 2008. *Marcellus Shale Drillers in Pennsylvania Amass 1614 Violations Since 2008: 1056 Identified as Most Likely to Harm the Environment*, http:// s3.amazonaws.com/conserveland/s3_files/585/report_draft10oct01_final.pdf?AWSAccessKeyId =1NXAG53SXSSG82H0V902&Expires=1373142144&Signature=E4nK1E053TJfAc6ZR3Ur 2mVoJOM%3D.

Pennsylvania Land Trust Association. 2008. *Marcellus Shale Drillers in Pennsylvania Amass 1614 Violations Since 2008: 1056 Identified as Most Likely to Harm the Environment*. Available at http:// s3.amazonaws.com/conserveland/s3_files/585/report_draft10oct01_final.pdf?AWSAccessKeyId =1NXAG53SXSSG82H0V902&Expires=1373142144&Signature=E4nK1E053TJfAc6ZR3Ur 2mVoJOM%3D.

Perrow, C. 2011. *Normal Accidents: Living with High Risk Technologies*. Princeton University Press, Princeton, New Jersey, 386 pp.

Pétron, G., G. J. Frost, B. R. Miller, A. I. Hirsch, S. A. Montzka, A. Karion, M. K. Trainer, C. Sweeney, A. E. Andrews, L. Miller, J. Kofer, A. Bar-Ilan, E. J. Dlugokencky, L. Patrick, C. T. Moore, T. D. Ryerson, C. Siso, W. Kolodzey, P. M. Lang, T. J. Conway, P. C. Novelli, K. A. Masarie, B. D. Hall, D. Guenther, D. R. Kitzis, J. B. Miller, D. C. Welsh, D. E. Wolfe, W. D. Neff, & P. P. Tans. 2012. Hydrocarbon emissions characterization in the Colorado Front Range: a pilot study. *Journal of Geophysical Research* 117; D4, doi: 10.1029/2011JD016360.

Pétron, G., G. J. Frost, M. K. Trainer, B. R. Miller, E. J. Dlugokencky, & P. Tans. 2013. Reply to comment on "Hydrocarbon emissions characterization in the Colorado Front Range—a pilot study" by Michael A. Levi. *Journal of Geophysical Research: Atmospheres*, 118(1): 236–242.

Phillips, N. G., R. Ackley, E. R. Crosson, A. Down, L. R. Hutyra, M. Brondfield, J. D. Karr, K. G. Zhao, & R. B. Jackson. 2013. Mapping urban pipeline leaks: methane leaks across Boston. *Environmental Pollution*, 173: 1–4.

Pimentel, D. 2006. Soil erosion: a food and environmental threat. *Environment, Development and Sustainability*, 8(1). 119–137, doi: 10.1007/s10668-005-1262-8.

Pipeline and Hazardous Materials Safety Administration (PHMSA), U.S. Department of Transportation. 2002. *Guidance Manual for Operators of Small Natural Gas Systems*. Available at http://www.phmsa.dot.gov/portal/site/PHMSA/menuitem.bdc7a8a7e39f2c55cf2031050248a0 c/?vgnextoid=a7c6ca170a574110VgnVCM1000009ed0/898RCRD&vgnextchannel=67027c2 cd44d3110VgnVCM1000009ed07898RCRD.

Podesta, J. D., & T. E. Wirth. 2009. *Natural Gas: a Bridge Fuel for the 21st Century*. Center for American Progress, Washington, DC, 11 pp. Available at http://www.americanprogress.org/wp-content/uploads/issues/2009/08/pdf/naturalgasmemo.pdf.

PPUC (Pennsylvania Public Utility Commission). 2012. *Unaccounted for Gas in the Commonwealth of Pennsylvania*. 16 pp. Available at http://www.puc.state.pa.us/transport/gassafe/pdf/UFG_Report_Feb2012.pdf.

ProPublica. 2008. *Buried Secrets: Is Natural Gas Drilling Endangering U.S. Water Supplies?* Available at http://www.propublica.org/article/buried-secrets-isnatural-gas-drilling-endangering-us-watersupplies-1113.

Radle, A. L. 2007. *The Effect of Noise on Wildlife: a Literature Review*. Unpublished Master's thesis, University of Oregon, Eugene, 16 p.

Rahm, B. G., & S. J. Riha. 2012. Toward strategic management of shale gas development: regional, collective impacts on water resources. *Environmenatal Science & Policy*, 17: 12–23.

Rahmstorf, S., F. Grant, & A. Cazenave. 2012. Comparing climate projections to observations up to 2011. *Environmental Research Letters*, 7(4): 044035, doi: 10.1088/1748-9326/7/4/044035.

Raymond, M. S., & W. L. Leffler. 2006. *Oil and Gas Production in Non-Technical Language*. PennWell Corporation, Tulsa, Oklahoma, 255 pp.

Reilly, S. 2012. Cornell studies diverge on drilling impact. Latest research disputes climate impact. *The Ithaca Journal*, January 10. Available at http://www.ithacajournal.com/article/20120110/ NEWS01/201100353/Cornell-studies-diverge-drilling-impact.

225

Resnikoff, M, E. Alexandrova, & J. Travers. 2010. *Radioactivity in Marcellus Shale.* Radioactive Waste Management Associates, New York, 29 May, available at http://www.nytimes.com/interactive/2011/03/01/us/natural-gas-documents-2.html#document/p50/a10108.

Revkin, A. C. 2012. A fresh scientific defense of the merits of moving from coal to shale gas. *The New York Times,* Dot Earth blog, February 29.

Revkin, A. C. 2013a. Another view on gas drilling in the context of climate change. *The New York Times,* Dot Earth, 29 July, available at http://dotearth.blogs.nytimes.com/2013/07/29/another-view-on-fracking-in-the-context-of-climate-change/?_r=0.

Revkin, A. C. 2013b. Two climate analysts fault gas leaks, but not as a big warming threat. *The New York Times,* Dot Earth, 1 August, available at http://dotearth.blogs.nytimes.com/2013/08/01/two-climate-analysts-fault-gas-leaks-but-not-as-a-big-warming-threat/?_r=0.

Richter, B. D., R. Mathews, D. L. Harrison, & R. Wigington. 2003. Ecologically sustainable water management: managing river flows for ecological integrity, *Ecological Applications;* 13: 206–224.

Rockström, J. W. Steffen, K. Noone, Å. Persson, F. S. Chapin, III, E. F. Lambin, T. M. Lenton, M. Scheffer, C. Folke, H. J. Schellnhuber, B. Nykvist, C. A. de Wit, T. Hughes, S. van der Leeuw, H. Rodhe, S. Sörlin, P. K. Snyder, R. Costanza, U. Svedin, M. Falkenmark, L. Karlberg, R. W. Corell, V. J. Fabry, J. Hansen, B. Walker, D. Liverman, K. Richardson, P. Crutzen, & J. A. Foley. 2009. A safe operating space for humanity. *Nature,* 461: 472–475.

Rogers, H. 2011. Shale gas—the unfolding story. *Oxford Reviews in Economic Policy,* 27(1): 117–143. Available at http://dx.doi.org/10.1093/oxrep/grr004.

Ropeik, D., & G. M. Gray. 2002. *Risk: A Practical Guide for Deciding What's Really Safe and What's Really Dangerous in the World Around You.* Mariner Books, New York, 485 pp.

Rowan, E. L., M. A. Engle, & C. S. Kirby. 2010. Inorganic geochemistry of formation waters from Devonian strata in the Appalachian Basin—preliminary observations from Pennsylvania, New York, and West Virginia. *Geological Society of America, Annual Meeting, Abstracts w/ Program,* no. 204-8. Available at https://gsa.confex.com/gsa/2010AM/finalprogram/abstract_174638.htm.

Rowan, E. L., M. A. Engle, C. S. Kirby, & T. F. Kraemer. 2011. *Radium Content of Oil- and Gas-Field Produced Waters in the Northern Appalachian Basin (USA)—Summary and Discussion of Data.* U.S. Geological Survey, Scientific Investigations Report 2011–5135, 31 pp. Available at http://pubs.usgs.gov/sir/2011/5135/.

Rowan, E. L., & T. F. Kraemer. 2012. *Radon-222 Content of Natural Gas Samples from Upper and Middle Devonian Sandstone and Shale Reservoirs in Pennsylvania: Preliminary Data.* U.S. Geological Survey, Open-File Report 2012–1159, 6 pp. Available at http://pubs.usgs.gov/of/2012/1159.

Ruddiman, W. F. 2013. The Anthropocene. *Annual Reviews of Earth and Planetary Science,* 41: 45–68.

Ryan, M. 2013. Electric sector sparking natural gas optimism. *Breaking Energy,* available at http://breakingenergy.com/tag/bnp-paribas/.

Sadiq, R., T. Husain, B. Veitch, & N. Bose. 2003. Evaluation of generic types of drilling fluid using a risk-based analytic hierarchy process. *Environmental Management,* 32(6): 778–787.

Sageman, B. B., D. J. Hollander, T. W. Lyons, A. E. Murphy, C. A. Ver Straeten, & J. P. Werne. 2003. A tale of shales: The relative roles of production, decomposition, and dilution in the accumulation of organic-rich strata, Middle-Upper Devonian, Appalachian Basin. *Chemical Geology,* 195: 229–273.

Santoro, R. L., R. W. Howarth, & A. Ingraffea. 2011. *Indirect Emissions of Carbon Dioxide from Marcellus Shale Gas Development.* Technical report, Agriculture, Energy, & the Environment Program, Cornell University, June 30. Available at http://www.eeb.cornell.edu/howarth/publications/IndirectEmissionsofCarbonDioxidefromMarcellusShaleGasDevelopment_June302011.pdf.

Schmoker, J. W. 1981. Determination of organic-matter content of Appalachian Devonian shales from gamma ray logs. *American Association of Petroleum Geologists Bulletin,* 65(7): 1285–1298.

Schon, S. C. 2011. Hydraulic fracturing not responsible for methane migration. *Proceedings of the National Academy of Sciences,* 108(37): E664.

Schrag, D. P. 2012. Is shale gas good for climate change? *Daedalus (American Academy of Arts and Sciences),* 141(2): 72–80.

Sempra, Inc. 2008. *Greenhouse Gas Life-Cycle Emissions Study: Fuel Life-Cycle of US Natural Gas Supplies and International LNG.* 68 pp. Available at http://www.adv-res.com/pdf/ARI_LCA_NOV_10_08.pdf.

Seto, C. 2011. Technology in unconventional gas resources. Supplemental Paper 2.3 in Moniz *et al.*, *The Future of Natural Gas—An Interdisciplinary Study*. Massachusetts Institute of Technology, Cambridge, Massachusetts, 33 pp. Available at http://mitei.mit.edu/system/files/Supplementary Paper SP_2_3_Unconventional_Technology.pdf.

Shindell, D. T. 2005. An emissions-based view of climate forcing by methane and tropospheric ozone. *Geophysical Research Letters*, 32 (4): L04803, 4 pp, doi: 10.1029/2004GL021900.

Shindell, D. T., G. Faluvegi, D. M. Kock, G. A. Schmidt, N. Unger, & S. E. Bauer. 2009. Improved attribution of climate forcing to emissions. *Science*, 326: 716–718.

Shindell D, J. C. I. Kuylenstierna, E. Vignati, R. van Dingenen, M. Amann, Z. Klimont, S. C. Anenberg, N. Muller, G. Janssens-Maenhout, F. Raes, J. Schwartz, G. Faluvegi, L. Pozzoli, K. Kupiainen, L. Höglund-Isaksson, L. Emberson, D. Streets, V. Ramanathan, K. Hicks, N. T. Kim Oanh, G. Milly, M. Williams, V. Demkine, & D. Fowler. 2012. Simultaneously mitigating near-term climate change and improving human health and food security. *Science*, 335: 183–189.

Shires, T., & M. Lev-On. 2012. *Characterizing Pivotal Sources of Methane Emissions from Unconventional Natural Gas Production: Summary and Analysis of API and ANGA Survey Responses*. American Petroleum Institute, and America's Natural Gas Alliance, Washington, DC, 48 pp. Available at http://www.api.org/~/media/Files/News/2012/12-October/API-ANGA-Survey-Report.pdf.

Skone, T. J., J. Littlefield, & J. Marriott. 2011. *Life Cycle Greenhouse Gas Analysis of Natural Gas Extraction & Delivery in the United States*. National Energy Technology Laboratory, Morgantown, West Virginia, DOE/NETL-2011/1522, 45 pp. Available at http://www.marcellus.psu.edu/resources/PDFs/NETLlifecycle.pdf.

Smith, D. R., C. D. Snyder, N. P. Hitt, J. A. Young, & S. P. Faulkner. 2012. Shale gas development and brook trout: scaling best management practices to anticipate cumulative effects. *Environmental Practice*, 14: 366–381.

Smolensky, N. L., & L. A. Fitzgerald. 2011. Population variation in dune-dwelling lizards in response to patch size, patch quality, and oil and gas development. *The Southwestern Naturalist*, 56(3): 315–324.

Soeder, D. J., & W. M. Kappel. 2009. *Water Resources and Natural Gas Production from the Marcellus Shale*. U.S. Geological Survey Fact Sheet 2009–3032, 6 pp.

Solomon, S., D. Battisti, S. Doney, K. Hayhoe, I. Held, D. Lettenmaier, D. Lobell, D. Matthews, R. T. Pierrehumbert, M. Raphael, R. Richels, T. Root, K. Steffen, C. Tebaldi, & G. Yohe. 2010. *Climate Stabilization Targets: Emissions, Concentrations and Impacts Over Decades to Millennia*. National Academy Press, Washington, DC, 190 pp.

Solomon, S., R. T. Pierrehumbert, D. Matthews, J. S. Daniel, & P. Friedlingstein. 2013. Atmospheric composition, irreversible climate change, and mitigation policy. Pp 415–436, in. *Climate Science for Serving Society: Research, Modeling and Prediction Priorities*, G. R. Asrar & J. W. Hurrell (eds). Springer Science+Business Media, Dordrecht, The Netherlands.

Stedman, R. C., J. B. Jacquet, M. Filteau, F. Willits, K. Brasier, & D. McLaughlin. 2012. Marcellus Shale gas development and new boomtown research: views of New York and Pennsylvania residents. *Environmental Practice*, 14(4): 382–393.

Steinbruner, J. D., P. C. Stern, & J. L. Husbands (eds). 2012. *Climate and Social Stress: Implications for Security Analysis*. The National Academies Press, Washington, DC, 252 pp.

Stephenson, T., J. E. Valle, & X. Riera-Palou. 2011. Modeling the relative GHG emissions of conventional and shale gas production. *Environmental Science and Technology*, 45: 10757–10764.

Strayer, D. L., & K. J. Jirka. 1997. *The Pearly Mussels of New York State*. University of the State of New York, State Education Department, Albany, New York, 113 pp.

Struchtemeyer, C. G., M. D. Morrison, & M. S. Elshahed. 2012. A critical assessment of the efficacy of biocides used during the hydraulic fracturing process in shale natural gas wells. *International Biodeterioration and Biodegradation*, 71: 15–21.

Susquehanna River Basin Commission. 2008. *Consumptive Use Mitigation Plan*. Publication no. 253, available at http://www.srbc.net/programs/docs/CUMP.pdf.

Sweeney, M. B., S. McClure, S. Chandler, C. Reber, P. Clark, J. Ferraro, P. Jimenez-Jacobs, D. Van Cise-Watta, C. Rogers, V. Bonnet, A. Shotts, L. Ritttle, & S. Hess. 2009. *Marcellus Shale Study Guides, 1-V.* League of Women Voters of Indiana County, Pennsylvania. Available at http://shale.palwv.org/?page_id=8.

Tollefson, J. 2013a. Methane leaks erode green credentials of natural gas. *Nature*, 493: 12.

Tollefson, J. 2013b. Oil boom raises burning issues. *Nature*, 495: 290–291.

Tour, J., C. Kittrell, & V. L. Colvin. 2010. Green carbon as a bridge to renewable energy. *Nature Materials*, 9: 871–874.

Townsend-Small, A., S. C. Tyler, D. E. Pataki, X. Xu, & L. E. Christensen. 2012. Isotopic measurements of atmospheric methane in Los Angeles, California, USA: influence of "fugitive" fossil fuel emissions. *Journal of Geophysical Research*, 117(D7): 2156–2202, doi:10.1029/2011JD016926. Available at http://dx.doi.org/10.1029/2011JD016360.

Trembath, A., & J. Jenkins. 2013. *Avoiding a Natural Gas Bridge to Nowhere*. The Breakthrough Institute, blog post, available at http://thebreakthrough.org/archive/avoiding_a_natural_gas_bridge.

URS Corporation. 2009. *Water-Related Issues Associated with Gas Production in the Marcellus Shale. Water Consulting Services in Support of the GEIS for Natural Gas Production*. NYSERDA Contract 10666, Fort Washington, Pennsylvania, 92 pp.

U. S. Department of Energy. 2006. Energy demands on water resources. Report to Congress on the interdependency of energy and water. U.S. Department of Energy, Washington, DC. Available at http://www.sandia.gov/energy-water/docs/121-RptToCongress-EWwEIAcomments-FINAL.pdf.

USGS (U. S. Geological Survey) Marcellus Shale Assessment Team. 2011. *U.S. Geological Survey Information Relevant to the U.S. Geological Survey Assessment of the Middle Devonian Marcellus Shale of the Appalachian Basin Province, 2011*. Open-File Report 2011–1298, U.S. Geological Survey, Washington, DC, 22 pp. Available at http://pubs.usgs.gov/of/2011/1298/.

USGS (U. S. Geological Survey) Oil and Gas Assessment Team. 2012. *Variability of Distributions of Well-Scale Estimated Ultimate Recovery for Continuous (Unconventional) Oil and Gas Resources in the United States*. Open-File Report 2012-1118, U.S. Geological Survey, Washington, DC. Available at http://pubs.usgs.gov/of/2012/1118/OF12-1118.pdf.

Veil, J. 2011. *White Paper on SPE Summit on Hydraulic Fracturing (Society of Petroleum Engineers, Houston)*. Available at http://www.spe.org/industry/docs/HFsummitwhitepaper.pdf.

Veil, J. A., M. G. Puder, D. Elcock, & R. J. Redweik. 2004. *A White Paper Describing Produced Water from Production of Crude Oil, Natural Gas, and Coal Bed Methane*. Argonne National Laboratory report under DOE (NETL), Contract W-31-109-Eng-38, 79 pp.

Venkatesh, A., P. Jaramillo, W. M. Griffin, & H. S. Matthews. 2011. Uncertainty in life cycle greenhouse gas emissions from United States natural gas end-uses and its effects on policy. *Environmental Science and Technology*, 45: 8182–8189.

Venkatesh, A., P. Jaramillo, W. M. Griffin, & H.S. Matthews. 2012. Uncertainty in life cycle greenhouse gas emissions from United States coal. *Energy Fuels*, 26(8): 4917–4923, doi: 10.1021/ef300693x.

Ver Straeten, C., G. Baird, C. Brett, G. Lash, J. Over, C. Karaca, T. Jordan, & R. Blood. 2011. The Marcellus Subgroup in its type area, Finger Lakes Area of New York, and beyond. Pp 23–86, in: *New York State Geological Association Field Trip Guidebook, Field Trip A-2*, New York State Geological Association 83rd Annual Meeting. Available at http://www.nysm.nysed.gov/staffpubs/docs/20398.pdf.

Vidic, R., S. L. Brantley, J. M. Vandenbossche, D. Yoxtheimer, & J. D. Abad. 2013. Impact of shale gas development on regional water quality. *Science*, 340(6134): 1235009, doi: 10.1126/science.1235009.

Walsh, B. 2011. Could shale gas power the world? *Time Magazine*, April 11. Available at http://www.time.com/time/magazine/article/0,9171,2062456,00.html.

Wang, G., & T. R. Carr. 2012. Methodology of organic-rich shale lithofacies identification and predition: a case study from Marcellus Shale in the Appalachian Basin. *Computers & Geosciences*, 49: 151–163.

Warner, N. R., R. B. Jackson, T. H. Darrah, S. G. Osborn, A. Down, K. Zhao, A. White, & A. Vengosh. 2012a. Geochemical evidence for possible natural migration of Marcellus Formation brine to shallow aquifers in Pennsylvania. *Proceedings of the National Academy of Sciences*, 109(30): 11961–11966.

Warner N. R., R. B. Jackson, T. H. Darrah, S. G. Osborn, A. Down, K. Zhao, A. White, & A. Vengosh. 2012b. Reply to Terry Engelder: potential for fluid migration from the Marcellus Formation remains possible. *Proceedings of the National Academy of Sciences*, 109(52): E3626.

Waxman, H. A., E. J. Markey, & D. DeGette. 2011. *Chemicals Used in Hydraulic Fracturing*. United

States House of Representatives, Committee on Energy and Commerce, Washington, DC, available at http://democrats.energycommerce.house.gov.

Weber, C. L., & C. Clavin. 2012. Life cycle carbon footprint of shale gas: review of evidence and implications. *Environmental Science and Technology*, 46: 5688–5695.

Wennberg, P. O., W. Mui, D. Wunch, E. A. Kort, D. R. Blake, E. L. Atlas, G. W. Santoni, S. C. Wofsy, G. S. Diskin, S. Jeong, & M. L Fisher, 2013. On the sources of methane to the Los Angeles atmosphere. *Environmental Science & Technology*, 46(17): 9282–9289, doi:10.1021/es301138y.

White, E. I. 2012. *Consideration of Radiation in Hazardous Waste Produced from Horizontal Hydrofracking*. Grassroots Environmental Education, Port Washington, New York, available at http://www.grassrootsinfo.org/pdf/whitereport.pdf.

Whiteley, T. E., G. J. Kloc, & C. E. Brett. 2002. *Trilobites of New York*. Cornell University Press, Ithaca, New York, 203 pp.

Whiteman, G., C. Hope, & P. Wadhams. 2013. Climate science: vast costs of Arctic change. *Nature*, 499: 401–403.

Wiggins, G. P., & J. McTighe. 2005. *Understanding by Design*. Association for Supervision and Curriculum Development, Alexandria, Virginia, 370 pp.

Wigley, T. M. L. 2011. Coal to gas: the influence of methane leakage. *Climatic Change*, 108: 601–608.

Wilber, T. 2012. *Under the Surface, Fracking, Fortunes, and the Fate of the Marcellus Shale*. Cornell University Press, Ithaca, New York, 272 pp.

Williams, J. D., M. L. Warren, Jr., K. S Cummings, J. L. Harris, & R. J. Neves. 1993. Conservation status of freshwater mussels of the United States and Canada. *Fisheries*, 18(9): 6–22.

Wood, R , P Gilbert, M. Sharmina, K. Anderson, A. Footitt, S. Glynn, & F. Nicholls. 2011. *Shale Gas: a Provisional Assessment of Climate Change and Environmental Impacts*. A report commissioned by the Cooperative and undertaken by researchers at the Tyndall Centre, University of Manchester, UK, 82 + v pp.

Wrightstone, G. 2009 Marcellus Shale—geologic controls on production. Extended abstract, prepared for oral presentation at AAPG Annual Convention, Denver, Colorado, June 7-10. Available at http://www.searchanddiscovery.com/documents/2009/10206wrightstone/.

Wunch, D., P O Wennberg, G. C. Toon, G. Keppel-Aleks, & Y. G. Yavin. 2009. Emissions of greenhouse gasses from an American megacity. *Geophysical Research Letters*, 36: L15810, doi: 10.1029/2009GL039825.

Yusuf, R. O., Z. Z. Noor, A. H. Abba, M. A. Abu Hassan, & M. F. Mohd Din. 2012. Methane emission by sectors: a comprehensive review of emission sources and mitigation methods. *Renewable and Sustainable Energy Reviews*, 16: 5059–5070.

Zalasiewicz, J., M. Williams, A Smith, T, L. Barry, A. L. Coe, P. R. Brown, P. Brenchley, D. Cantrill, A. Gale, P. Gibbard, F. J. Gregory, M W. Hounslow, A. C. Kerr, P. Pearson, R. Knox, J. Powell, C. Waters, J. Marshall, M. Oates, P. Rawson, & P Stone. 2008. Are we now living in the Anthropocene? *GSA Today*, 18(2):4 8, doi: 10.1130/GSAT01802A.1.

Zalasiewicz, J., M. Williams, W. Steffen, & P. Crutzen. 2010. The new world of the Anthropocene. *Environment Science & Technology*, 44(7): 2228–2231, doi: 10.1021/es903118j.

Zeller, T., Jr. 2011a. Studies say natural gas has its own enviromental problems *The New York Times*, April 11. Available at http://www.nytimes.com/2011/04/12/business/energy-environment/12gas.html?ref=tomjrzeller&_r=0.

Zeller, T., Jr. 2011b. Methane losses stir debate on natural gas. *The New York Times*, Green Blog, April 12. Available at http://green.blogs.nytimes.com/2011/04/12/fugitive-methane-stirs-debate-on_natural-gas/?ref=tomjrzeller.

Zeller, T., Jr 2011c. Cornell gas study stirs heated debate. *The New York Times*, Green Blog, April 18. Available at http://green.blogs.nytimes.com/2011/04/18/cornell-gas-study-stirs-heated-debate/?ref=tomjrzeller.

Ziman, J. M. 2000. *Real Science. What It Is and What It Means*. Cambridge University Press, Cambridge, United Kingdom, 412 pp.

INDEX

The letter "f" following a page number indicates association with a figure on that page.

231

241

CONTRIBUTORS

Don Duggan-Haas received his bachelor's degree in Physics from State University of New York-Geneseo and his Ph.D. in Curriculum, Teaching, and Educational Policy from Michigan State University. He is currently Senior Education Research Associate at the Paleontological Research Institution in Ithaca, New York.

Robert M. Ross received his bachelor's degree in Geological Sciences from Case Western Reserve University, and his Ph.D. in Earth and Planetary Sciences from Harvard University. Since 1997, he has overseen the education program at the Paleontological Research Institution in Ithaca, New York, most recently as Associate Director for Outreach.

Warren D. Allmon received his bachelor's degree in Earth Sciences from Dartmouth College and his Ph.D. in Earth and Planetary Sciences from Harvard University. Since 1992, he has been Director of the Paleontological Research Institution in Ithaca, New York and, since 2008, the Hunter R. Rawlings III Professor of Paleontology at Cornell University.

Kelly E. Cronin received her bachelor's degree in Biology from Cornell University. From 2008 to 2013, she worked in a variety of positions at the Paleontological Research Institution in Ithaca, New York, most recently as Climate and Energy Programs Manager. She is currently a graduate student in Earth Sciences at the University of North Carolina at Wilmington.

Trisha A. Smrecak received her bachelor's degree in Geology from St. Lawrence University and her master's degree in Geology from the University of Cincinnati. From 2008 to 2011, she was Global Change and Evolution Projects Manager at the Paleontological Research Institution in Ithaca, New York. She is currently a graduate student in Geological Sciences at Michigan State University.

Sara Auer Perry received her bachelor's degree in Geology from Michigan State University, and master's degrees in Geology from the University of Oregon and Childhood Education from Ithaca College. From 2008 to 2011, she was Geoscience Education Resource Developer at the Paleontological Research Institution in Ithaca, New York. She is currently an educator in the Ithaca City School District.